BookEnds

THE CHANGING MEDIA ENVIRONMENT OF AMERICAN CLASSROOMS

The Hampton Press Communication Series
MEDIA ECOLOGY
Lance Strate, supervisory editor

Mediating the Muse: A Communications Approach to Music,
Media, and Cultural Change
Robert Albrecht

Online Connections: Internet Interpersonal Relationships
Susan B. Barnes

Bookends: The Changing Media Environment of the American
Classroom
Margaret Cassidy

Walter Ong's Contribution to Cultural Studies:
The Phenomenology of the Word and I-Thous Communication
Thomas J. Farrell

The Power of Metaphor in the Age of Electronic Media
Raymond Gozzi, Jr.

An Ong Reader
Walter Ong, Thomas J. Farrell, and Paul A. Soukup (eds.)

No Safety in Numbers: How the Computer Quantified Everything
and Made People Risk Aversive
Henry J. Perkinson

The Media Symplex: At the Edge of Meaning in the Age of Chaos
Frank Zingrone

forthcoming

Cybermedia and the Ecology of Digital Media
Lance Strate and Susan B. Barnes (eds.)

The Legacy of McLuhan
Lance Strate and Edward Wachtel (eds.)

BookEnds

THE CHANGING MEDIA ENVIRONMENT OF AMERICAN CLASSROOMS

MARGARET CASSIDY
ADELPHI UNIVERSITY

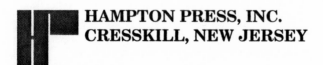

HAMPTON PRESS, INC.
CRESSKILL, NEW JERSEY

Printed in the United States of America

Library of Congress Cataloging-in-Publication Data

Cassidy, Margaret.
    Bookends : the changing media environment of American classrooms / Margaret Cassidy.
        p. cm. -- (The Hampton Press communication series. Media ecology)
    Includes bibliographical references and index.
    ISBN 1-57273-492-2 -- ISBN 1-57273-493-0
        1. Education--Effect of technological innovations on--United States. 2. Educational technology--United States. 3. Information technology--United States. I. Title. II. Series.

LB0128.3C33 2004
371.33'5--dc22

                                                        2004040571

Hampton Press, Inc.
23 Broadway
Cresskill, NJ 07626

FOR MARK

CONTENTS

ACKNOWLEDGMENTS

Above all, I want to thank my husband, Mark Hudson, for his endless support. His patience and good humor throughout this process, which happened to coincide with the births of our son, Justin, and daughter, Molly, were remarkable. It is hard to imagine how I could have finished this project without him.

I am grateful to Lance Strate, series editor for the Media Ecology Series of which this book is a part, not only for his help in developing this manuscript and shepherding it through the production process, but for the many ways he has helped me build my career over the years.

I must also thank Devin Thornburg, of New York University's Metropolitan Center for Urban Education. He read several drafts of the manuscript, and suggested directions I never would have thought of taking with it. Sometimes I felt he understood the book better than I did.

Finally, I wish to acknowledge the National Endowment for the Humanities, whose Summer Stipend award helped support my research for this book.

INTRODUCTION

The life for which the American schools should now prepare their pupils is an utterly different life from that for which the schools were preparing the children forty years ago—or even twenty years ago. All the scenes have shifted within a single generation.

—Charles W. Eliot (1903)

Harvard President Charles Eliot was describing a shift in the character of American life that began in the mid-19th century largely due to rapid technological change. He went on to identify such inventions as the telephone, telegraph, steam engine, and electric light as some of the revolutionary technologies of his time from which "immeasurable benefits have flowed,"[1] arguing that schools had to change to keep up with changing times. In such a tumultuous age, he argued, a proper education would reduce violent crime, drunkenness, and gambling. It would elevate people's impoverished taste in reading and theater, and make them less susceptible to medical quackery. It would reduce the divorce rate, and ensure that people would be qualified to exercise their suffrage rights wisely.

---
[1]Eliot, 1903, p. 67

There is much in his basic argument that sounds familiar. Today, Americans largely continue to believe that education is the solution to society's ills. Although confidence in public schools is not as high now as it was in other eras, faith in education as the answer to a myriad of problems remains strong. The particular problems that Americans expect schools to solve today have changed as have some of the means by which they expect schools to solve those problems. However, the basic beliefs underlying those expectations have remained essentially the same, including the belief that unprecedented technological change demands that schools alter their practices to prepare children for the new, technologically different world they are inheriting. It hardly needs to be pointed out that today one of the most often cited reasons for bringing new media into schools is to prepare children for lives in this *information age*, although people might disagree on what *preparation* might entail and what exactly an *information age* is. What is less known is that this has been a standard argument about education and media for at least 100 years, made in much the same way and the same spirit throughout that time.

It has been a characteristically American response to new media to see them as reasons for changing schools, and to hope that their introduction into classrooms can revitalize education in one way or another. Hopes for the educational potential of new technologies abounded throughout the 20th century and continue to dominate policy talk. Film was so vast in "its possibilities for the instruction . . . of humanity that did it not already exist we should, if we possessed enough imagination, pray for its invention."[2] Once fully understood, films would "no doubt, be considered as necessary a part of school equipment as are textbooks, maps, charts, and blackboards."[3] Radio was described as "the greatest implement of democracy yet given to mankind,"[4] sure to raise the human mind "to an entirely new level of precision and efficiency."[5] Television was hailed as "the power tool of education,"[6] "the greatest vital force in modern education,"[7] and "the most exciting educational voyage since our nation embarked on the

[2]Forman, 1935, p. 1
[3]Ellis and Thornborough, 1923, p. vi
[4]Robinson, 1930, p. 3
[5]Darrow, 1932, p. ix
[6]Conrad, 1954, p. 373
[7]Long, 1952, p. 417

universal education of its citizens."[8] Computer-assisted instruction would provide "a much broader learning experience than other mass communications instructional media"[9]; it was predicted to "march relentlessly into our instructional lives."[10] Each of these media was embraced by many education reformers of its day and argued to be compatible with then-current ideas about pedagogy, curriculum, and the purposes and priorities of schooling. Yet despite some high hopes about the potential uses of these media in schools, they rarely saw extensive use in typical classrooms.

It is rather striking that schools have had and continue to have such an allergic reaction to newly introduced communication technologies. Some are tempted to condemn public schools altogether as reactionary organizations that never change and that doom our children to an anachronistic education. Along those lines, there is an analogy, popular among educational technology advocates, drawn between doctors and teachers: If a doctor and teacher from 100 years ago were somehow to be transported through time to the present day, the doctor would be utterly at a loss in an operating room. Technological advances have been so profound that little remains of the earlier practices of that profession. However, the argument goes, the teacher (unfortunately) could walk into a modern day classroom and scarcely miss a beat so similar are today's schools to those of a century ago.

As popular as this frozen in time conception of schools might be, it can be misleading, and it gets in the way of our understanding the nature of change in educational policies and practices. It implies that reform is cyclical and futile, that educational fads fly in and out of currency without leaving a trace, only to be replaced by new, equally futile and ineffective plans for change. Yet schools today are *not* the same as schools of a century ago, although some—even many—features have proved durable (for good or ill). For example, the time from which our time-traveling schoolmarm came was one when there were still nearly 200,000 one-room schoolhouses, where children of all ages were educated together in a nongraded setting. A century ago, the total number of days of schooling received by the average American in his lifetime was under 1,000, and the school curriculum was generally confined to the 3Rs. Barely 10% of children

[8]Morehead, 1955, p. 179
[9]Filep, 1967, p. 102
[10]Goodlad, 1968, p. 7

ages 14 to 17 attended high school, and the junior high school had not yet been invented. School segregation was legal, child labor or the care of infant siblings kept many poor children out of school altogether, and women were generally forbidden to continue teaching after they married. In other words, things have not been so static in American public education as some wish to believe. That is not to say that schools are, in fact, quickly and dramatically changing institutions that barely resemble their counterparts of a century ago or that similar problems and situations never cycle back around. It is that when those issues reappear, as they frequently do, they do so in new times with new social conditions and debates, and schools that are not precisely the same as the ones in existence last time. Consequently, what has changed in society and in schools sometimes has an important effect on what the outcome of each new stab at reform will be.

All the more interesting, then, that the story of new media in schools is so strongly characterized by recurring themes. Each of the media discussed in this book was celebrated for its educational potential despite coming on the scene in different times, characterized by somewhat different social and political concerns, ideas about teaching and learning, and conceptions of what schools are for. One might be tempted to predict that these differences would make for different outcomes. Instead the story of educational technologies emerges as one where the same kinds of hopes have been followed by the same kinds of problems over and over again throughout the 20th century.

The differences in these various attempts to bring new communication technologies into the school environment are in the details—for example, in the particular social problem people hoped to solve by using a new technology in schools—*not* in the basic, underlying assumptions—for example, that social problems can be addressed by using technology in schools. We need to be more consciously aware of the assumptions being made today about technology and education so that we can think harder about their validity and usefulness. A good place to start—and it sometimes seems a rare one—is in the past, where we are not quite so emotionally invested in what people were thinking and doing, and are therefore more likely to establish some critical distance. From there, with any luck, we can apply our newly honed skills in critical distance to the present, along with some different ideas against which we can compare our own. What is more, we come back to the present with a better understanding of where our ideas came from, what circumstances brought them into being in the first place, and how they have changed over time.

In particular, ideas about educational technology cannot be properly understood without some understanding of how American ideas about progress, technology, and education have been interrelated throughout the nation's history. American history is characterized by a profound faith in progress, particularly in technological progress, and by a deep belief that progress can be achieved through education. Understanding this faith, however it may have been changed and compromised over the centuries, goes a long way in clarifying why Americans continue to invest their hopes in educational technology, despite the evidence that has accrued over the years that might have challenged those hopes.

The myth of progress has often been promoted (consciously or otherwise) in the telling of American history in general, and of American educational history in particular. As education historian David Tyack pointed out, histories of American public education have traditionally served the purpose of telling "a triumphant 'house history'. . . . The major purpose of educational history was to give teachers and administrators a greater sense of professional esprit and identity,"[11] not to question the fundamental assumptions or conflicts embedded in the story of American public education. More recently, the tone of scholarship concerning the history of education has shifted to include more critical examinations of curriculum, pedagogy, and literacy.[12] Educational sociologists have explored alternatives to the view that schooling helps promote and sustain a society of equal opportunity, offering instead the argument that schools often serve to reinforce existing inequalities and maintain a status quo that perpetuates the dominance of a small, but powerful, ruling class.[13] These types of approaches to the examination of American public education can go a long way in informing the history of educational technology and should be used to provide some much-needed context.

The story of educational technology must be more thoroughly and deliberately intertwined with these other ideas about school reform if the repeated attempts to transform schools with technology are to be more adequately understood. That is, what happens to new

---

[11]Tyack, 1974, pp. 8-9
[12]See, for example, Apple, 1988; Freire and Macedo, 1987; Katz, 1987; Tyack, 1974; Tyner, 1999
[13]Hurn, 1993

media in schools is—and always has been—mediated by theories of curriculum and pedagogy, prevailing beliefs about the purposes of schooling, and the relationship between technology and the work of teachers. The meanings and motives that teachers attach to communication technology have a lot to do with the way such media are used in schools, as is the perception teachers have of the role they have been able or permitted to play in deciding how and why technology is brought into or excluded from schools.

Connecting the story of educational technology to other mediating factors is an important step toward demythologizing technology—toward understanding the choices that affect the way technology is brought into people's lives and social institutions. Otherwise it is tempting to attribute a degree of agency or destiny to technology that obscures the many interrelating elements that come into play. This process is particularly important in any consideration of American public education, where an obsessive focus on technology's wonders and perils has nearly monopolized recent conversations about school reform, leaving many substantive issues outside the parameters defined by the technology conversation. It has also tended to promote the belief that new technology has some sort of inherent destiny to do good, to usher in a new educational age, to transform the experience of teaching and learning—if only we put enough of it in schools. Such grandiose claims tend to mask the real work involved in accomplishing school reform (technological or otherwise) while scapegoating teachers, who are often seen as standing in the way of these powerful new tools for educational progress. They also sidestep any critical examination of the powerful commercial, economic, governmental, and military interests involved in putting new media in schools, all of which tend to work against the idealistic vision of schools as democratic institutions and technology as an agent of democracy.

Those who are in a position to direct the development of new media are also in a position to shape those media in ways that favor some individuals, groups, power structures, and ways of knowing and interacting over others. Education scholar Hank Bromley describes how "tools can be flexible but only within certain limits, because their design inevitably favors some applications and prohibits others. . . . Once a piece of technology has been designed, its predispositions are locked in."[14] With that possibility in mind, it becomes crucial to be

---

[14]Bromley, 1998, pp. 3-4

more aware of the process by which new media come into being, and
the role of human agency in determining what each new medium will
become.

There is also a degree to which media environments, regardless of who shaped them and how they came into being, exert a force
on the relationships, interactions, and habits of mind of all those
functioning within those environments. Media scholars Lance Strate
and Susan Barnes describe how "as an environment, media set the
stage on which human agents act. They fix the parameters, enabling
certain 'effects' while discouraging others, and providing the raw
materials out of which historical events are made."[15] They distinguish between the cultural studies approach to media and the media
ecological approach—two views that are compatible with one another, and both of which are crucial to understanding the process by
which new media are (or are not) incorporated into a society's educational institutions. Where critical and cultural studies tend to focus
on how media are used and shaped by those in power to maintain
that power, a media ecological approach regards the media environment as "the ground for the exercise of power and the dissemination
of ideology."[16] That is, although media ecology acknowledges human
agency in technological change and considers media to be but one of
many influences in an environment, it also suggests that the biases
and influences of the media environment are not entirely under the
control of those acting within it. At times, the media environment
contributes to the maintenance, alteration, or elimination of social
institutions and practices despite what a particular individual or
group might desire or seek to accomplish.

One can go so far as to argue that the whole idea of *school* is,
in part, the product of the biases of a particular media environment—one that is proving highly resistant to the introduction of new
media. Oral cultures tend not to have separate educative institutions, choosing instead to distribute the process of education throughout the society. It is generally with the development of writing and
literacy that societies come to believe that they must create schools to
equip young people (at least some of them) to use the dominant symbolic forms of their age. The invention of the printing press, and the
ensuing widespread availability of print media, once again shifted

---

[15]Barnes and Strate, 1996, pp. 183-184
[16]Barnes and Strate, 1996, p. 184

conceptions of education, and we have largely inherited the conception of education that emerged in an era dominated by typography. Media historian Robert Logan links media environments and education systems in *The Alphabet Effect*:

> The Gutenberg print revolution inspired a new form of education in which the printed book served as the principal focus of instruction. The educational goals and values of today's school system are a product of that print mentality. They have been devised to instruct youngsters to operate in the print environment.[17]

American public education was founded in a typographic age and was meant to prepare people to function in a media environment dominated by print. It focused on the development of literacy and numeracy skills, those skills being the ones required for informed participation in civic life, as well as for personal fulfillment in a predominantly Protestant religious climate that considered Bible reading to be central to religious practice. Certainly the practices and priorities of public schools today are different in many ways from their earlier ancestors, but public schools to this day retain in their basic structures many biases of the typographic era in which they were created. Advocates of new media today love to predict the abandonment of the book, the shift from books to digital resources, and they are not necessarily wrong in advocating that shift. However, they rarely give sufficient consideration to the dominance of print and the print mindset in education, and it is possible that the relative lack of success achieved by new media-oriented school reformers throughout the 20th century is due, in part, to this fundamental oversight.

This durability and dominance of print media in schools cannot be ignored. Unless we understand this aspect of educational institutions better, we can never really understand much about how new media fit into those institutions. It is not merely a matter of delivering the existing curriculum through new media; it is a matter of understanding how the schools we have inherited were built around the medium of print, and how one cannot consider the content of educational media apart from the form of those media. It is both the content and form of media that encourage or discourage certain relationships, power structures, and habits of mind in the people who do most of their knowing through those media. The form a medium

---

[17]Logan, 1986, p. 239

takes can privilege some people over others and some ways of knowing over others. Consequently, the media environment of schools and the information configurations it establishes are important to understand. Equally important is an awareness of who has what interests in maintaining or changing those configurations, and how they might be able to orchestrate or resist changes in the form and content of the school media environment.

John Dewey understood how the form and content of the educational experience are inseparable. He insisted that educational innovations cannot survive as simple add-ons to the existing system—that, as such, they will surely be marginalized or sloughed off. He argued that the organization of schools, the seemingly neutral, innocuous ways in which schools are put together and kept going, were well suited for the established curriculum and hostile to the ideas he was trying to introduce. Without changing the form of schools, he argued, one can never change the content or character of instruction. Dewey was half a century ahead of McLuhan in insisting that the medium is the message or at least that the medium is a rather important factor in determining what messages are conveyed and how they are understood. In much the same way that Dewey showed how school methods and organization perpetuate a particular way of learning, we need to understand how new media favor certain ways of knowing over others, and how they relate to the existing media biases in schools. That is, we need to know more about the epistemological biases of educational media and the ways in which we internalize the tools and symbol systems of our culture and use them to structure our thinking.[18]

Dewey also understood an issue about human communication that may prove central to an understanding of the media's role in American public education. Communication scholar James Carey considers Dewey's work to be the natural starting point for the study of communication because Dewey was aware of two necessary functions of communication that Carey later described as the *transmission* (or transportation) and the *ritual* functions. The transmission function, which Carey says dominates the American sensibility, focuses on the goal of moving a message accurately and efficiently

---

[18]See Postman and Weingartner, 1969, for a comparison of Dewey and McLuhan, and Postman, 1985, for an elaboration on epistemological biases of media. See also Salomon, 1988, and Vygotsky, 1978, on the process of internalizing tools.

from its source to its intended recipient. In contrast, the ritual function is "directed not toward the extension of messages in space but toward the maintenance of society in time; not the act of imparting information but the representation of shared beliefs."[19] Each serves an important purpose in social functioning and cohesion, but Dewey and Carey argue (Carey deliberately and consciously, Dewey more indirectly) that Americans have tended to neglect the ritual function to the detriment of civic participation and the proper functioning of the democratic process.

In many respects, attempts to introduce new media to schools have been dominated by conceptions of education that focus on the effective, efficient transmission of information to students. For that matter, American public education more generally has tended to be dominated by such a view despite strands and movements in pedagogy, curriculum, and learning theory that have advocated something different. The conception of communication dominating educational practices, then, is another important factor to keep in mind in any attempt to understand how new media fit into the school environment.

In other words, telling the story of educational technology is not merely the process of setting down a timeline of machinery invented, introduced into schools, experimented with, and either adopted or set aside. This book is about some of the ideas and events that provide the context for present-day discussions about educational media. It is about the hope Americans have invested in progress through education and technology, the form and content of education and media, and the ways in which media both influence and are influenced by school reformers and their ideas about what schools are for. What is happening in school reform today has deep historical roots. Our circumstances might not be the same as those who came before us, but their ideas and experiences have shaped our own—often without our knowing it—and we would do well to better understand our inheritance.

---

[19]Carey, 1989, p. 18

1

PROGRESS, TECHNOLOGY, AND EDUCATION IN AMERICAN HISTORY

That the present is an "age of progress," is generally admitted. We see this spirit in the new discoveries which science and art are daily developing, making known the secrets of nature, unravelling the mysteries of ages . . . and thus affording new proof of the truth of history and revelation. We see progress . . . in the wonders of the telegraph, by which places, however, remote, are brought within whispering distance, and which already nearly encircles the earth by its magic power. . . . We see it in the improved school house, convenient furniture, apparatus and books. . . . But we see it more completely in the progress of Christianity, and in the general diffusion of the blessings of our holy religion, which teaches us to regard all men as brethren, and breathes peace on earth and good will to men."

—J.W. Bulkley, Superintendent of Common Schools,
City of Brooklyn (1867)

It is a well-established notion that Americans have long been known for their faith in progress. The American vision of the United States as a special place with a special purpose has made its way through several centuries to the present, however remade for different eras or challenged by particular periods in the nation's history. Closely linked to that faith in progress are equally powerful beliefs in both education and technology as agents of progress; progress, education, and technology have together come to constitute something of an American trinity.

Although we live today in a world profoundly different from that of the founding of the nation, the remnants of the ideas on which the nation was founded can be found in American belief systems and continue to show themselves in the character of American educational institutions. It is important to make more conscious and explicit the origins of those beliefs, and the impact they have had on those institutions—in particular, on the ways in which new technologies are brought into them. For good or ill, efforts to introduce new technologies into schools have not usually gone well if one measures the success of an educational innovation by the extent to which it becomes a regular part of classroom practice. Yet hope to change schools with technology remains one of the most prominent elements of educational policy talk. How does that make sense?

On closer inspection, it makes perfect sense. What would be more sensible to a people who believe in progress, education, and technology to repeatedly attempt to achieve progress with educational technology? If that belief system is long established and largely unquestioned, why would those people ever really doubt that although individual efforts along these lines might fail and periods of setback might occur, the basic premises are sound and should continue to be followed? A good place to begin, then, is by looking more closely at how these ideas of progress and technology became intertwined in the history of American public education.

AMERICANS AND PROGRESS

A popular belief originating in the colonial period was that America had a destiny of inevitable progress. In *The Idea of Progress in America*, Arthur A. Ekirch described this idea of progress as "the most popular American philosophy, thoroughly congenial to the ideas and interests of the age."[1] The North American continent boasted an

---

[1] Ekirch, 1969a, p. 267

abundance of natural wonders and exotic phenomena, which became points of pride and identity for colonists. Early 20th-century education reformer David Snedden described this sentiment well:

> American peoples, almost from the time of their first settlements, have given expression to a large number and variety of intensively hopeful aspirations. All the conditions surrounding the seeking of fortunes in a new land, and in a land designed ultimately to confer large new types of security, wealth, and other good things, have led inevitably to the development of an optimism of glowing hopes and even of utopian expectations.[2]

The intense sense of optimism brought to North America by European colonists carried powerfully into the early national period and became a well-known characteristic of what has become known as the American character.

A deeply religious significance went along with the idea of progress. Part of the idea of the American utopia was the notion that America was the chosen nation destined to fulfill the prophecies of the Book of Revelations, in which Satan is defeated for 1,000 years and, ultimately, forever. John Adams expressed the sentiment in the following way:

> I always consider the settlement of America with reverence and wonder, as the opening of a grand scene and design in Providence for the illumination of the ignorant, and the emancipation of the slavish part of mankind all over the earth.[3]

In *Redeemer Nation: The Idea of America's Millennial Role*, Ernest Tuveson argued that the American belief in progress had its religious origins in a Protestant worldview that believed in human agency—in particular, in bringing about the millennium. It would come through hard work and preparation, and it would happen in this world, not in some heavenly afterlife. He described the conditions that seemed and have remained favorable for instilling in Americans a sense of their destiny:

> The eighteenth, nineteenth, and twentieth centuries would certainly be unique in both importance and character. Protestants

---

[2]Snedden, 1927, p. 20

[3]Tuveson, 1968, p. 25

who lived in these centuries accordingly might be expected to live through the most terrible yet the most inspiring days anyone had known since the Resurrection. And it seemed logical that to some nation or nations would be assigned leadership in finishing God's great plan. Sure enough, an age of revolution ensued—in science and technology as well as in government. A hemisphere, hitherto unknown, came into the forefront of history. And bestriding it, was a new nation. The United States hardly needed to identify itself as the appointed agent of the Apocalypse; it seemed as if the stage manager of Providence had summoned the American people from the wings of the stage of history.[4]

So the stage was set, and Americans adopted and cultivated a sense of themselves as saviors of the world and bound for greatness. That is not to say that belief in progress has gone unchallenged or unmodified. Wars, economic depressions, disparities between rich and poor, violations of civil rights, and technological catastrophes all diluted or changed the American idea of progress, although one could argue that none of them destroyed the basic faith in progress for most Americans, and some of them were used as exceptions to prove the rule or rationalized as tests the millennial nation had to undergo. Moreover, at the same time as these things happened, so did major accomplishments that helped restore people's faith in progress. Historian and cultural critic Neil Postman describes how 19th-century Americans found inspiration in new ideas and achievements of the age:

It would be possible to write a whole book—in fact, several—on how and why faith in progress could be maintained, although for different reasons, by both rationalists and romantics. . . . Rationalists would find evidence in the obvious advances in science and technology, increased political and religious freedom, the decline of monarchies, the rise of republics, and the "proof" that Darwinian evolution gave to the doctrine of progress. Romantics, for all of their skepticism, could take heart from examples of moral progress, such as the decline of slavery, the elevation of women, the growth of the concept of childhood, and a new appreciation of nature.[5]

---

[4]Tuveson, 1968, p. 46

[5]Postman, 1999, p. 34

The idea of progress has been powerful enough to remain lodged in the sensibilities of many Americans as an integral component of their worldview, despite events that have challenged it over the ages.

More recently, the 20th century brought its share of accomplishments that served to reinforce the idea of progress, such as Lindbergh's flight, the New Deal, space travel, and the fall of the Berlin Wall. Although modern life has often been regarded as a time of disillusionment, of recognition that progress is not inevitable, it has also been thought of as a time of nearly limitless possibility. In *Redeeming Modernity: Contradictions in Media Criticism*, Joli Jensen describes how "progress, like modernity, is Janus-faced—it is both the wondrous possibility and the terrifying prospect of 'the new.'"[6] Despite that Americans have paid a high price for progress, there remains, to borrow Jensen's words, a "positive, booster version of modernity"[7] in circulation that sustains many Americans through periods of crisis. Out of every such period comes a renewed faith in the promise of the future, and the belief that America has a noble purpose to fulfill for itself and the world.

This optimistic view of modernity is particularly focused on technology as an agent of progress. Jensen describes how this view "defines contemporary life as an arena of scientific discovery that makes possible an extraordinarily desirable future."[8] Like progress more generally, technological progress has not been without its setbacks—sometimes of catastrophic proportions. Still it remains a common response to such crises to seek a technological solution, thus reaffirming the traditional faith that technology is a central agent in progress.

AMERICANS AND TECHNOLOGICAL PROGRESS

It is interesting that American descriptions of the millennium often included prophecies of technological and scientific progress; some millennialist thinkers interpreted the Biblical prophecy that "many shall run to and fro, and knowledge shall be increased" as meaning

---

[6]Jensen, 1990, p. 84

[7]Jensen, 1990, p. 90

[8]Jensen, 1990, p. 90

that the millennium would be characterized by increased travel and rapid acquisition of information. Tuveson wrote that "in this millennialist utopia, it is interesting to see how often the words 'comfort' and 'convenience' appear; and in this attitude, which also appears in most accounts of the millennium later, we have perhaps one source of the almost religious fervor of Americans for . . . technological improvement."[9] Indeed, it is impossible to understand the American idea of progress without considering American attitudes toward technology so often regarded as a critical component (or the equivalent) of progress.

Americans have particularly expressed great pride in their technological accomplishments and have fancied those accomplishments as having near-religious (if not outright religious) significance. A kind of transcendence through technology has been for centuries one of America's "central ideas about itself,"[10] according to David Nye, author of *The Technological Sublime*. Nye describes the experience of the sublime as "an essentially religious feeling, aroused by the confrontation with impressive objects."[11] Americans were quick to embrace technology as a crucial component of progress and as a symbol of national greatness. In *Technology and American Society: A History*, G. Cross and R. Szostak argue that "in this near worship of the technological 'sublime,' the United States had no peers. . . . Americans have long loved their machines. That affection was perhaps an inevitable offspring of an ambitious and individualistic nation cutting its way through a wilderness."[12]

The negative effects of technological change were not unknown to Americans; they were aware of the havoc that industrialization was wreaking on European cities. As early as 1787, Thomas Jefferson was calling in his *Notes on the State of Virginia* for Americans to "let our work-shops remain in Europe. . . . The mobs of great cities add just so much to the support of pure government, as sores do to the strength of the human body."[13] Despite Jefferson's admonitions, Americans managed to fashion an image of their industrializing nation that rendered them "exempt from history," to use

---

[9]Tuveson, 1968, p. 62

[10]Nye, 1994, p. xiv

[11]Nye, 1994, p. xiii

[12]Cross and Szostak, 1995, pp. 141, 147

[13]Jefferson, 1955, p. 165

James Carey's words. Carey described how Americans rationalized their belief that they would derive only good from technology:

> The controlling metaphor that invoked this promised land was Nature, the healing power of an unsullied virgin wilderness. . . . Machinery was to be implanted into and humanized by an idealized rural landscape. The grime, desolation, poverty, injustice, and class struggle typical of the European city were not to be reproduced here. America's redemption from European history, its uniqueness, was to be through unblemished nature, which would allow us to have the factory without the factory system, machines without a mechanized society.[14]

Fascination with technology intensified in the 19th century. In *The Idea of Progress in America*, Ekirch wrote:

> With the rise of an industrialized, urbanized society, science . . . became the chief authority for a belief in the idea of progress . . . even before the Civil War, science was the magic power by which it was felt that progress, if not inevitable, could at least be made highly probable.[15]

This pre-Civil War belief in the magic power of technology was well expressed by Thomas Ewbank, Commissioner of Patents from 1849 to 1852. He wrote of inventors:

> It is they who, by discovering new physical truths, are establishing the grandest of moral ones—*Perpetual Progress*—illimitable advancement in social, civil, and intellectual enjoyments. . . . Though not suspected, the power of inventors over human affairs is already supreme; machinery even now governs the world, though the world does not acknowledge it.[16]

Characteristic of the response to new technologies was a sense of awe, the combination of fascination and fear so characteristic of the experience of the sublime.[17] Technology was seen as an agent of morality, unity, and democracy—all high on the agenda of 19th-cen-

---

[14]Carey and Quirk, 1989b, p. 118

[15]Ekirch, 1969a, p. 267

[16]in Ekirch, 1969a, p. 128

[17]Nye, 1994, chapter 1

tury Americans, a population that was diversifying, growing, and spreading out.

Americans had good reason to embrace faith in technology as an organizing narrative. Early American society was very diverse, and lacking uniform religious beliefs, citizens of this new nation needed some shared way to ascribe transcendent significance to lives and events. According to Nye, for early Americans, the powerful impression made by their spectacular technological accomplishments may have served in part as a substitute for any single, defining set of religious beliefs. They could experience communal transcendence through shared participation, if not shared consensus about the meaning of the experience.[18]

Technology was an integral element in the plans of certain 19th-century American utopian thinkers. Although they did not constitute a formal movement per se, their work embodies certain common ideas, enough for historian Howard Segal to identify the salient features of what he called *technological utopianism*. In particular, he described how technological utopians differed from other utopian thinkers in their belief that utopia could actually be achieved in this world, and that it would be through American invention and technological innovation that it would happen. In *Technological Utopianism in American Culture*, Segal described how technological utopians "made technological progress equivalent to progress itself rather than merely a means to progress, and they modeled their utopia after the machines and structures that made such technological progress probable."[19] Although these writers were by no means numerous, "their message was widely and warmly received. . . . Their collective vision appeared in a cultural context predisposed for various reasons to accept its principal themes."[20]

Of all forms of technology, electricity was particularly fascinating to Americans, "invoked as the panacea for every social ill and the key to a whole range of personal transformations."[21] It generated ideas of "electrical cocktails" to improve health, jewelry fashioned from electric lights, and instant gratification through electric push-

---

[18]Nye, 1994

[19]Segal, 1985, pp. 74-75

[20]Segal, 1985, p. 102

[21]Nye, 1994, p. 143

buttons.[22] In *When Old Technologies Were New*, Carolyn Marvin describes how it became popular to believe that electricity was the "mysterious vital force at the root of life,"[23] and that it was the therapeutic agent in all manner of medicines, lotions, teas, and apparel, including electrified hats to cure baldness and corsets with electrical alarms that went off if suitors pressed them too hard. People with magical electrical powers were popular in circuses, and lighting displays became a standard feature of fairs and other celebrations.

Henry Adams, great grandson of John Adams, epitomized this American fascination with technology. In *The Education of Henry Adams* (an autobiography written in the third person and first published postmortem in 1918), he described Americans' inability to derive inspiration from traditional sources, but rather to find it in technology. Adams was particularly taken by electricity, describing the dynamo—the electrical generator—as the epitome of the technological sublime:

> . . . to Adams the dynamo became a symbol of infinity. As he grew accustomed to the great gallery of machines, he began to feel the forty-foot dynamos as a moral force, much as the early Christians felt the Cross. . . . Before the end, one began to pray to it; inherited instinct taught the natural expression of man before silent and infinite force.[24]

Of all things electrical, electronic means of communication were especially exciting to Americans; Marvin documents how "a favorite light sport in popular and professional journals was to detail ways in which timely and imaginative applications of new technologies would unravel social difficulties by opening up new avenues of information."[25] In 1851, Presbyterian clergyman Robert Baird wrote of new communication technologies:

> What elements of power are here entrusted to us! . . . these means of communication over sea and land,—through the broad earth,—who does not hear the voice of God in all these? [26]

---

[22]Marvin, 1988, p. 123

[23]Marvin, 1988, p. 129

[24]Adams, 1999 (originally published 1918), p. 318

[25]Marvin, 1988, p. 66

[26]in Ekirch, 1969a, p. 121

From their earliest days, electronic media were seen as a moral force for good that would bind Americans together and foster understanding among a diverse population.

These new forms of communication were regarded as critical to the survival of the nation. No one had ever attempted to create a republic on such a grand scale in terms of geography and population, and there was a great deal of uncertainty as to the viability of such a union. James Carey expresses this challenge well:

> How was this continental nation to be held together, to function effectively, to avoid declension into faction or tyranny or chaos? How were we, to use a phrase of that day, "to cement the union"? To make it all to simple, the answer was sought in the word and the wheel, in transportation and transmission, in the power of printing and civil engineering to bind a vast distance and a large population into cultural unity or, as the less optimistic would have it, into cultural hegemony.[27]

Of all the inventions hailed to unite the nation and promote moral progress, the telegraph reigned supreme. This sentiment was reflected in the *Report of the Commissioner of Patents* in 1844, the year the first telegraphic message was sent:

> Among the most brilliant discoveries of the age, the electromagnetic telegraph deserves a conspicuous place. Destined as it is to change as well as hasten transmission of intelligence, and so essentially to affect the welfare of society, all that concerns its further developments will be hailed with joy.[28]

Telegraph documentarians Charles Briggs and Augustus Maverick described in 1858 how, to Americans of the time, "the Telegraph has more than a mechanical meaning; it has an ideal, a religious, and a prospective significance, far-reaching and incalculable in its influences."[29] Samuel Morse wrote in an 1855 letter to a friend that the telegraph would "bind man to his fellowman in such bonds of amity as to put an end to war."[30] Minister Horace Bushnell wrote in 1847,

---

[27]Carey, 1989, p. 5

[28]Ekirch, 1969, pp. 109-110

[29]Charles Briggs and Augustus Maverick, *The Story of the Telegraph and the History of the Great Atlantic Cable*, 1858, in Czitrom, 1982, p. 188

[30]in Ekirch, 1969, p. 110

"the sooner we have railroads and telegraphs spinning into the wilderness, and setting the remotest hamlets in connexion and close proximity with the east, the more certain it is that light, good manners and Christian refinement, will become universally diffused."[31] Daniel Czitrom, whose work on the telegraph draws from that of James Carey, documents the way in which "the presumed annihilation of time and space held a special meaning for a country of seemingly limitless size. . . . Americans generally hailed the telegraph as a means of forging the Republic closer together, a vital political consideration as millions moved to the West."[32] In other words, the hope was that the telegraph was destined to bring unity, morality, and Christianity to all.

Faith in electricity and electronic means of communication persisted even when Americans became disillusioned by other technologies that had been a source of inspiration. As the 19th century progressed, the effects of industrialization—from which Americans had declared themselves immune—were being acutely felt in American cities. Technology had not lived up to its apparent promises. However, according to James Carey and John Quirk, the result was not an abandonment of faith in technology so much as a shift to faith in a technology that had not yet disappointed:

> But reality was unable to reverse rhetoric, and in the last third of the nineteenth century, as the dreams of a mechanical utopia gave way to the realities of industrialization, there arose a new school of thought dedicated to the notion that there was a qualitative difference between mechanics and electronics, between machines and electricity, between mechanization and electrification. In electricity was suddenly seen the power to redeem all the dreams betrayed by the machine.[33]

Americans' faith in electricity and electronic media (to the point of utopian fantasies) was not without qualification. New communication technologies elicited a variety of fears and anxieties. For example, some nineteenth century neurologists expressed concern that the telegraph would speed up the acquisition of information so much that it would overload the brain's circuitry; they feared a type of nervous

---

[31]in Cremin, 1980, p. 47

[32]Czitrom, 1982, pp. 11-12

[33]Carey and Quirk, 1989b, p. 121

exhaustion caused by the sped-up lifestyle brought on by new technologies.[34] Parents were afraid that traditional social distinctions and hierarchies would be challenged by the telephone's tendency to weaken their control over their children's social interactions.[35] Some concerns approached apocalyptic proportions, revealing "the fear that man was throwing nature wildly out of balance"[36] and that nature would exact its revenge. A number of prominent American authors of the time, including Thoreau, Hawthorne, Melville, and Henry Adams, questioned the value of technological progress, and their skepticism was evident in their writings.

Despite these concerns, the dominant attitude toward technological progress in the United States was generally positive; Ekirch described the critical stance of writers like Thoreau as "out of joint with the times."[37] Americans were less inclined to criticize technology than people of other nations; Cross and Szostak argued that "so pervasive was the American infatuation with technology that Americans were slow to develop a critique of the impact of technology on nature, work, and, more broadly, society and the human spirit."[38] Where the British were, according to Nye, "prone to view industrialization in terms of satanic mills, frankensteinian monsters, and class strife,"[39] Americans were more inclined to focus on the potential of technological change to morally uplift them and their fellow citizens.

Like the attitude toward progress more generally, the American attitude toward technological progress has been challenged particularly in the 20th century. It is clear that technology has the potential to be the undoing of the world, and that it has already taken a horrific toll on some people and places. At the same time, it has dramatically improved the health, safety, and comfort of many people, and Americans generally retain the belief that further-improved technology is a viable solution to the problems—technological and otherwise—that the nation faces. Carey and Quirk argue that, "while the favored symbols of technological progress have changed—satellites, spaceships, computers, and information utilities

---

[34]Czitrom, 1982, pp. 20-21

[35]Marvin, 1988, chapter 2

[36]Marvin, 1988, p. 121

[37]Ekirch, 1969a, p. 182

[38]Cross and Szostak, 1995, p. 135

[39]Nye, 1994, p. 54

having replaced steam engines and dynamos—the same style of exhortation to a better future through technology dominates contemporary life."[40]

Technology has been used to renew Americans' faith in progress at times when that faith was in question. For example, Franklin D. Roosevelt's New Deal exemplified not only a general renewal of American optimism, but a renewal of optimism through technology-based projects.[41] Cold war anxieties were allayed by the spectacular technological achievements of the space race and reinforced the good-versus-evil, millennial tone to technological progress. As Tuveson argued, the idea of the United States as the *redeemer nation* became even more important in the cold war, with the proliferation of nuclear weapons. They seemed to leave the nation with no choice: save the world or face annihilation. In particular, it was the prospect of being technologically inferior to the Soviets that redoubled the American commitment to technology as the key factor in progress, and that made technology seem to be the primary factor in the preservation of the American way of life.

Although the cold war era is in the past, the threat of destruction remains real and, with it, the American sense that the future of the world is in their hands perhaps more so than ever before. Although this conception of the American destiny is argued by many to be corny, imperialistic, and/or oppressive, it is one that remains resonant with many Americans, and it is summoned up on a regular basis to garner support for political policies, particularly when they involve military action. Despite its imperfections, it still carries weight with many people and remains a dominant feature of the general notion of the "American character."

Overall, then, Americans have long regarded technology as a potential agent of improvement in happiness, morality, unity, and democracy, and continue to do so. James Carey argues that

> All of the claims that have been made for electricity and electrical communication, down through the computer and cable, satellite television, and the Internet, were made for the telegraph with about the same mixture of whimsy, propaganda, and truth. Cadences change, vocabulary is subtly altered, examples shift,

---

[40]Carey and Quirk, 1989a, p. 177

[41]Ekirch, 1969b

the religious metaphors decline, but the medium has the same message.[42]

Much the same can be said for the way in which Americans have regarded education. It, too, has been a critical component in the American idea of progress, called on to serve a variety of functions in the improvement of the nation. It has been expected to cultivate morality, promote cultural unity and uniformity, protect and advance democracy, and engineer consensus among diverse people—in short, to be a key agent of progress. Moreover, one of the primary means through which educators have attempted to fulfill these expectations has been through the use of the new technology of the day, be it outline maps or the Internet. Albeit an "imperfect panacea,"[43] to borrow an expression from education historian Henry Perkinson, public education, mobilizing the new technology of the day, continues to inspire Americans as a means of achieving personal and national progress.

AMERICANS, PROGRESS, AND PUBLIC EDUCATION

Americans were not the first to promote mass education or public schooling. However, the United States was different in that it was founded on a belief that if properly educated, citizens could rule themselves. This belief, coupled with the millennial spirit of the early national era, created a sense of urgency and importance around education that was different from other nations and other times. From the beginning of nationhood, American was heavily invested in the idea that progress and education were inextricably intertwined, and this belief has persisted to the present day. It was heightened by the popularity of pragmatism in the late 19th century—a philosophy that emphasized the need to put ideas to work toward the improvement of daily life, to translate thought into action. The pragmatic orientation encouraged people to believe that their own individual effort could make a real difference in the world. Pragmatism was formulated and popularized most notably by William James, Charles S. Peirce, and John Dewey, Dewey being the one who applied it most directly to education.

[42]Carey, 1997, p. 44

[43]Perkinson, 1968

Although the belief systems underlying pre-20th-century optimism about public education as an agent of progress have been challenged and modified, that optimism has by no means vanished from the American sensibility. If anything, some would argue, it has intensified. For example, Henry Perkinson argued that Americans have so equated schools and progress that they expect their schools to solve every imaginable problem they might encounter.[44]

Throughout the history of American public education, school reformers have cited changes in communication technologies as a rationale for changes in education. In many respects, the earliest schools in America were a response to the media environment of the day, assigned, as they were, the task of providing children with the basic literacy and numeracy skills those children would need to function in a typographic era. Historically, a popular argument for reforming education has been the changing demands of life brought about by technological change, and it has been standard to argue that the new communication technology of the day should be brought into schools to support school reform.

Each of the next five chapters examines a particular 20th-century educational technology in some detail, along with the school reform movements in circulation at the time the technology under examination came on the scene. First, a brief look at the history of American public education, and the media and materials used in schools, is in order as a way to establish some context and foreshadowing of what is to come in subsequent chapters.

EARLY AMERICAN EDUCATION

American public schools are largely a product of the quest for progress, with a millennial tone underlying their establishment. Education historian Lawrence Cremin pointed out that the mottoes chosen for the national seal were *Annuit coeptis* ("He has favored our undertaking") and *Novus ordo seclorum* ("A new order of the ages has begun"). "A new era," Cremin wrote, "under the watchful eye of Providence, proclaimed in Virgilian rhetoric—nothing could be more representative of the way in which Americans thought about them-

---

[44]Perkinson, 1968

selves and their destiny as a people."[45] This destiny, however, could not be left to chance, and education was considered to be one of the most important institutions to build to secure the nation's future and its excellence. An editorial in the November 1854 issue of *New York Teacher* read:

> If we revert to the past, we see that little more than two centuries have elapsed since progressive enterprise lifted the light of civilization, and commenced its progress within the present limits of the United States. "Young America" has progressed with a giant step hitherto unparalleled and unprecedented in the annals of history—the wonder of the nation—and the admiration of the world. . . . We must educate, *we must educate*, or we must perish by our own prosperity. . . . There can be no work of more transcendent importance or more directly claiming the attention of all, than the proper instruction and education of the rising generation.[46]

Another article in that same issue summed up the basic millennial rationale for free public schools: "The destiny of the world depends upon the future course of America. The destiny of America depends upon the general intelligence of the people, and the general intelligence of the people depends upon our common schools."[47] Under the circumstances, it stands to reason that a great deal of energy was devoted to conceptualizing and developing American educative institutions.

The fact that Americans have always felt strongly about education does not mean that they have always had, desired, or even approved of free public schooling. Education in the early national period took place in a wide variety of ways depending on geographical region, who was to be educated, and for what purpose one was to be educated. For example, New England Puritans were adamant about education because of their desire to establish universal literacy—out of concern that their carefree children, in an age of high infant mortality, had no time to lose in the quest to serve a wrathful God. Under the circumstances, they felt the need to teach sufficient literacy skills for Bible study.[48] By contrast, in the South in the late 18th century, education was less about religion and more about the

---

[45]Cremin, 1980, p. 17

[46]"The demands of the age," 1854, pp. 114-116

[47]"The influence of education," 1854, p. 76

[48]Tyack, 1967, chapter 1

training of gentlemen. Planters, as individuals or small groups, sometimes hired a tutor to instruct their sons as part of their gentlemanly training. However, there was little emphasis on formal schooling due, in part, to the distribution of the educative function among a variety of experiences, and partly because the low population density of the southern states made it difficult to establish schools.[49]

Early advocates of mass schooling, such as Thomas Jefferson, Noah Webster, and Benjamin Rush, generally promoted the idea of such education in the spirit of equipping citizens to fulfill their role in a democratic society. They believed that citizens needed adequate literacy skills to access and analyze political information and issues available primarily through the printed word. They were also concerned with the proper education of leaders, believing in a natural aristocracy, where those most qualified to be leaders would be identified and educated accordingly. (The assumption followed that the rest of the citizens would recognize the abilities of these select few and elect them to office.) As a result, they conceived of schooling as a two-tiered system—one for the masses and one for future leaders. These men generally supported disenfranchisement of the illiterate.

These early advocates of public education were also greatly concerned with cultivating an American sensibility—with establishing Americans' sense of nationhood and common identity and purpose. According to education historian David Tyack, they promoted "the paradox that the *free* American was the *uniform* republican."[50] They wanted to homogenize Americans through schooling, particularly through the use of American textbooks that promoted what they deemed to be American values. Such texts as those of Noah Webster were designed to accomplish this purpose, seeking to standardize American English in spoken and written form. They presented American history as a story of the heroic deeds of godlike figures and American government as the greatest ever conceived. For example, a section of Noah Webster's "Federal Catechism" describes different forms of government, such as aristocracy, monarchy, and democracy; the final passage reads as follows:

> A representative republic, in which the people freely choose deputies to make laws for them, is much the best form of government hitherto invented.

---

[49]Tyack, 1967, chapter 2

[50]Tyack, 1967, p. 86

Q. *Which of the forms or kinds of government is adopted by the American States?"*

A. The states are all governed by constitutions that fall under the name of representative republics.[51]

Webster's texts sold in huge quantities, with sales of over 20 million of his speller alone.

The ideas of these early advocates of free public education were not quickly or enthusiastically adopted. Jefferson's proposal for public education in Virginia was not accepted by the state legislature, and it would be some time before Americans were convinced that education should take place in state-supported, free schools available to all children. Heading into the 19th century, Americans had many different ways to educate themselves, including newspapers and other printed materials, apprenticeships, libraries, and fairs. They also had lyceums, first organized by Josiah Holbrook in 1826, officially defined at the time as:

> a literary club of almost any description, a literary association or a society for debate or lectures; and to these objects may be added literary contributors or correspondents, exertions for the popular diffusion of the arts or sciences, the improvement of taste by the embellishment of village scenery, rural architecture, or the promotion of education in schools.[52]

Besides the availability of a variety of learning opportunities other than school, many Americans regarded formal schooling with a measure of distrust. The self-educated American—Benjamin Franklin being the epitome—was a popular image, and any schooling beyond the 3Rs was often held in disdain as a sign of aristocratic snobbery. The American folk hero was more "the unlettered backwoodsman who pretended to be the goat of the fop or lawyer and then slyly turned the tables on him,"[53] not the bookish intellectual.

The first completely free schools in the United States were available only to the destitute, established as charity schools to educate poor children. For the most part, private institutions set up these schools in the 1790s and early 1800s. For example, the Free School Society of New York was established in 1805 to educate desti-

---

[51]in Tyack, 1967, p. 190

[52]Jackson, 1940, p. 103

[53]Jackson, 1940, p. 12

tute children in New York City who were not covered by any religious society. The goal of those who founded these schools was to reduce crime and poverty by setting young urban children, generally the children of immigrants, on the *right* path by providing them with *proper* moral education in their early formative years and instilling in them the value of industry and hard work.

Free schooling for the poor was made financially possible by the use of the Lancasterian monitorial system of instruction, where one teacher could manage a class of hundreds, with the more advanced students acting as teaching assistants. Its emphasis on discipline and order was believed to provide proper moral training to children who were believed to come from homes lacking such training. Education historian Joel Spring describes how this process was supposed to work:

> The Lancasterian system was supposed to help the pauper child escape poverty and crime by imparting formal knowledge and by instilling the virtues needed in the world of work. Within this framework of reasoning, the qualities of submission, order, and industriousness made the child moral by making him or her useful to and functional in society.[54]

Early free schooling depended on the Lancasterian system because of its affordability. However, by the 1830s, the system fell out of use because of the severity of its authoritarian approach. Education historian Michael Katz describes how workingmen's associations, in particular, objected to the system, understanding that those who designed it did so not "for their own children or for the children of their friends. Rather, they attempted to ensure social order through the socialization of the poor in cheap, mass schooling factories."[55]

Those who established pauper schools may have been motivated by genuine concern for the well-being of poor children. However, their tone was often patronizing, thus alienating those they were trying to serve. For example, a book written to promote the free schools of New York City demonstrated the sometimes condescending character of the rhetoric employed to persuade parents to send their children to school, telling parents that others will question the character of their children if they do not send their children to school. However,

---

[54]Spring, 1986, p. 55

[55]Katz, 1987, p. 28

the book argued, if they do send their children to school, people will "think well of *the child and parent both*, and be much more ready to believe other good things that may be told them about your son or daughter."[56] The book went on to invoke the fear of death in parents:

> And believe me, this is a thing of no small importance in this changing and dying world. For you know not how soon your children may be left without your care, to get along as well as they can; when, under the blessing of God, every thing may depend upon their *character*, and the favorable opinion that kind and respectable persons may form of them.[57]

Despite such injunctions, many parents would not or could not send their children to pauper schools. In some cases, pride was an issue; parents were reluctant to accept charity or did not want to send their children to school in tattered clothes. In other cases, families simply could not afford to forego the income from their children's labor, and there was not sufficient time in the day for children to be both students and wage earners.

In retrospect, charity schools clearly had their flaws. Overall, the most significant contribution of these schools to the future form and purpose of public education, according to Joel Spring, was that "they embodied the belief that education could end poverty and crime in society,"[58] setting the stage for a persistent faith in public schools to solve a myriad of social problems.

The transition to widespread acceptance and support of free public schools for all children, not just the destitute, took place in the period from 1825 to 1850 depending on where in the country one happened to be. Although common schooling ultimately had strong support in all regions, that support generally only came after long struggles by its advocates.

THE STRUGGLE FOR COMMON SCHOOLS

The story of American common schools is an interesting one in that quite disparate groups of people somehow came to share the belief

---

[56]Welter, 1971, p. 64

[57]Welter, 1971, p. 64

[58]Spring, 1986, p. 56

that this institution was in their best interest. Different groups of Americans supported common schooling for different reasons; others opposed the idea entirely. However, what is remarkable about the common school movement is that ultimately most Americans did come to embrace it even if they never came to a consensus about the exact reason that such schools should exist.

One important early impetus driving the development of public schools was religion. The predestination of Calvinism had not left much room for individual work toward salvation, but as Calvinism receded the belief emerged that one could earn salvation through good deeds and self-improvement. In *The American Common School: An Historical Conception*, historian Lawrence Cremin characterizes this shift as follows:

> While the older theological systems had insisted that life in this world was simply a preparation for life in the next, humanitarian optimism now saw man fulfilling his destiny in the here and now. Predestination gave way to unbounded possibilities for individual and social progress.[59]

If people were to fulfill their destiny during their Earthly life, it seemed to follow that they would need to educate themselves as part of the process of self-improvement.

The campaign to evangelize the West flourished in the 1830s, when Protestant preachers went west to fight barbarism and create virtuous citizens. They hoped to promote literacy so that all Americans would choose to instruct and elevate themselves in the manner befitting a nation with such lofty ideals. They were also concerned about the recent influx of Catholic immigrants and how such newcomers might threaten national progres. In *America's Struggle for Free Schools*, Sidney Jackson documents how "America was warned that the 'Papists' were sweeping the Mississippi Valley and that they would soon be in a position to topple over everything the worthy citizen held dear."[60] Cremin describes how groups like the American Bible Society and the American Sunday-School Union held revival meetings, distributed Bibles, and established Sunday schools with the result that:

---

[59]Cremin, 1951, p. 17

[60]Jackson, 1940, p. 43

by the 1840s and 1850s, a generalized Protestant piety had become an integral part of the American vernacular, and the responsibility for teaching that piety to all Americans had become the central task of a newly constructed configuration of educative institutions. The piety that emerged was an embracing one, popular in character and millennial in orientation; and its substance and spirit were shared by an extraordinary variety of sects, denominations, and utopian communities.[61]

The generalized Protestant tone to common schooling would ultimately become a bone of contention in American public education, but the fact remains that the goal of spreading Protestant morality was a fundamental purpose behind the common school movement.

Another major factor in building support for common schooling was the shift in the Jacksonian era toward a people's democracy. The early national period was essentially aristocratic. With suffrage often tied to property ownership or payment of taxes, the vast majority of citizens were not eligible to vote. However, in the 1820s, Jacksonian democrats rejected all forms of elitism or aristocracy, promoting instead the idea that any citizen was eligible for public office. As Cremin pointed out, "By the age of Jackson, it was a foregone conclusion that the common man was to rule American society."[62]

This shift showed itself in changing attitudes toward schooling. Schools were increasingly regarded as equalizers, not as selectors. In *American Writings on Popular Education*, R. Welter argues that in a fairly short time, "most Americans came to insist that education must be available on equal terms to all if it were to be truly effective in serving their political and social values."[63] In the process, they became more and more inclined to favor state-controlled and state-funded schools.

A more conservative version of this same story is that those who resisted the shift from republicanism to democracy intensely feared rule by the masses. They, too, supported common schooling, but not in the spirit of encouraging any citizen to rise to a position of leadership. Rather, according to Cremin, they regarded common schooling "largely as a propaganda agency to save society from the

---

[61]Cremin, 1980, p. 18

[62]Cremin, 1951, p. 17

[63]Welter, 1971, p. lvi

'tyranny of democratic anarchy.'"[64] To them, schooling would counter-
act the "incipient radicalism of the lower classes"[65] by pacifying them
with a more or less illusory means to upward mobility.

　　The common school movement (or as some refer to it *crusade*)
is most commonly associated with a group of reformers, such as
Horace Mann and Henry Barnard, who managed, according to David
Tyack, "to articulate and focus the generalized American belief in
education and to make it relevant to the aspirations and anxieties of
the age."[66] Joel Spring describes how these reformers had a "utopian
vision of the good society created by a system of common schooling,"[67]
hoping that bringing children from a variety of backgrounds together
in a common schoolhouse would create greater understanding among
them, promoting national unity. This unity would enhance America's
progress; as secretary of the Massachusetts Board of Education,
Horace Mann wrote in his 1848 report:

> in universal education, every "follower of God and friend of
> human kind" will find the only sure means of carrying forward
> that particular reform to which he is devoted. In whatever
> department of philanthropy he may be engaged, he will find that
> department to be only a segment of the great circle of benefi-
> cence, of which *Universal Education* is centre and circumference;
> and that it is only when these segments are fitly joined together,
> that the wheel of Progress can move harmoniously and resistless-
> ly onward.[68]

The overtly millennial rhetoric of these reformers was picked up by
school administrators of the time. For example, part of a principal's
address, given on the day his school opened in 1842, went as follows:

> Who shall say, but that an all-wise Providence has designed, that
> as Fulton was the first to discover and apply steam to locomotion;
> almost annihilating distance, and bringing the distant parts of
> the earth together; so the county bearing his name shall be the
> favored spot to put into operation a nobler and more powerful
> engine, destined to elevate the character of our common schools,

---

[64]Cremin, 1951, p. 30

[65]Cremin, 1951, p. 29

[66]Tyack, 1967, p. 124

[67]Spring, 1986, p. 89

[68]Mann, 1848, p. 135

and make them what they ought to be, the safe guards of our
dear bought liberties, and precursors of a moral and intellectual
millennium.[69]

One of the primary goals of common school crusaders was to
bring order to American schooling. They believed that they could
standardize and systematize public education by establishing state
systems of education, normal schools for the training of teachers, and
graded schools. David Tyack describes their vision as follows:

> The division of labor in the factory, the punctuality of the rail-
> road, the chain of command and coordination in modern business-
> es—these aroused a sense of wonder and excitement in men and
> women seeking to systematize the schools. They sought to replace
> confused and erratic means of control with careful allocation of
> powers and functions within hierarchical organizations; to estab-
> lish networks of communication that would convey information
> and directives and would provide data for planning in the future;
> to substitute impersonal rules for informal, individual adjudica-
> tion of disputes; to regularize procedures so that they would
> apply uniformly to all in certain categories; and to set objective
> standards for admission to and performance in each role, whether
> superintendent or third-grader. Efficiency, rationality, continu-
> ity, precision, impartiality became watchwords of the consolida-
> tors. In short, they tried to create a more bureaucratic system.[70]

Horace Mann and the other common school crusaders were
motivated less by an interest in cultivating the academic skills of the
masses than by their concern that disorder threatened society and
their belief that the salvation of society required not only intellectual,
but moral education in an organized system of public education.
Earlier and less successful common school advocates, like Thomas
Jefferson, argued that public education was necessary to create citizens who possessed the capacity to protect themselves from the
potential abuses of their government. These new reformers offered a
different argument: The danger to the people was not their government, but themselves. Ignorance bred vice, violence, and barbarism,
and it would be the purpose of public schools to teach the restraint

---

[69]Annual Report of the Superintendent of Common Schools, State of New York,
1843, p. 172

[70]Tyack, 1974, pp. 28-29

needed to maintain social order. Part of their vision of common schooling was moral education in Protestant Christian principles, which, they believed, would diminish criminal acts.

The idea of schools as civilizers resonated with schoolmen of the day, one of whom argued that education "saves us from many consequences of blind frenzy, unbridled passions, and destructive outbreaks of vice and crime."[71] Another wrote that "you will find that State or community in which the cause of education has reached the highest stage of advancement the most law-abiding and order-loving. Lawlessness is the legitimate offspring of ignorance."[72] Yet another believed that "We owe two-thirds of our crime, and we will not say how much of our misery, to popular ignorance."[73] He went on to argue that schools should teach discipline, hard work, and "the cheerful submission to lawful authority."[74] Certainly public schools were meant partly to cultivate the intellect. Yet as Katz argues, perhaps more important was their responsibility "to shape behavior and attitudes, alleviate social and family problems, and reinforce a social structure under stress. The character of pupils was a much greater concern than their minds."[75]

This purpose of schooling was a good fit with a society concerned about the problems growing in its cities and fearful that the stability of society was threatened by urban poverty and crime. It helped persuade those citizens who were opposed to taxation for the education of "other people's children," arguing that those children were potential criminals and that educating them would protect the taxpayer from becoming a victim of these people's crimes. Common schooling was pitched to the middle and upper classes as a way to maintain order and prevent violent uprising from the urban poor. The idea of schools as an economical way to fight crime was well expressed in a report by New York City Superintendent S. S. Randall:

---

[71]Twelfth Annual Report of the Board of Education of the City and County of New York, 1854

[72]Annual Report of the Superintendent of Public Instruction of the State of New York, 1867, p. 260

[73]Packard, 1969 (originally published 1866), p. 7

[74]Packard, 1969 (originally published 1866), p. 7

[75]Katz, 1987, p. 23

For every school house we build and fill with the youth of our
city, of every class and every grade, we reclaim from the ranks of
future pauperism and crime, and add to the available industry,
wealth and order of the community as many of our future citizens
as we thus provide with the means of instruction; and for every
hundred dollars we appropriate to this object, we not only save
thousands in future inevitable expenditures for the prison, the
almshouse and the gallows, but we augment the industrial,
social, civil, moral and religious resources of the community to an
incalculable extent.[76]

It is impossible to consider the argument favoring common
schooling as a source of moral education without acknowledging *who*
was believed to be in need of such an education. The 1830s and 1840s
were a time of massive immigration, particularly from Ireland and
Germany, which prompted a surge of nativism in the United States.
In that spirit, common schools were promoted as a way to create a
more homogeneous culture by Americanizing immigrant children.
Lawrence Cremin documented the way in which the Jacksonian period inspired a deep sense of American destiny and progress toward a
great future, but how these new immigrants were seen as a threat to
that progress. The loyalty of these immigrants—particularly the
Roman Catholics—was questioned to the point that fearful nativists
formed the Native American Party in the 1850s.[77] In the nativist
spirit, public schools were called on to teach immigrant children the
fundamental principles of American democracy. Additionally, the
idea of common schooling—that is, schooling that brought children of
many backgrounds together in the same schools—was promoted as
the way to cultivate in immigrant children a sense of American identity. Common school advocate Calvin Stowe expressed this view as
follows:

it is necessary that [immigrants] become substantially Anglo-
Americans. Let them be like grafts which become branches of the
parent stock; improve its fruit, and add to its beauty and its
vigor; and not like the parasitical misseltoe, which never incorpo-
rates itself with the trunk from which it derives its nourishment,
but exhausts its sap, withers its foliage, despoils it of its strength,

[76]Annual Report of the Superintendent of Public Instruction of the State of New
York, 1867, pp. 204-205

[77]Cremin, 1951, p. 24

and sooner or later by destroying its support, involves itself in ruin.[78]

Among the "principles of American democracy" that common schools were to promote were morality, obedience, and righteous and industrious living—qualities that many people feared were lacking in immigrant children. There existed widespread fears that immigrant children were depraved and susceptible to the corrupting influences of their families and communities, which were seen as rife with laziness, intemperance, and crime. One purpose of common schooling was to separate children from their families so as to steer them onto the *right* path. Additionally, some hoped that stubborn parents could be indirectly Americanized through their children. Popular textbooks contributed to the cause of Americanization by portraying the United States in such a way as to promote patriotism, often to the detriment of other cultures.

As can well be imagined, this aspect of common schooling was deeply problematic. To fulfill this function, educators had to teach children not to respect or emulate their parents. They drove a wedge between immigrant parents and children, creating a powerful sense of ambivalence on the part of those parents. On the one hand, these schools were ruining their relationships with their children; on the other hand, an education seemed to be the opportunity their children needed to live successful lives. Many immigrant groups responded by establishing private schools devoted to preserving their cultural heritage and passing it onto their children, but there were not enough of these schools to serve all such children. Consequently, most immigrant children continued to be educated in public schools.

In a different spirit, workingmen's organizations of the period promoted the cause of common schooling as a way to equalize opportunity for their children, thus shifting the character of agitation for common schooling. These newly enfranchised citizens criticized existing systems of education as undemocratic. They felt that the stigma and humiliation of charity schools effectively prevented poor children from being educated, and thus made academies and colleges (many of which received public funds) accessible only to wealthy children. They argued that the only way to eradicate aristocratic tendencies in American society was to provide a common education for all children.

---

[78]in Tyack, 1967, p. 149

Workingmen's groups were not generally critical of the social order per se, and they did not seek to take anything away from the upper classes. Rather, they wanted their children to have a fair shot at the kind of success that those of the upper classes enjoyed. To them, common schooling was not so much a way to control the masses of poor citizens as it was a means to personal economic advancement.[79]

In summary, then, arguments in favor of common schooling ranged from conservative fears—focused on maintaining social order in a time of intense social upheaval from urbanization, industrialization, and immigration—to more liberal hopes of equalizing opportunity and leveling class differences. There were also those who opposed free public education altogether. Outright opposition to common schooling came from diverse sources. For example, those who objected to the expenditure of public funds on education included both farmers and wealthy urbanites, both groups questioning the value they personally could derive from public schools. Some middle- and upper-class citizens feared that common schooling might create social unrest by educating people beyond their proper station in life.[80] Similarly, some proslavery Americans argued that if slavery were to be abolished, education by social class would be a necessity or there would be no effective laboring class.[81] Americans in northern states, although generally opposed to slavery, sometimes opposed common schools that defined *common* as *integrated*.

Some of the most intense opposition to common schooling came from Roman Catholics, who objected to the overtly Protestant tone of common school instruction. They engaged in sometimes violent protests, calling for offensive passages to be expunged from textbooks. The following is an example of a passage deemed anti-Catholic from an 1828 reader:

> Huss, John, a zealous reformer from Popery, who lived in Bohemia, towards the close of the fourteenth, and the beginning of the fifteenth centuries. He was bold and persevering; but at length, trusting himself to the deceitful Catholics, he was by them brought to trial, condemned as a heretic, and burnt at the stake.[82]

---

[79]Tyack, 1967

[80]Welter, 1971, p. xx

[81]Welter, 1971, p. 199

[82]in Welter, 1971, pp. 104-105

Catholics also objected to the use of the King James Bible in public schools. During the 1850s, state legislatures were bombarded with petitions from Catholic voters calling for the exclusion of this Bible from common schools. To some extent, the objections of Catholics were accommodated. Many Catholics also pressed for public funds for their own private schools, rather than seeking to change the Protestant tone of public schools.

So there were many objections to common schools. Moreover, even those who supported common schools did so for different—sometimes incompatible—reasons. More significant, however, is the fact that within a relatively short time, most Americans came to embrace the idea, and it quickly became the norm for children to be educated in the common schools in their communities.

Despite the growing importance ascribed to public education at the time, most schools were far from the romanticized image many people have today of the pristine, pleasant, one-room schoolhouse of yesteryear. Early common schools were often something of a disgrace. Reports of 1843 and 1845 of the school superintendents of the various counties of the State of New York (a state arguably in the forefront of the development of public education) included repeated accounts of deplorable conditions in many of their schools. These schools were typically one-room, framed-wood constructions placed on plots of land without much (or any) play space; the scarcity of cleared land often resulted in the placement of schools on swampy ground or close to a highway. Schools rarely had adequate ventilation, heat, or seating. Superintendents' reports sometimes estimated the quantity of oxygen consumed by the schools' occupants and marveled that people could stay alive in them. They frequently commented on the backless benches on which students sat, often much too high or too low for children, or on floorboards in such disrepair that children would fall through them. A full 65% of New York's common schools at that time had no outhouses, the facilities of the other schools being generally dilapidated.[83] In 1845, New York's Montgomery County superintendent's sentiments were representative of his colleagues' views:

> a due regard to truth compels me to say that a large number of
> our school houses are so unpleasantly located, so imperfectly and

---

[83]Annual Report of the Superintendent of Common Schools, State of New York, 1843 and 1845

inconveniently constructed, and so destitute of every appendage usually deemed necessary for comfort and convenience, as to be emphatically a disgrace to a civilized and refined people.[84]

The poor condition of common schools was not restricted to any particular region. Report after report by state and district superintendents found a sizable percentage of schools unfit for occupation. T. J. Connatty, a member of a Pennsylvania teachers' association visiting committee, had the following remarks about the schools he saw in Pennsylvania in 1853:

> In nine out of fifteen schools visited by me I have seen such an absence of order and methodical arrangement, such a confusion of text-books and classes, such a violation of the plainest principles of mental and physical hygiene, as to render it, to me, exceedingly problematical whether the evil would not overbalance the good accruing to scholars. Nay, I am convinced, that in some instances, the pupils received positive detriment from their school relations.[85]

A report from Massachusetts found the following:

> most of our schoolhouses are, year by year, growing worse. Few scholars would be attracted by an old, dilapidated building, destitute, externally, of paint, except perhaps a dingy coat of red, the playgrounds crowding so closely on the highway that it is impossible to distinguish one from the other; with no shade trees except perhaps the use of one borrowed of some neighbour across the way, with an interior begrimed with the smoke and dust of the last twenty years, rickety seats and desks, pannel-less and latchless doors, chairs broken and perhaps without backs, and everything offensive to the eye.[86]

Attendance at early common schools was typically not good. Early common school advocates generally opposed compulsory attendance laws, in part, because such laws seemed a state intrusion into parents' rights and, in part, because they hoped they could create schools whose atmosphere was inviting enough to avoid coerced attendance. Typically, a large majority of school-age children would

[84]Annual Report of the Superintendent of Common Schools, State of New York, 1845, p. 221

[85]*Pennsylvania School Journal*, vol. 1, no. 15 (March 1853), p. 363

[86]Packard, 1969 (originally published 1866), p. 146

be registered in school and attend for part of the year, but much lower percentages of children attended consistently throughout the school year. For example, in New York in 1843, of 601,765 children ages 5 to 16, 598,749 were registered in school, but fewer than half attended regularly.[87] In Massachusetts, out of 209,929 children ages 4 to 16 in 1848, 160,952 were registered in summer schools and 178,776 in winter schools. However, the average attendance for both summer and winter was about 40,000 less than the enrollment numbers.[88]

Poor attendance made it difficult to operate schools for a term of any substantial length. For example, according to an 1853 issue of the *Pennsylvania School Journal*, the average school term in Pennsylvania at the time was a mere 5 months, and state law required only 3 months.[89] F. A. Packard reported in his 1866 book, *The Daily Public School in the United States*, that although Ohio law in the 1860s required a minimum school term of 6 months, their average daily attendance of 57% resulted in many schools staying open only 4 or 5 months, and some as few as 3.[90]

It was popular for school administrators to blame parental indifference or ignorance for low attendance rates. For example, an 1853 letter to the editor of the *Pennsylvania School Journal* reads:

> It is a lamentable fact that very many of our citizens know so little about the manner in which our Common Schools should be conducted, that they cause a great part of the Teacher's labors to be in a manner lost. . . . By visiting the schools they might obtain considerable information, yet their visits are like angel's, "few and far between". . . . But whilst the cause of education has many trials and difficulties to overcome, yet we rejoice to know that it is making such rapid progress in its onward march.[91]

However, there was more involved than mere lack of interest. In rural areas, parents needed their older children to work on family farms, particularly in the summer. In cities, many children worked in

---

[87]Annual Report of the Superintendent of Common Schools, State of New York, 1843, p. 4

[88]Mann, 1848, p. 32

[89]Nineteenth annual report of the supt of common schools for the commonwealth of pa for the year ending june 1852

[90]Packard, 1969 (originally published 1866), p. 46

[91]Jackson, 1853, p. 433

factories. Children as young as 7 or 8 often worked long hours, making it impossible for them to attend school. One of the arguments advanced by workingmen's groups in favor of common schooling was linked to their push to limit child labor on the grounds that child factory workers were unable to derive the benefit from publicly funded schools. Even when the children of the urban poor were not employed outside the home, many of them had to forego an education so their parents could work. Common schools generally did not enroll young children, so many families relied on older children to care for infant siblings while parents worked.

Poor attendance made it difficult to keep good teachers. Given the brevity of school terms, teaching positions were not full-time jobs. Another issue affecting the high turnover in teachers was the common practice of *boarding around*, where teachers were housed by their students' families, spending a week or two with each over the course of the school year. These living arrangements did not make for a desirable lifestyle for long, so many schoolhouses would go through several teachers during a single school term.

Prior to the development of common schools, and in the early decades of common schooling, most teachers were men. Teaching was something they could do between harvests, or while on break from their own schooling. However, a variety of factors converged in the mid-19th century that led to the dominance of women in the teaching profession. First, in some areas, the Civil War depleted the supply of young men.[92] Second, industrialization and urbanization created exciting new career opportunities for young men, and they no longer needed or desired teaching positions. Third, the growth of common schooling and the rapid influx of immigrants created a need for a huge number of teachers. The supply of male teachers simply did not suffice; moreover, women could be paid a fraction of men's salaries, and so it was cost-effective to employ women as teachers.[93]

Around the time of the popularization of common schooling, then, came arguments that women were more appropriate for the teaching profession than men. It became customary to assert that young, unmarried women possessed the character traits befitting someone with the charge of moral instruction, and that the job would prepare them for their future mothering roles.

---

[92]Packard, 1969 (originally published 1866), p. 73

[93]Hoffman, 1981

It is hard to know how much the arguments in favor of female teachers stemmed from a genuine belief that women were well suited for the job and how much derived from simple necessity. In *Woman's "True" Profession: Voices from the History of Teaching*, Nancy Hoffman documents how women generally chose the profession for a variety of personal and professional reasons, but rarely out of a personal love of children or a desire to cultivate their maternal instincts.[94] That is not to say that these teachers did not like children, but that their purposes were not necessarily the ones ascribed to them by school administrators at the time.

The feminization of teaching was a double-edged sword of sorts for women and public education. It provided them with professional opportunities, but it also contributed to the standardization and deskilling of the profession, where women teachers in the new, graded school were subject to the strict control of the building principal, who was generally a man. In the words of David Tyack, "thus was stamped on mid-century America not only the graded school, but also the pedagogical harem."[95] Whatever the justification or impact of the shift, by 1880, the vast majority of teachers were women.

Another factor contributing to the feminization of teaching was the changing conception of childhood, which generated new ideas about pedagogy and curriculum. Declining infant mortality rates and conscious choices to limit the size of families contributed to a shift where parents' emotional bonds with their children intensified.[96] The softening of attitudes toward children was a good fit with the new educational ideas of Johann Heinrich Pestalozzi and Friedrich Froebel, both of whose works were popularized in the United States in the 19th century. Pestalozzi (1746–1827), born in Zurich, placed a great deal of emphasis on the home as the starting point of education and on the importance of the mother and maternal nurturing of the child. Pestalozzi emphasized sensory experience in the education of young children. He believed that all knowledge derives from sensory experience, and that children, therefore, should learn through direct experience, manipulation of objects, and activity. He was critical of the passivity of books, advocating instead the use of such materials as woodcuts, cardboard cutouts of shapes, maps, movable letters

---

[94]Hoffman, 1981

[95]Tyack, 1974, p. 45

[96]Katz, 1987, p. 11

pasted on cards, and counting with real objects. These ideas were known to American educators by the 1840s, becoming the basis of *object teaching,* where students used hands-on materials in class and carried into the 20th century through the visual education movement and the pedagogical progressive reformers.[97]

Like Pestalozzi, Froebel (1782–1852) emphasized activity and discouraged introducing young children to reading. He insisted on the educative value of play and designed a system of early childhood education for the physical, intellectual, and moral development of the child. Froebel's system began with the presentation to children of a series of objects that he called *gifts.* The gifts included such objects as colored balls, wooden shapes, interlocking cubes, and wire rings. The idea was that the children would improve their observation skills, understanding of the relationship between parts and wholes, and understanding of interconnections. After the gifts came *occupations,* which were activities like needlework, sewing, clay modeling, and paper folding, through which children would learn to work with solid forms and textures. Finally came songs, games, gardening, and other group activities, designed to involve children in making individual contributions to group efforts. In particular, each child was to tend a small garden, observing the parallels between its development and the child's. Like Pestalozzi, Froebel also believed that teachers should be women, embodying the ideals of motherhood.[98]

The kindergarten was brought from Germany to the United States in the 1850s by students and followers of Froebel. Although the kindergarten was promoted for children of all classes, and private, tuition-charging kindergartens were established, the main thrust of the kindergarten movement in the United States came in the form of charity kindergartens for children of the urban poor. Not unlike the arguments for charity schools, these kindergartens were promoted on the grounds that slum children were subject to damaging influences in their first 7 years before they entered primary school and could be saved from a future of ignorance, crime, and/or intemperance by going to kindergarten.[99]

There were certainly some kindergarten advocates who adopted a patronizing or derisive tone toward the children they

---

[97]Pestalozzi, 1977 (translated from 1898 edition)

[98]Lilley, 1967

[99]Ross, 1976

sought to educate. Some people argued that kindergartens should adapt children to the norms of middle-class society, teaching them manners and cultivating a sense of industry. However, kindergarten teachers (*kindergartners*) often had an intense involvement in local communities and earned a fair degree of trust from students' parents. Kindergartens generally met in the morning, and teachers would spend their afternoons conducting home visits and *mothers'* meetings, and arranging for social services for children and families. In *The Kindergarten Crusade: The Establishment of Preschool Education in the United States*, E. D. Ross likened the job of kindergartner to settlement worker. In fact, many settlement houses established kindergartens as a way to gain the trust of the community.[100]

Toward the end of the 19th century, kindergartens became a part of primary schools. Although they lost some of their characteristic qualities in the process—in particular, their emphasis on community work—they also influenced the character of primary instruction, bringing to it a deemphasis on stillness and obedience and a new emphasis on activity, songs, art, and physical education. They were also an important precursor to the child-centered progressive reforms of the early 20th century.

In summary, the 19th century brought with it large changes in who was to be educated, and who was to do the educating. There were also changes in the structure of schools, the curriculum to be taught, and the curricular materials to be used. One of the goals of the common school crusaders was to establish a graded system of instruction, where children would be taught in groups of similar age and ability. Such a system, they believed, would mobilize some of the more successful features of industrial operations in the quest to make education more effective and more efficient. Although graded schooling was nearly impossible in small, rural schools, it was adopted fairly quickly by schools in cities and towns large enough to organize themselves in graded fashion, so that by the 1860s most schools in such locations were graded schools.[101]

The move toward graded schools was aided by an 1848 invention of John Philbrick, known today as the *egg crate school*. He designed a four-story school with 12 classrooms and a large auditorium, where each teacher would be assigned to a single classroom and

---

[100]Ross, 1976, p. 45

[101]Tyack, 1974, p. 45

teach only students of a particular grade. The entire operation would be overseen by a building principal.[102] This general structure of schools was widely adopted and characterizes American public school buildings to the present day.

The desire to make education more uniform and systematic carried into curricular content and materials as well. Early common schooling focused on literacy and numeracy skills, with smatterings of subjects like geography and science. For the most part the curriculum and the textbook employed were one and the same; as David Tyack describes, most teaching was conducted by rote recitation, so "the textbook was in large degree the curriculum; children studied books rather than subjects."[103] The children of a particular region or even of a single school did not necessarily study the same books; a persistent problem was that teachers had to work with whatever books children happened to own and bring to school, so there was little uniformity to the texts in use. This lack of uniformity was addressed largely by the growth of a national textbook industry aided by the growth of railroads. With the expansion to regional or national markets, publishers built into their books, and therefore propagated, according to David Tyack, "a common denominator of thought and feeling"[104] that stressed the fulfillment of the American dream through perseverance, frugality, and obedience. They emerged at approximately the same time as an entire genre of rags-to-riches children's literature became popular, the best known stories of this genre being those by Horatio Alger.[105]

The most popular of the textbooks written in this style were the McGuffey readers, of which some 122,000,000 copies were sold between 1836 and 1920. Children in the McGuffey stories who exhibited those desirable traits of hard work, virtue, and restraint were handsomely rewarded, whereas transgressors tended to find themselves maimed or otherwise severely punished for their mistakes. For example, one reader includes the story of "The Passionate Boy," in which an ill-tempered boy tries to throw a hot iron at his brother, only to burn himself in the process. The iron "burnt his hand so much, that all the skin came off, to his fingers' ends, and he suffered

---

[102]Tyack, 1974, p. 44

[103]Tyack, 1967, p. 178

[104]Tyack, 1967, p. 182

[105]Cawelti, 1965

so much pain that he did not know what to do with himself."[106] In another story, a boy named George is given a dollar as a new year's present. He goes outside, throws a snowball, and accidentally breaks a window of a neighbor's house. He then decides to do the honest thing by telling the man in the house and giving the man his dollar. The man turns out to be a rich merchant, who is so impressed by George's honesty that he brings George to live and work with him, and George becomes rich.

In similar fashion, heroes of American history were elevated to a stature befitting a chosen nation. Lawrence Cremin describes this characteristic of the McGuffey readers as follows:

> George Washington, for example, was often compared to Moses. The events of American history were portrayed as developments in a holy design, Columbus having been guided by the hand of Providence and the Revolution having been brought to a successful conclusion by the Intervention of God. And the significance of American history was equated with "the divine scheme for moral government."[107]

Cremin borrows this last phrase from a McGuffey reader, illustrating the ties made in those readers between religious destiny and American history.

These texts also served the purpose of promoting a generalized Protestant faith. An 1844 advertisement for McGuffey's Eclectic Fourth Reader promised that the book was "decidedly moral and religious."[108] The Puritanism that had dominated earlier texts was gone, but not the religious focus. According to David Tyack, "God became less the fearsome Judge than the Divine Underwriter who insured that the virtues of hard work, truthfulness, obedience, sobriety, and kindness would pay off both here and in the hereafter."[109]

As the century progressed, textbooks increasingly portrayed the typical American as White, middle class, and Protestant and presented unfavorable stereotypes of other groups. Many contained good literature and provided children with an opportunity to escape to a fantasy world through reading. However, critics argue that the textbooks

---

[106]Tyack, 1967, p. 214

[107]Cremin, 1980, p. 73

[108]Tyack, 1967, p. 179

[109]Tyack, 1967, p. 179

also contributed to the social conditions that caused poor children to live under such harsh circumstances. Tyack argues that "textbooks so selected their themes as to disguise the real world, not to reveal it; to repress anxieties, not to confront them; to foster complacency among established groups rather than to include the dispossesed."[110]

Textbooks were not the only books available to children; many common schools established libraries to further promote literacy and learning. However, it is not clear that these libraries saw much use. Many reports of the first half of the 19th century point out that the books sat collecting dust or were never taken out of their original packages in the first place. Moreover, school administrators were not always pleased with some of the purchases made for those libraries, believing that many books, particularly novels, were *pernicious* (a favored adjective among school administrators) and had to be kept from children. Salvation was at stake here, according to the 1843 report of the New York State Superintendent of Common Schools:

> Like the vestal fire, the virgin purity of the juvenile mind should be scrupulously guarded and maintained; and no false appetites, superstitious fears, morbid sensibilities nor factitious desires should be allowed to germinate. The correct moral training of the youthful mind, is fraught with as high and holy a promise at least for this life, as was the annunciation of salvation, "peace on earth and good will to men." And hence, the vast importance, which in the estimation of the Superintendent is justly attached to the *kind of books* which are placed in the hands of susceptible and inexperienced childhood.[111]

Of particular concern, it seems, was a book called *Thaddeus of Warsaw*. Other books frequently deemed pernicious by school administrators and removed from school libraries were *Wonders of the Universe, The Pirate's Own Book, Arabian Night's Entertainment, The Vicar of Wakefield, Tales of the Ocean*, and *Captain Kyd*.

In addition to the use of books, common schools were sometimes equipped with other types of materials. Educational *apparatus,* as it was referred to in the 19th century, consisted primarily of blackboards, maps, globes, and perhaps some measuring devices. The

---

[110]Tyack, 1967, p. 184

[111]Annual Report of the Superintedent of Common Schools, State of New York, 1843, p. 12.

degree to which schools possessed these appurtenances varied widely, but even in those days educational apparatus was promoted by
administrators as a symbol of educational progress and was sometimes provided even when more basic needs were lacking. According
to the 1843 and 1845 New York State Superintendent's reports,
schools more often had blackboards than outhouses or adequate ventilation. District superintendents, while acknowledging the difficult
conditions under which teachers were working, also criticized them
for lacking interest in this important innovation or for using it poorly, and thus wasting taxpayers' money.

    It seems that blackboards were just beginning to find their
way into school houses in the 1840s and that their use was spotty.
Various superintendents in the State of New York expressed their
dismay in their 1843 reports over the slow acceptance of this new
resource:

> Black-boards are frequently found, where there has been no
> chalk in the school house for months together, and frequently
> where they have chalk, the blackboard is hardly used for the pur-
> pose of illustration or demonstration three times a year.[112]
> (Jefferson County)

> Another very common defect, I have discovered among teachers, is
> a lack of ingenuity or inclination, to exercise their schools upon the
> black-board. It is true, there are but few of our houses furnished
> with this useful and necessary appendage; but among those that
> *have* them, I find but *few* teachers who know *how* to *use* them. . . .
> It seems to be very hard also, to convince parents that the black-
> board is of any use whatever in a school house; and they are many
> times horror-stricken, when asked to tax themselves seventy-five
> cents to furnish an article, which I deem indispensable to a school
> room.[113] (Oswego County, emphasis in original text)

> [Blackboards] are in use in about one-half of the schools, but . . .
> are not employed to the extent or with that benefit they should
> be, owing to the ignorance of the teachers of the unlimited aid

---

[112]Annual Report of the Superintedent of Common Schools, State of New York,
1843, p. 12.

[113]Annual Report of the Superintedent of Common Schools, State of New York,
1843, p. 195.

which they afford in the instruction of youth, and of their proper
and timely uses.[114] (Schenectady County)

Many teachers cannot conceive what use can possibly be made of
a black-board, or any other apparatus, as they have no idea of
giving any explanations, and cannot believe that children ought
to be taught in any other way than from books, and in the most
antiquated manner.[115] (Tompkins County)

There were counties where blackboards were being produc-
tively used, most praised by the Livingston County superintendent in
his 1845 report (in this case, on the teaching of geography):

In this noble and interesting study, full as much, if not more than
in any other, oral instruction with a globe, and a skillful use of
the chalk and board, is highly useful, and, I might say, indispensable. . . . In our best schools the blackboard is used in geography
altogether. . . . Let a class be placed before the board, and let one
be requested to draw an outline of the country under consideration—another to locate its bays and gulf—a third, its rivers . . .
and the numerous years of study, now thrown away upon it, will
store the mind with a vast fund of useful knowledge. Mapping on
the board led to drawing on paper, and for the last year and a
half, very many of our schools have been engaged in that interesting exercise.[116]

In the same year, the Onondaga County Superintendent was
also pleased with his cutting-edge teachers:

The blackboard is just beginning to be appreciated by some of our
best teachers. It should be deemed an indispensable auxiliary in
teaching every branch of instruction, from the alphabet to the
most abstruse sciences. And with the blackboard . . . oral instruction should be universally adopted, as the main means of imparting instruction.[117]

[114]Annual Report of the Superintedent of Common Schools, State of New York,
1843, p. 305.

[115]Annual Report of the Superintedent of Common Schools, State of New York,
1843, p. 365.

[116]Annual Report of the Superintedent of Common Schools, State of New York,
1843, pp. 204–205.

[117]Annual Report of the Superintedent of Common Schools, State of New York,
1843, p. 258.

It took several decades for teachers to settle into using this innovation, but it appears that by the 1860s blackboards were a standard feature in common schools, and they saw plenty of use. Articles appeared in education publications over the next few decades describing how to make good use of blackboards. For example, W. Bertha Hintz, of Boston's Normal School, recommended using the blackboard to draw pictures to illustrate lessons in language, reading, geography, arithmetic, and morality:

> Blackboard sketches are particularly useful in general animal lessons, in which more animals would be needed than could be brought into the schoolroom. . . . In the little moral lesson the attention of the children can be better held, because they are helped by the blackboard sketches to picture conditions, scenes, and things more vividly, and when a conclusion is drawn, will feel it more keenly, and be more strongly impressed.[118]

It is also worth mentioning that the use of the blackboard was compatible with Pestalozzian pedagogy. He strongly advocated the use of slates by children because mistakes could easily be erased, and children would not become demoralized by their mistakes.[119] The increasing acceptance and use of the blackboard might also have a connection to the shift from solitary book study to whole-class instruction in graded classes. Blackboards were certainly used for individual work, but they were particularly good resources to support whole-class lectures and demonstrations.

So the common school movement was making substantial headway by the middle of the 18th century, having rallied many different kinds of people to its cause and developed a variety of methods and materials. However, escalating tensions leading to the Civil War slowed the progress of public education. Much of what had begun in the first few decades of the common school movement would not really come into its own until after the war was over.

---

[118]Hintz, 1888, pp. 114–116
[119]Pestalozzi, 1977, p. 197

COMMON SCHOOLS AFTER THE CIVIL WAR

By the time of the Civil War, although common schooling had flourished and improved unevenly, the general American consensus was
that progress was, indeed, tied to education—in particular, to public
education. The Civil War was a huge blow to Americans and their
belief in the inevitable progress and bright future of the nation. Still,
after the war, faith in progress and education were reaffirmed and
showed themselves in such places as explanations of the causes of the
war and hopes of emancipated slaves for a better future.

The northeast had led the nation in the establishment of
common schools. For a variety of reasons, including a different conception of the purpose of education and a dispersed population,
southern states did not generally have common schools before the
Civil War. Therefore, a popular northern explanation for the war was
that it was southerners' inadequate education that enabled savvy
leaders to rally citizens behind a cause they never would have supported had they been educated well enough to really understand the
issues. In a way, then, the catastrophe of civil war served as a reaffir-
mation of the value of common schooling for many northerners.[120]

Faith in education was also clear in the actions of emancipated slaves, who clamored for education. It showed itself in postwar
debates over whether the newly emancipated could exercise their
right to vote responsibly, being uneducated, or whether suffrage
rights should be withheld until they achieved some measure of literacy. These debates generally came down on the side of giving freed
slaves the right to vote, trusting that the education they were going
to receive would quickly bring them to a degree of learnedness adequate to ensure responsible citizenship.[121] Changes to southern
schooling during Reconstruction, although laden with conflict, also
had the ultimate effect of spreading common schooling throughout
the South, although sparse populations made it extremely difficult to
establish and maintain such schools.

One important issue to be resolved after the Civil War was
that of the rate-bill system. Public schools were still not entirely free
in some states. Instead, deficits in school budgets were made up by
charging parents a fee based on the number of children they had in

---

[120]Welter, 1971, p. xxvii
[121]Welter, 1971, p. 216

school and the number of days attended. Many parents simply stopped sending their children to school on whatever day in the term they would otherwise have to start paying for their children to attend.[122] In other words, common schools still had an air of pauper schools about them. By the end of the 1860s, the rate-bill system had been abolished in all states that had once employed it.

The question of compulsory education moved to the forefront after the Civil War. Many people remained opposed to the idea, which at the time seemed a terribly undemocratic intrusion of the state into family life. With a regular attendance rate of about 40% in 1867, the New York State Superintendent wrote "that invitation and persuasion are more in accordance with the spirit of republican institutions than the exercise of compulsory powers," arguing that "if schools were more attractive, and teachers more skilled and cheerful, children would voluntarily attend."[123] Perkinson points out that, "only after the Civil War, when the rise of the cities created fears for the stability of society, do we find any widespread effort to secure effective compulsory education laws."[124]

Many states had enacted compulsory attendance laws, which included restrictions on child labor, but such laws were rarely enforced. Gradually, however, these laws were amended to further limit child labor, both by age of the child and the number of hours children could work, and to require that children be educated—and prove a degree of literacy—before they could be permitted to work. The education requirement addressed concerns about social stability because without it unemployed children might spend their days on the streets engaging in criminal or otherwise disruptive acts. By the beginning of the 20th century, compulsory attendance laws were much stricter and more often enforced than they had been in the past. That is not to say that they were always strictly enforced, but there was significant movement in that direction.

Another feature of education in the latter half of the century was a proliferation of educational gadgets, devices, and accessories, such as writing tablets, anatomical charts and paper models, stencils, relief maps, slate globes (to draw on), microscopes, and ther-

---

[122]Packard, 1969 (Orginal publication 1866)

[123]Annual Report of the Superintedent of Common Schools, State of New York, 1867, p. 29

[124]Perkinson, 1968, p. 77

mometers. For example, the February 2, 1888, issue of the *Journal of Education* described a "truly ingenious device" to facilitate the teaching of reading; it was a frame, 2 feet square, with three apertures, into each of which a strip of letters could be inserted, permitting the user to spell words. The advantages, according to this author, were that only one word at a time could be shown, unlike wall charts or primers, and the teacher was freed from the job of writing many words on the blackboard.[125] A variety of devices of this sort appeared in education journals of this era, promoting their value in classroom instruction. A particularly interesting ad appeared in the October 11, 1888, issue of the *Journal of Education* for the Kodak camera, promising "a new phase of photography" with this new $25 camera that "may be used by anybody." Although cameras were not widely used by teachers, new photographic and lithographic techniques of this time made various types of art reproductions and other pictures available for school use.

The latter decades of the 19th century were a time of increasing organization and systematization of education—of districts, curriculum, teacher preparation and certification, and classroom methods and materials. These new educational gadgets were in keeping with the interest of schoolmen to streamline and standardize education, and to apply the methods of industry and business to make education more efficient.

The increasing variety of educational materials also may have been inspired by the popularity of the pedagogies of Pestalozzi and Froebel, both of whom deemphasized the book in favor of other kinds of curricular materials. Their stress on sensory experience and manipulation of concrete objects may have inspired an interest in expanding educational resources beyond books. As the 19th century progressed, teachers made increasing use of various nonprint media and materials with their students with the popularization of object teaching, which was brought to the United States in the 1860s and came to dominate teacher preparation in normal schools.[126]

Although fairly short lived, popularization of the theories of Johann Friedrich Herbart also might have contributed to an interest in the use of educational technologies in the late 19th century. He advocated a more scientific approach to education, encouraging the

[125]Klemm, 1888, p. 70

[126]Perkinson, 1968, p. 77

careful sequencing of instruction so as to permit students to relate new ideas to old and assimilate them into their understanding.[127] John Dewey argued that Herbart's main contribution "lay in taking the work of teaching out of the region of routine and accident."[128] In that spirit, apparatus designed to standardize or systematize the teaching process might have seemed in keeping with trends in learning theory at the time.

By the turn of the century, much of what is associated with public education to the present day, particularly at the elementary level, was already in place. However, the early 20th century was a time of dramatic changes in public education, as school districts expanded through centralization, student enrollments swelled, and the number of years spent in school increased.

PUBLIC EDUCATION IN THE 20TH CENTURY

A dominant strand of education reform at the turn of the century was centralization and standardization. From the 1890s to the 1920s, urban elites (such as businessmen and educational administrators) sought to centralize school control. They were met with hostility by local community members, who wanted to retain control over their schools. David Tyack describes the conflict as follows:

> Community control of schools became anathema to many of the educational reformers of 1900, like other familiar features of the country school: nongraded primary education, instruction of younger children by older, flexible scheduling, and a lack of bureaucratic buffers between teacher and patrons.[129]

These reformers sought to load school boards with successful businessmen, who they believed would run schools efficiently and act dispassionately in the best interests of the community. They also promoted the consolidation and centralization of school districts, believing that the same methods that had worked well for the corporate world would work well for schools. In the late 1890s, New York,

---

[127]Perkinson, 1968

[128]Dewey, 1916, p. 83

[129]Tyack, 1974, p. 10

Baltimore, and St. Louis centralized their schools, followed by many
other metropolitan areas in the first two decades of the 20th century.

    The turn of the century marked the substantial growth of
the secondary school population, which rose from 360,000 in 1890 to
2,500,000 in 1920. The first high school was established in Boston in
1821; gradually the idea spread to other states. Many people resisted the idea of tax-funded public high schools, which seemed beyond
the level of education a community had the obligation to provide free
to all children. However, the 1874 "Kalamazoo decision," in which
the people of Kalamazoo sued their village for establishing a public
high school, helped establish support for high schools. In this decision, Michigan Supreme Court Justice Thomas M. Cooley expressed
the view that the state constitution's provision for free schools
included high schools. His decision promoted high schools both for
practical and classical, or college-prep, education, helping to establish the idea of the high school as a rung in the educational ladder
leading to college.

    Most public high schools originated in local academies, which
were generally established out of a sense of local pride; they were
good for a town's image. Academies varied widely in their character
and academic offerings. Colleges and universities at the time primarily drew from local communities for their students, so the lack of uniformity of the academies was not particularly problematic. However,
as colleges began to look farther from their immediate surroundings
for students, they increasingly sought control over secondary education through new entrance exams and forms of accreditation.[130] In
the process, the conception of high school as a rung in a continuous
educational ladder from primary school to college was strengthened.

    This conception of the high school was further promoted by
the report of the "Committee of Ten," a group formed by the National
Education Association in 1892 and chaired by Harvard president
Charles Eliot. At issue was the lack of uniformity of college admis-
sion requirements. The Committee recommended that colleges have
flexible admissions requirements and accept a high school education
consisting of 16 units of 120 classroom hours (courses offered five
periods weekly for a full academic year) in one subject each. These
units came to be known as *Carnegie units* because the Carnegie foun-

---

[130]Tyack, 1967, p. 10

dation funded the work of the Committee of Ten. The Carnegie Foundation provided an incentive to colleges and universities who accepted this plan by making such acceptance one of the conditions a college had to meet for its retiring faculty to qualify for pensions from the Foundation. Shortly after 1909, the year in which the Carnegie Foundation began funding the Committee of Ten's work, most high schools had adopted the Carnegie unit,[131] thus standardizing many aspects of high school education nationwide.

The Committee of Ten advocated what has come to be known as a *humanist* model of education, advocating a rigorous liberal arts education for all students, not just those bound for college. They stressed the importance of mental discipline, in line with the theories of *faculty psychology*, summarized by education scholar Elliot Eisner as follows:

> faculty psychologists viewed the brain as consisting of a variety of intellectual faculties. These faculties, they held, could be strengthened if exercised in appropriate ways with particular subject matters. Once strengthened, the faculties could be used in any area of human activity to which they were applicable. Thus, if the important faculties could be identified and if methods of strengthening them developed, the school could concentrate on this task and expect general intellectual excellence as a result.[132]

In keeping with this view of learning, the Committee of Ten recommended an abstract, verbal curriculum including foreign languages, mathematics, physical geography, botany, geology, physics, anatomy, English, and history.

The Committee of Ten's recommendations were made at a time of intense debate about what the curriculum should include. Educators grappled with the question of what constitutes a democratic education—the same education for all students or different experiences tailored to children's particular interests, abilities, or limitations?

Some people, like Eliot and the members of the Committee of Ten, believed that the same education that would prepare a student for college would prepare that student for life, and so all children should receive a broad liberal education. That was not to say that all

---

[131]Perkinson, 1968, pp. 135–137

[132]Eisner, 1997, p. 69

students should take precisely the same classes. Eliot is perhaps best known for introducing the elective system to Harvard during his presidency and for advocating similar changes in high schools. However, Eliot and other humanists focused on the liberal arts and sciences, not on vocational education or courses, which wandered too far from traditional academic disciplines.

Other school reformers saw the humanists as out of joint with the times, believing that the rapidly changing world in which they were living demanded dramatic changes in the curriculum. The criticisms of these reformers were part of the larger Progressive movement, which called for increased public participation in politics and government, and reasserted the need for schools to play a central role in preparing Americans for civic participation.

Progressive education reformers were by no means a uniform lot. What they shared was the view that rapid change, particularly technological change, was altering the character of modern life in ways that demanded changes in schools. They recognized the increasing interconnectedness of the world; progressive reformer Elwood Cubberley wrote in 1909 that "the world has become very much smaller than it used to be, and its parts have become interdependent to an extent never known before."[133] They also shared the belief that public education was going to have to assume many responsibilities formerly addressed by other people or institutions.

Beyond the recognition that change was needed, the different strands of progressive education reform varied widely. One group, which is often referred to as the *administrative progressives* (or *social efficiency experts*), were the reformers who sought to centralize school districts and put school boards under the control of businessmen and urban elites. They focused on the application of Frederick Taylor's newly popularized principles of scientific management to education and the use of newly developed methods of intelligence testing to sort and track students. Impressed by the efficiency of industrial operations and centralized bureaucratic structures, they sought to apply the methods of industry to education. They promoted what they called *scientific curriculum making*, developed by John Franklin Bobbitt and W.W. Charters among others. Scientific curriculum making borrowed from Taylorism in the way it focused on systematizing the curriculum through the statement of clear educational objectives,

---

[133]Cubberley, 1909, pp. 56–57

the breaking down of the material to be learned into small components, and the careful sequencing of instruction so as to maximize
and streamline learning. These reformers sought to eliminate waste
from the curriculum, sorting human capital by ability and probable
future occupation, and providing precisely the education required for
those occupations. They were hugely successful in their endeavors. In
The Struggle for the American Curriculum, 1893–1958, H. M.
Kliebard describes this time in the history of education as "a veritable orgy of efficiency."[134]

The efficiency movement was aided by several other developments of this period. Educational psychologist Edward Lee
Thorndike popularized the idea of *connectionism,* imagining the mind
to be a kind of machine with millions of tiny circuits that needed to
be properly connected up. He challenged faculty psychology by arguing that intelligence was fairly fixed—that a student's intellect was
improved not by any particular curriculum, but by that person's
native intelligence. Moreover, his research suggested that what students learned in the context of one discipline did not transfer to other
contexts. In that case, there was little reason to provide everyone
with a liberal education designed to teach students how to think
because it seemed people could not "learn how to learn"; instead, they
should receive training in the specific skills they would require for
the life they were likely to live. As Eisner describes, "If Thorndike
was right, if transfer was limited, it seemed reasonable to encourage
the teacher to teach for particular outcomes and to construct curriculums only after specific objectives had been identified."[135] Thorndike's
theories were used to legitimize the administrative progressives'
push for curriculum revision.

Another development aiding the efficiency movement was the
proliferation of intelligence testing popularized during World War I
as a way to facilitate the training of soldiers. Efficiency advocates
embraced intelligence testing as a scientific system of mental measurement that would effectively sort students by ability.
Furthermore, it helped justify such sorting by providing proof that
students' destinies had been properly determined according to their
abilities, and that the American ideal of individual opportunity was
still viable.

---

[134]Kliebard, 1995, p. 81

[135]Eisner, 1997, p. 70

A big issue for educators in the first decades of the 20th century, and one addressed in a particular way by the administrative progressives, was a new wave of immigrants arriving in record numbers from the Mediterranean and eastern Europe. Recent developments in intelligence testing had produced scientific evidence that people of these backgrounds were genetically inferior, prompting a new surge of nativism and a renewed fervor to educate and Americanize the children of these immigrants. Administrative progressive Ellwood Cubberley expressed a popular sentiment as follows:

> These southern and eastern Europeans are of a very different type from the north Europeans who preceded them. . . . Their coming has served to dilute tremendously our national stock, and to corrupt our civic life. . . . Everywhere these people tend to settle in groups or settlements, and to set up here their national manners, customs, and observances. Our task is to break up these groups or settlements, to assimilate and amalgamate these people as part of our American race, and to implant in their children, so far as can be done, the Anglo-Saxon conception of righteousness, law and order, and popular government . . . [136]

This wave of immigration provoked tremendous fear among people of the middle and upper classes that their way of life was in danger. They were afraid of these newcomers, who they believed had weak family structures and lacked restraint, virtue, industry, and temperance. The immigration acts of 1921 and 1924, establishing immigration quotas, were particularly aimed at immigrants from eastern and southern Europe.

Administrative progressives argued that schools needed to focus on becoming more organized and efficient to deal with growing immigrant populations. Socializing these children, they argued, would require systematic effort. They advocated an orderly, tightly structured, factory-like school atmosphere to train these children to be orderly, punctual, and suitable for factory work. David Tyack describes how schoolmen "talked more in terms borrowed from business and social science. . . . They argued that the structure of schools should correspond with that in large corporations."[137] Their push to centralize school districts also came largely out of a distrust of immi-

---

[136]Cubberley, 1909, pp. 56–57

[137]Tyack, 1974, pp. 75–76

grants and local control of schools by immigrants. When school boards were elected by citywide voting, it was easier to secure the election of White, middle-class, Protestant elites who might not receive many votes in the district they were going to serve, but whose counterparts in other districts would surely elect them.[138]

The administrative progressives' conception of a democratic education was one with a differentiated curriculum that provided students with the specific kind of knowledge or skills they would need for the future occupation they were most likely to have. Elwood Cubberley promoted this idea as follows:

> Our city schools will soon be forced to give up the exceedingly democratic idea that all are equal, and that our society is devoid of classes . . . and to begin a specialization of educational effort along many new lines in an attempt better to adapt the school to the needs of these many classes in the city life.[139]

Administrative progressives were particularly enthusiastic supporters of vocational education, which emerged early in the 20th century as schools were increasingly seen as existing primarily for job preparation. It was in this same period that the junior high school was created as a new institution for a newly conceived category of life: adolescence. It was in this life stage that vocational tracking was to take place, and the junior high school was assigned that responsibility. Meanwhile, it was hoped that the social aspects of secondary education would contribute to students' sense of community and group loyalty, preparing them to be good workers.

The social efficiency orientation was heavily criticized by reformers taking other approaches to progressive education most particularly because it sought to adapt people to a society that, as it stood, did not always function in their best interests. However, the instability of the times went a long way toward swaying citizens to prefer the stability offered by this orientation than the upheaval demanded by those reformers with large-scale social criticism and change in mind.

Another strand of progressive education reform was that of the developmentalists, led by G. Stanley Hall, a pioneer in adolescent psychology. A leader of the child-study movement, Hall is credited

---

[138]Nasaw, 1979, p. 109

[139]Spring, 1986, p. 201

with the invention or discovery of adolescence. He promoted the junior high school as a place to address the particular needs of adolescents, who were newly regarded as having sexual and social drives different from younger and older children. Joel Spring describes how it became popular to conceive of adolescence as the time when children's impulses

> could be captured and directed toward socially useful projects such as helping the poor, the community, or the nation. . . . On the other hand, when youth of the 1920s adopted the style of the Jazz Age, the popular press warned of the imminent collapse of civilization.[140]

The American public was preoccupied with concerns about juvenile delinquency and sought to channel the excessive sexual and destructive energies of adolescents into productive, wholesome activities. Responsibility for containing adolescent impulses was assigned to the junior high school—an institution specifically designed with adolescents in mind. In agreement with the administrative progressives, Hall believed that the junior high school should direct students on different paths depending on their probable future occupations. In the process, it was hoped that teenagers' threat to social stability would be minimized by directing their attention in socially useful ways.

Then there were the progressive reformers that most people think of when the term *progressive* is used, who are referred to here as *pedagogical progressives*, or *child-centered progressives*. Their orientation derives from Hall and the child-study movement in the sense that they stressed the importance of providing developmentally appropriate experiences for children and starting from children's interests and questions. In other ways, child-centered progressivism traces back to John Dewey, who argued that education should be meaningful to children in the present, not merely preparation for the future. He envisioned the school as a miniature community, where children would learn in a social context and in the context of activities relevant to that community. Dewey was critical of the rigid separation of disciplines, arguing that specific skills like reading or math should be learned as outgrowths of meaningful activities, not as intellectual exercises for their own sake. In line with his philosophy of instrumentalism, an outgrowth of pragmatism, Dewey also

---

[140]Spring, 1986, p. 201

believed that an important purpose of education was the improvement of society—that intellectual development would lead to meaningful social action. These ideas ran counter to those of the efficiency advocates, particularly their emphasis on standardization, precision in instruction and testing, and maintenance of the status quo.

Many people embraced progressive education as Dewey defined it, although they often misunderstood Dewey and his intentions. *Progressive* came to be applied to all kinds of ideas and practices, many of which were misinterpretations or oversimplifications of Dewey's theories. Dewey criticized what child-centered progressivism became in the 1920s, when it was largely depoliticized by shedding all concern for schools acting as agents of social change. In the 1930s, a change of leadership, coupled with a dramatic shift in the political sensibilities of Americans, restored some of the political activism of this form of progressive education reform. It was in this era that *social meliorists*, the most prominent being George S. Counts, brought to progressive education a scathing critique of capitalism and its injustices. This orientation found an audience in disillusioned 1930s Americans, leading to the huge popularity and widespread adoption of the social studies textbooks written by Harold Rugg, containing clear anticapitalist themes. However, American involvement in World War II made such criticism seem unpatriotic, and the postwar Red Scare was directed heavily toward this style of progressive education. By the 1950s, progressive education was under severe attack, blamed for nearly everything that was believed to be wrong with American public education.

Meanwhile, high school enrollments were bulging. During the Depression era, new legislation was passed to restrict child labor and remove young people from the labor market. At the same time, new efforts were made to make high school seem appealing to teenagers so they would stay in school and leave jobs open for adults. In that spirit, the curriculum of high schools was expanded in the hope of lowering the dropout rate. In the 1929-1930 school year, 51.3% of Americans ages 14 to 17 were enrolled in secondary schools; by 1939 to 1940, that percentage had risen to 73.3.

The expanded curriculum was part of a new model for the comprehensive high school, the model for which derived from the 1918 report from the National Education Association on *The Cardinal Principles of Secondary Education*. This report promoted a large high school with a differentiated curriculum that included sub-

jects outside the traditional academic disciplines in the hope of satisfying the needs of those students who were neither college-bound nor
in a vocational track. The comprehensive high school was to offer the
best of both worlds in education, in the sense that students could
receive an education tailored to their needs, but the school would
retain its democratic orientation by bringing different tracks of students together for extracurricular and nonacademic activities.[141]

A post-World War II addition to the comprehensive high
school, and to the attempt to keep teenagers in school appeared in
the form of *life-adjustment education*, promoted by Charles Prosser
in a 1945 report to the U.S. Office of Education. Prosser's report
became most famous for his argument that the 20% of American students who were in college-preparatory tracks and the 20% in vocational tracks were adequately served by their high schools, but that a
full 60% of students were being neglected by a curriculum that had
little to offer them. Life-adjustment education sought to correct this
deficiency by responding to those students' *felt needs*, offering courses
in subjects that had direct application to their life experiences.[142]

At the same time as these changes were taking place in 20th
century public education, the vast new media industries of film and
radio were growing. These media attracted the attention of education
reformers, who often found film and radio to be compatible with their
ideas about how schools should change. For example, film and radio
were both promoted, in part, for their potential to make instruction
more efficient. Advocates argued that these media would distribute
the best teachers to all students, improve the skills of classroom
teachers, and transmit the curriculum more quickly and accurately
than conventional instruction. Both could be used to centralize and
standardize the curriculum.

Film and radio were also promoted by child-centered progressives. Their sensory appeal was said to capture students' interest and
increase motivation. They could be used to connect children to the
world outside the classroom, bringing experts and important events
to children of all geographic regions. They were compatible with the
principles of life adjustment education in that they presented information differently—and perhaps more appealingly—than traditional
texts.

---

[141]Kliebard, 1995

[142]Kliebard, 1995

Each of these media has an entire chapter devoted to it in this book, so the point here is not to describe in detail the ways in which each was applied to education, or how successful those applications were. For the moment, suffice it to say that new media were seen as a match with agendas for school reform and were brought into schools in the context of those agendas. Similarly, they tended to vanish from schools as the agendas they were introduced to support were replaced by new ideas about what was wrong with schools and what needed to be done.

A major shift in educational policy took place after World War II, when cold war anxieties, coupled with intense school over-crowding and teacher shortages, dominated the rhetoric of school reform. As the United States lagged behind the Soviet Union in the space race, comparisons were often made between American and Soviet education. American schools were criticized for being anti-intellectual, for having erred on the side of vocational preparation and neglecting serious academic training, and, according to H. M. Kliebard, "the 1950s became a period of criticism of American education unequaled in modern times."[143] Critics like Arthur Bestor and Mortimer Smith slammed progressive education, accusing it of being *regressive* instead. They condemned life-adjustment education for dumbing down all of education and leading to the abandonment of serious intellectual inquiry and activity in schools. They advocated the return to traditional liberal education, especially for the most gifted students, who were called on in particular to become engineers, mathematicians, and researchers.

Part of the hostility toward progressivism (which by this time had become the standard way to refer to child-centered progressivism) was due to the fact that some of its leaders, particularly the social meliorists, were known or suspected communists. They had called for schools to be agents of change and critics of capitalism and the social inequities it produced. Dewey had visited the Soviet Union and reported back that he liked some of what he saw in their schools. At a time when citizens' groups were fighting to purge schools of all traces of communist sympathy, the idea that the philosophies of these reformers be practiced in schools was intolerable.

The cold war era marked the entry of the federal government into educational policy to an unprecedented degree. The National

---

[143]Kliebard, 1995, p. 22

Science Foundation (NSF) was created in 1950 to spearhead massive curriculum revision, particularly in math and science, and the National Defense Education Act (NDEA) of 1958 provided funds for improving instruction in math, science, and foreign languages. In *The Sorting Machine Revisited: National Educational Policy Since 1945*, Joel Spring argues that the goal of such initiatives as the NSF and NDEA was "to align the curriculum of the public schools with the needs of American foreign policy . . . for the purpose of educating more scientists and engineers to compete in the military weapons race with the Soviet Union."[144]

Meanwhile schools' failure to integrate after the 1954 *Brown v. the Board of Education of Topeka, Kansas* decision was a glaring reminder of the racial injustice in American society. Criticisms of schools as discriminatory institutions arose in large part from the civil rights movement, but also in relation to the cold war climate, in the sense that it was increasingly difficult to promote the virtues of America to the world when such obvious inequities existed, were sanctioned by law, and were being viewed on television in the United States and abroad. Schools were slow to integrate until the passage of both the Civil Rights Act of 1964 and the Elementary and Secondary Education Act (ESEA) of 1965. The former required the withholding of federal funds from schools that failed to abide by the mandates of civil rights legislation, and the latter provided the funds that schools would not want withheld from them.

The ESEA was framed in the new spirit of compensatory education, which was meant to address the educational needs of culturally deprived children by supplementing their education in ways that would make them competitive with more affluent children. The hope was to break the cycle of poverty for the underprivileged by getting them started in school on an equal footing with other children. The Economic Opportunity Act of 1964 established the Head Start program for poor preschoolers, and the Elementary and Secondary Education Act of 1965 included provisions for improving the education of children living in poverty.

Audiovisual media were promoted for schools in line with the spirit of both cold war preparedness and compensatory education. Television was promoted primarily as a way to address the overcrowding of schools that was seen as a threat to national security (in

---

[144]Spring, 1989, p. vii

that American children were believed to be receiving a substandard education). Many instructional TV projects were conducted in the hope of spreading out master teachers to more students and bringing subject area specialists to students and teachers alike. In an age when it was believed that students had far more to learn than earlier generations, television seemed to offer the promise of delivering instruction more efficiently. Moreover, as knowledge in a field changed, TV lessons could be changed simply by changing the script, thus revising the curriculum much more rapidly (if not more effectively) than through conventional instruction.

A major shift took place in the application of new technology to instruction with the development of automated systems of instruction in the 1950s and 1960s. Programmed texts, teaching machines, and (slightly later) computer-assisted instruction were all created by psychological researchers who were trying to understand the process of human learning, which, at the time, was explained primarily by the principles of behaviorism. Behaviorist theories were designed into these machines and, through the machines, applied to instruction. In other words, these educational technologies differed from earlier ones in that they actually embodied dominant learning theories of the age, where earlier media had simply been applied to the pedagogical styles of their time.

Like television, automated instruction was promoted in line with both cold war school reform and compensatory education. Automated instruction was particularly appropriate for cold war reform agendas because it originated in military research laboratories and was designed as part of larger efforts to apply the military systems approach to education. It seemed especially good for instruction in the key subjects of math, science, and foreign languages, and its focus on individualizing instruction was a good match with the interest in paying special attention to separating out talented youth and allowing them to work at an accelerated pace. In the spirit of compensatory education, automated instruction was promoted for its capacity to allow slower learners from disadvantaged backgrounds work at their own pace from a patient, nonjudgmental teacher. Additionally, given that automated instructional programs were designed so as to minimize student errors, the hope was that all students would achieve mastery of subjects learned through automated systems, thus equalizing learning to an unprecedented degree.

Both instructional television and automated instruction
declined in popularity as the tone of educational policy shifted once
again—this time, with a shift back to the kind of progressive pedagogy promoted by Dewey and the child-centered reformers. A wide
variety of new forms of school organization were experimented with
in this period, all sharing the general belief that traditional schooling
was too authoritarian and that the traditional curriculum neither
acknowledged the needs or interests of learners nor permitted students to learn through the processes of inquiry and discovery. Free,
open, and alternative schools were all promoted in this period as a
response against the rigidity and bureaucracy of postwar education.

Some of the neoprogressive reformers of the 1960s were also
media scholars, bringing critiques of contemporary media into school
reform movements. In particular, Teachers College professor Louis
Forsdale took an interest in the work of Canadian scholar Marshall
McLuhan, inviting him to New York in 1955 to present his work at a
Teachers College seminar on media and education. From there,
McLuhan's controversial views attracted the attention of the
National Council of Teachers of English (NCTE), which, according to
McLuhan biographer Philip Marchand, "remained one of McLuhan's
chief platforms"[145] for many years. McLuhan also became known to
the National Association of Educational Broadcasters (NAEB)
through its president, University of Illinois professor Harry Skornia,
who invited McLuhan to be the keynote speaker at the NAEB's annual convention in 1958. In 1959, the NAEB commissioned McLuhan to
develop an 11th-grade media literacy curriculum, funded by the
National Defense Education Act. The NAEB wished this curriculum
to provide teachers and students "familiarity with the various and
often contradictory qualities and effects of media."[146]

What McLuhan produced baffled those who had commissioned the project. His perspectives on media were unlike any that
had preceded him. Although his NAEB report "caused no great
stir,"[147] according to Marchand, it was significant in that the ideas in
the report became the basis of two of McLuhan's best-known books:
The Gutenberg Galaxy: The Making of Typographic Man (1962) and
Understanding Media: The Extensions of Man (1967). McLuhan is

---

[145]Marchand, 1998, p. 143

[146]Marchand, 1998, p. 147

[147]Marchand, 1998, p. 160

perhaps best known for pointing out that electronic media were challenging the ways of knowing and the habits of mind characterized by print media. From there, he called on schools to acknowledge that the world in which students were immersed was no longer one dominated by print.[148] In *Understanding Media*, McLuhan argued:

> The young today live mythically and in depth. But they encounter instruction in situations organized by means of classified information—subjects are unrelated, they are visually conceived in terms of a blueprint. Many of our institutions suppress all the natural direct experience of youth, who respond with untaught delight to the poetry and the beauty of the new technological environment, the environment of popular culture. It could be their door to all past achievement if studied as an active (and not necessarily benign) force.[149]

Although McLuhan's ideas baffled many, they captured the imagination of Teachers College graduate students Neil Postman and Charles Weingartner, who came to know him through Professor Forsdale. Postman's first book, *Television and the Teaching of English* (1961), had been commissioned by the NCTE Committee on the Study of Television, for which Forsdale was chairman. In it he argued for school reform to respond to changes in the media environment, referring to some of the same major shifts in media history that McLuhan emphasized. Later in the 1960s, Postman and Weingartner drew on McLuhan's work in their popular book, *Teaching as a Subversive Activity*. They used McLuhan's concept of rearview thinking to describe the ways in which schools were preparing students to function in a media environment that no longer existed. The new media environment, they argued, required "a whole new repertoire of survival strategies,"[150] which meant that a whole new kind of education was needed. They also borrowed McLuhan's characterization of media as environments that act on their inhabitants in unnoticed ways, applying that idea to the ways in which schools have a hidden curriculum that structures what can be learned, and how it will be learned, more powerfully than any overt curriculum or curricular goals. In particular, they criticized the structure of conventional

---

[148]McLuhan, 1962

[149]McLuhan, 1967, p. 100

[150]Postman and Weingartner, 1969, p. 7

schooling for working against the cultivation of the inquiry method, which they believed was the most important form of thinking to encourage in students.

The school experiments of the 1960s—media related or otherwise—were relatively short lived. New research was suggesting that compensatory education was not working, and conservative reformers voiced concern that the effort to equalize education had only watered it down and lowered academic standards and achievement. This swing in educational policy produced the Back to Basics movement of the 1970s, when the focus of schools shifted back to basic skills and core academics. That movement set the stage for early 1980s attacks on schools, the most famous of which came in the form of the report *A Nation at Risk: The Imperative for Educational Reform*. This report stated plainly that "the educational foundations of our society are presently being eroded by a rising tide of mediocrity that threatens our very future as a Nation and a people."[151] The report threatened that "our once unchallenged preeminence in commerce, industry, science, and technological innovation is being overtaken by competitors throughout the world. . . . We have, in effect, been committing an act of unthinking, unilateral educational disarmament."[152] The recommendations of the report are apparent in a variety of reform efforts since its publication, including the focus on holding schools accountable for student achievement, increased involvement of business and industry in public education, and aggressive implementation of information technology into schools.

In the 1990s, a large thrust of education reform was for the development of detailed learning standards at the local, state, national, and international levels. Six national education goals came out of a 1989 meeting of governors and other political leaders, and the National Education Goals Panel (NEGP) was created in 1990 to monitor national progress toward meeting those goals. Shortly thereafter, President Bush promoted "America 2000," legislation identifying education goals to be met by the year 2000, which was passed into law in 1994, under President Clinton, as the "Goals 2000: Education America Act." This law supported the development of state learning standards, assessments aligned to those standards, and mechanisms for holding schools accountable for meeting those stan-

---

[151]National Commission on Excellence in Education, 1983, p. 5

[152]National Commission on Excellence in Education, 1983, p. 5

dards. Since that time, standards-based reform and its associated methods of accountability have dominated the rhetoric of education reform. The standards movement is not without its critics, nor is it the only set of ideas about school reform in circulation. However, it is the language of the standards movement that is most fluently spoken by politicians and educational policymakers at the present time.

While schools were going back to basics and moving toward the development of learning standards, changes in computer media were taking place as well. In the late 1970s and early 1980s, the push for computer literacy spread through schools, sometimes suggesting that along with the new focus on the old basics should come the addition of this *new basic.* Seymour Papert's *microworld* program, *Logo,* also became popular in schools, providing a programming language that allowed children to manipulate a graphical *turtle* on the screen.

Although *Logo* had a period of popularity in schools, cognitive psychologists were shifting their focus to the question of learning transfer and the conditions that facilitate transfer, and they criticized *Logo* for teaching skills outside of the context in which those skills would ultimately be used. They called for learning to be situated, both in terms of the task environment and the social context of learning, and *Logo* did not seem to be an appropriate tool for situated learning. Instead they developed new cognitive tools, designed to be used in the contexts and in the ways they felt were critical to effective learning. In the 1990s, their ideas have been brought into schools in the standards movement's emphasis on the cultivation of higher order thinking skills, such as critical thinking and problem solving. They are also promoted in the spirit of constructivist education, which derives from Piaget, Papert, and the situated learning theorists, stressing that children learn by actively constructing their own knowledge and understandings of the world.

Today a wide variety of new technologies are promoted for an equally wide variety of educational purposes. Educational technology is promoted for improving basic skills as well as cultivating higher order skills. It is hailed for improving standardized test scores and creating the kind of education that would do away with standardized tests. It is presented as a way to make learning more efficient and more messy. It is great for individualized instruction; it is great for collaborative instruction. It will lure students to school earlier in the morning and keep them there later at night; it will reduce the amount

of time spent in school. It will improve traditional literacy skills; it
will render traditional literacy skills obsolete. Americans might not be
entirely sure what exactly they want educational technology to do, but
they seem to want it in schools one way or another. Perhaps it is this
lack of consensus about the details that explains the popularity of the
rationale of "preparing students for the Information Age"—its meaning is vague enough to secure widespread consensus, and it is hard to
make a reasonable argument that America's children should go
unprepared for the age in which they live or that they can be prepared
for it without bringing its key components into their classrooms.

In other words, the ideas Americans have today about technology and education are not unlike the ideas of earlier generations.
The particular reform agendas, pedagogical styles, and learning theories change, but the idea of applying new media to them does not. As
we see in chapters 2 to 6, such application does not necessarily guarantee that school reform will work, but the tone of the rhetoric of
school reform remains insistent in promoting new media as central
components in the improvement of education.

CONCLUSION

American public education has gone through and continues to undergo a variety of permutations in form, purpose, scope, and method.
Public education has always been a subject of debate and disagreement, with some ideas dominating and others providing resistance
and counterargument. The story of American public education is a
story of the interaction of the agendas and ideologies of a variety of
different interest groups. At any given time, there are a number of
ideas in circulation. One might seem to dominate, but there are
always dissenting views, and whose views are translated into actual
school practices varies over time.

What seems to remain fairly consistent in the story of
American public education is the passion people have invested in it,
if not the consensus they have reached about it. On a whole,
Americans have long believed and continue to believe that education
is important, that it serves a vital purpose, and that it is a requirement for all kinds of personal and social improvement. That is not to
say that all Americans agreed on what kind of education was best,

who was entitled to what kind of education, or what kind of progress it would facilitate. Still the general faith in progress through education has persisted through the ages, however employed to justify a variety of (sometimes incompatible) purposes of schooling.

It is hard to imagine a major national issue that the schools have not taken up or that they have not been asked to address. The details change, but the issue is essentially the same. Americans tend to believe in the idea of progress (although individual definitions of progress vary), and they want schools to play a leading role in furthering progress. American ideas about progress tend to be strongly tied to technology, and so technological change is used as a rationale for education reform as well as a component in such reform. Rather than choose something else to believe in, the tendency has been to shift attention and hope from one educational technology to another as one disappoints and a new one, with new promise, emerges.

Every major new medium of the 20th century followed a similar pattern with respect to its application to education. Each of the next five chapters examines a major 20th century medium (film, radio, TV) or group of related media (automated instructional systems, contemporary digital media) in terms of the ways in which these media were brought into discussions of school reform, placing educational media movements in the context of the educational policies and philosophies, curricular and pedagogical concerns of the times in which they took place. Chapter 7 then points out some of the common themes in the stories of these different media, taking a new look at contemporary discussions once they have been placed in their historical context. In particular, today's conflicts over the nature of teaching and learning; the influence of commercial, government, and military forces on public education; and the effects of new media on children were foreshadowed in earlier debates about earlier media. These conflicts are pointed out in each chapter and are applied to the contemporary situation at the end of the book.

FILM

When could an educator count upon so much! The screen becomes one of the most powerful single instruments in the education of our population.

—Henry James Forman, *Our Movie Made Children*
(1935)

It is hard to imagine the thrill of early motion pictures. For the first time, people could watch the events and actions of people separated from them by space and time. As a form of entertainment, films were a huge and rapid success, in the first decade of the 20th century in small, storefront nickelodeons, and then in the teens in movie palaces, modeled on the most luxurious of concert halls. By 1935, the average weekly movie audience in the United States was 77,000,000, one third of whom were children and adolescents.[1]

Many of the earliest film pioneers had educational purposes in mind for their invention, including Thomas Edison, who began producing films for classroom use in 1911 and was quoted as saying

---

[1]Forman, 1935, p. 10

that "films are inevitable as practically the sole teaching method,"[2] and that "our school system will be completely changed in ten years."[3] Although those purposes were quickly eclipsed by the theatrical film industry, many educators had an intense interest in using film in schools. In 1923, William Jennings Bryan addressed the Visual Instruction Association of New York, saying, "The motion picture is the greatest educational institution that man has known and it won't be long before every school in the country will use motion pictures because there isn't anything good that can not be taught by films."[4] Educators interested in educational film set about forming professional organizations, seeking funding, and developing projects in keeping with their hopes. The New York City schools were the first to use films systematically in 1920, described in a 1923 handbook on educational film as "setting a pace and a standard for other schools of the country."[5] They were followed by cities like Chicago, Detroit, Newark, and Philadelphia; by 1923, 40 cities were doing so.

Advocates of educational film met with their share of obstacles, including conflicts with theatrical film makers, transition to sound film, equipment problems, and fears that film did more harm than good to children. The Depression came at a bad time for them. Although the military training films of World War II revived interest in the instructional use of film, and some educational films continued to be made for several decades, interest in transforming schools with film had largely faded by the end of the 1950s and could not be revived by later advances in film technology nor by shifts in school reform.

HOPES AND PLANS FOR EDUCATIONAL FILM

In many respects, the story of educational film is tied into the story of progressive education. Advocates of educational film tended to promote it, consciously or unconsciously, in ways that fit either with the views of the child-centered progressives, whose greatest period of

---

[2]Ellis and Thornborough, 1923, p. 34

[3]quoted in Saettler, 1990, p. 98 (Originally in the New York *Dramatic Mirror*, 7/9/13)

[4]Ellis and Thornborough, 1923, p. 65

[5]Ellis and Thornborough, 1923, p. 32

popularity corresponded roughly to the time that educational film peaked or with the administrative progressives, whose goals were temporarily slowed by child-centered progressivism, but ultimately came to dominate American educational policy.

As noted in chapter 1, reformers of the progressive era had a variety of ideas about what needed to happen to public education. They generally agreed on the premise that the conditions of contemporary life demanded changes in education, and they were aware of the impact that new communication technologies, in particular, were transforming the way people lived and interacted. One of the arguments in favor of visual instruction—the origin of instructional film— was that it would help children cope with an increasingly stressful information environment. Dudley Grant Hays, Director of Visual Instruction for the Chicago schools, expressed this view as follows:

> Only through careful training can pupils be led to see quickly and accurately things that flit before their vision. With the multiplicity of things pressing upon them for attention, we must so train them that they may readily trace out the connecting links between causes and effects, and enable them to do accurate reasoning.[6]

A popular belief held that the sensory onslaught brought on by new communication technologies required preparation and training, and that schools had to help children develop good judgment skills so as not to be overwhelmed.

Beyond the notion that a changing world called for changes in schools, progressives largely parted company. Two of the main categories of progressive thought were those referred to now as child-centered progressives and administrative (or social efficiency) progressives. Child-centered progressivism is most commonly associated with John Dewey, at least for the purpose of locating its origins and its early inspiration. Although it ultimately deviated in many ways from Dewey's philosophy, to the point that he sharply criticized what it had become some decades later,[7] child-centered progressivism is generally characterized by an emphasis on a curriculum emerging from children's natural curiosity and interests, connecting school experiences with the world outside the classroom, learning through collaborative activities and projects, and thinking of education as

---

[6]Hays, 1923, p. 60

[7]Dewey, 1938

serving students in the present—not as narrow vocational preparation for their future lives as adults. This view took the position that extrinsic motivations and punishments were unnecessary if students were engaged in activities that were meaningful to them and originated in their questions and concerns.

Coming out of the child-centered progressive movement was the *project method* developed by William Heard Kilpatrick and popularized in his widely read 1918 article in the *Teachers College Record*.[8] Like Dewey, Kilpatrick was critical of the *cold storage* conception of education, where the purpose of schooling was to have students store information away, year after year, to retrieve it someday as adults. Instead, Kilpatrick advocated purposeful activity by students who would be engaged in meaningful projects during class time. Within a short time, the project method was popularized in teacher education, expanding by the 1930s into what was known as the *activity* or *experience* curriculum.

The application of film to child-centered progressivism came through the visual instruction movement, which began in the early 20th century. At that time, visual education bureaus were established in many city school systems, the first being Chicago in 1895.[9] Visual education became enough of a movement to warrant the formation of professional associations. The National Academy of Visual Instruction was formed in 1920 to distribute films, establish standards for the use of film, and organize state associations. In 1932, it merged with the NEA Department of Visual Instruction, which had been established in 1923.[10] The Visual Instruction Association of America was formed at the 1922 NEA meeting out of the already existing Visual Instruction Association of New York.[11] Its purpose was primarily to promote visual education. To that end, it gave demonstrations at major education conferences across the nation. In 1935, the Educational Motion Picture Project of the American Council on Education was formed, serving as a clearing house for information on the use of films in the classroom, offering conferences, publishing books, and conducting research.[12] Colleges and universities offered

---

[8]Kilpatrick, 1918

[9]Dale et al., 1937, p. 33

[10]Saettler, 1990, p. 144

[11]Ellis and Thornborough, 1923, p. 33

[12]Dale et al., 1937, pp. 106–107

courses in visual education, the first course in educational film being offered by Columbia University in their 1921 summer session,[13] and university extension departments distributed slides and films to schools. Some districts had their own film and slide libraries. For example, in the mid-1930s, the Department of Visual Instruction for the Chicago schools had 150,000 slides, 2,500 reels of 16-mm film, and 400 silent film projectors for distribution to Chicago schools.[14]

One feature of child-centered progressivism that visual instruction could address was its emphasis on sensory experience in learning. Although pictures and silent films engaged no more senses than print media did, their focus on image over text was seen as a desirable addition to the sensory experiences of students. Dewey believed that "the image is the great instrument of instruction,"[15] not only in terms of its potential to convey meanings to children, but because he believed it was through the development of images of their own that children learned:

> Much of the time and attention now given to the preparation and presentation of lessons might be more wisely and profitably expended in training the child's power of imagery and in seeing to it that he was continually forming definite vivid, and growing images of the various subjects with which he comes in contact in his experience.[16]

It was a popular argument of the visual education and child-centered progressive movements that children learned best through the eye, that they learned better through images than through lectures, and that they learned best when a variety of senses were engaged—when they were furnished with "an abundance of experience in sense perception to be used in reflecting, reasoning and imaging."[17] An article in a 1927 issue of *Educational Screen* argued that, "the present theoretical basis for the use of the educational film—and for visual instruction generally—may be summed up in the belief that sense perception is the basis of all knowledge."[18]

---

[13]Ellis and Thornborough, 1923, p. 45

[14]Dale et al., 1937, pp. 106–107

[15]Dewey, 1997, p. 21 (originally published in 1929)

[16]Dewey, 1997, p. 22 (originally published in 1929)

[17]Hays, 1923, p. 60

[18]Horm, 1927, p. 411

Educational film was also promoted for its ability to make visible that which is otherwise undetectable by the human eye. In a 1923 educational film handbook by Don Carlos Ellis and Laura Thornborough, film was said to disclose "a whole new world for observation and study."[19] For example, slow motion and time-lapse techniques could demonstrate scientific concepts that could not be visualized in any other way. Films were made using this technique to show such things as surgical procedures, the workings of machines, military tactics, and sports.[20]

Another goal of child-centered progressivism that visual education—and film in particular—could serve was that of bridging the gap between the classroom and the outside world. Film more generally was celebrated by some, and condemned by others, for democratizing all kinds of knowledge and cultural experiences, by bringing experiences to the masses who would otherwise have no access to them. Specific to education, a frequently cited advantage of film was its potential to "expand the experiences of the pupils by bringing to them the whole wide world"[21] and "to clarify, to illuminate, and to project the imagination into a world beyond the classroom."[22] An article in a 1933 issue of *School and Society* claimed:

> [film will bring] the voice and knowledge of teachers in university and school, from workshop and mart, from places of healing and fields of play, from music chambers and art galleries and a thousand other spheres, and so will gladden the people with the light of knowledge.[23]

Motion pictures would bring the best teachers to all students by preserving them on film; it would also democratize education by providing "equally good teachers for all pupils."[24] For example, Ellis and Thornborough's handbook describes how "a great surgeon performs a marvelous operation. . . . Students all over the world may now witness the unusual operation performed over and over again by

---

[19]Ellis and Thornborough, 1923, p. 5

[20]Orndorff, 1923, pp. 79–80

[21]Ellis and Thornborough, 1923, p. 59

[22]Anderson, 1948, p. 11

[23]"Children and the films," 1933, p. 25

[24]Lewin, 1927, p. 452

the expert. . . . The work of the great surgeon becomes an immortal teacher of thousands."[25] Finally, it would cultivate a sense of citizenship in students. In the foreword to *The Cinema in School* (1935), John Grierson advocated film for "bringing alive to children . . . the life and composition of the community as they see it on their doorsteps and under their doorsteps."[26]

Educational film was most heavily promoted and experimented with in the period after World War I—a time when Americans were particularly aware of the dangers inherent in a world lacking international cooperation and understanding. Some advocates of educational film argued that film was far better than textbooks in illustrating the everyday lives of people of other cultures, thus contributing to greater understanding of different cultures and nationalities. Ellis and Thornborough expressed this view as follows:

> The factors tending towards a better common understanding between the nations and peoples of the world will be the strongest guarantees of peace in the years to come. . . . As a fitting culmination to these centuries of growth [of visual education] has at last come the "visual textbook," as the pedagogical film is now sometimes called, bringing the wide world to the child, making him know at first hand, as it were, and better understand the people of other countries, their problems and their aspirations; causing him to recognize the brotherhood of man; broadening his viewpoint and his sympathies even as does travel and association with nature.[27]

A similar view would be expressed fervently toward radio in the World War II era and toward later media in other tumultuous times.

One of the Payne Fund studies, a series of research studies that is described in greater detail later in this chapter, found that films had dramatic and enduring effects on children's attitudes toward people of other races and nationalities. For example, children who held the Chinese in low esteem were shown a film that portrayed the Chinese positively. Afterward the children's attitudes improved, and that improvement endured over time. By the same token, however, after seeing "Birth of a Nation," children who were not particularly racist expressed more racist attitudes and continued to do so over

---

[25]Ellis and Thornborough, 1923, pp. 61-62

[26]Grierson, 1935, p. 7

[27]Ellis and Thornborough, 1923, pp. 258–259

time.[28] Henry James Forman, whose book summarized this research, reminded readers that, "during the War . . . motion pictures were in use by virtually all belligerents as an instrument of propaganda."[29] Having been through a war more horrific than any preceding it, and believing that it was aided by film, using film to make the right impression on children was a high priority for Americans at that time.

As mentioned earlier, child-centered progressives placed a huge emphasis on student involvement and engagement in learning. One of the most popular arguments in favor of using instructional films was that they energized students' interest in learning and inspired them to actively pursue learning. In a 1927 issue of the *Journal of Education*, A. E. Winsip praised a series of educational films produced by George Eastman for being "question creators," ideal for generating valuable class discussions.[30] Many articles about educational film stressed the importance of involving students in the activity and initiating discussions that draw on children's powers of observation and get beyond the mere acquisition of facts from the films. Chicago superintendent William Bodine claimed that, "progressive education calls for picturized pedagogy. . . . Travel films will be the progressive geography of the future."[31] Audiovisual education advocate Charles Hoban promoted the use of films in line with contemporary pedagogy by using films to help students relate their school experiences to their larger communities, as well as blur the boundaries between separate academic subjects.[32]

Although film making by students was not a common occurrence in schools, it fit in well with conceptions of learning as an active process involving collaborative projects and interdisciplinary studies. Some teachers had students produce film dramatizations of works of literature they had studied; others filmed safety or health lessons. Some schools used film as an extension of the school newspaper, where students created newsreels about school and community events. Such work required students to research, write, design sets and costumes, act, direct, film, and edit. It also gave them a finished product that they could admire and share with classmates, parents,

---

[28]Forman, 1935, pp. 123–131

[29]Forman, 1935, p. 122

[30]Winsip, 1927, p. 533

[31]Ellis and Thornborough, 1923, p. 96

[32]Hoban, 1946, p. 77

and community members.[33] This use of film was fundamentally different from the showing of educational films produced by commercial, theatrical, or educational film companies, in that it put students and teachers in the active role of choosing film content and creating films of their own.

A criticism of child-centered progressives was that traditionally presented academic knowledge was too abstract. Similarly, advocates of visual instruction made frequent reference to their belief that learning was most effective when it began with concrete ideas and experiences and moved to the abstract.[34] Pictures and films were promoted as ideal starting points for learning, particularly with young students.

Films were sometimes used as a component in the project method. As mentioned earlier, this method treated the curriculum as a series of projects, where the teacher helped students plan, carry out, and evaluate their projects. Through this method, Kilpatrick popularized some of Dewey's ideas, including the interdisciplinary treatment of learning and the emphasis on student activity and problem solving. For example, a New York City fourth-grade class in a progressive school used an Eastman teaching film, *Clean Face and Hands*, as part of a hygiene unit. They also built their own health kits for use at home and wrote letters to purchase soap and paper towels for their classroom (bringing math and writing into the project).[35] Another New York City class, while studying the African Congo, borrowed materials from the American Museum of Natural History such as baskets, jewelry, and axes; they also viewed relevant films and slides.[36] An Illinois class studied the Panama Canal by constructing salt relief maps, viewing stereographs (three-dimensional photos), presenting oral reports, and viewing a film.[37] A Pasadena, California, first-grade class studied food by examining actual heads of wheat and other grains; germinating a grain of wheat; visiting a flour mill, a bakery, and an ice plant; viewing a film on dairying; and writing a class book about their experiences.[38]

---

[33]See Dale et al., 1937, for accounts of student film making.

[34]Hoban, Hoban, Jr., and Zisman, 1937; Freeman, 1924; Weber, 1928

[35]Dale et al., 1937, p. 170

[36]Dale et al., 1937, p. 160

[37]Myers, 1928

[38]Cook, 1931

In the 1920s and 1930s, many schools across the nation engaged in curriculum revisions to incorporate some of the principles of child-centered progressivism. Sometimes those revisions were accompanied by efforts to integrate new media, such as film, into the curriculum. For example, the Santa Barbara, California, schools embarked on curriculum reform in the 1930s and collaborated with the Committee on Motion Pictures in Education in their effort to use film to achieve some of their new goals.[39] Their film projects are an interesting illustration of the compatibility of film and child-centered progressivism. For example, a first-grade teacher struggling with a particularly lethargic class discovered that the children perked up when she introduced films about animals into their activities. They would participate in active discussions after viewing the films; they wrote stories, drew pictures, and composed songs and poems inspired by their film viewing. In the 1941 report on the Santa Barbara film projects, Marjorie Riedel described how the films were "the instruments which drew out of the youngsters a spirit of interest in and cooperation with the world about them. . . . Above all, the films helped to create a happier working attitude in the room and to develop a splendid spirit of cooperation."[40]

Another teacher had the challenge of working with a class where the majority of students had limited proficiency in English, being largely of Mexican or Japanese descent. After a disappointing field trip designed to learn about sea birds, the teacher found a film on the topic that excited the children. They were eager to discuss the film and searched the library for books related to the subject of the film. They took more trips, built birdhouses, developed a system for classifying birds, and extended their activities to study other kinds of animals. In this case, the teacher believed that films helped inspire children to work on areas where they had great difficulties—in particular, in observation and classification skills and in language abilities.[41]

Yet another teacher's challenge was to teach safety education, which was of particular concern in a school situated near railroad tracks and a major highway and that had a high incidence of student violations of safety rules. Up to this point, students had been disregarding safety rules. This teacher selected several films on top-

[39]Bell et al., 1941, pp. 3–9
[40]Riedel, 1941, pp. 19–23
[41]Denno, 1941, pp. 25–38

ics like bicycle safety and made them the focus of a safety unit. The students took such an interest that they appointed themselves school bicycle inspectors and developed a safety checklist to inspect other children's bicycles.[42]

In contrast to child-centered progressivism, the administrative progressives were focused on efficiency, organization, cost-effectiveness, and standardization. They were interested in Frederick Taylor's principles of scientific management, which involved conducting careful task analysis and breaking down procedures into their smallest units, then seeking to eliminate waste in the performance of those procedures. These reformers sought to eliminate waste in education, particularly waste of instructional time. Their conception of education was one where the purpose of schooling was to prepare students, as efficiently as possible, for their probable future roles in society. They advocated the use of intelligence testing to sort students by ability, then deliver to them only that knowledge they would be likely to need in the future toward which they appeared to be headed. They adhered to the new views emerging from educational psychology, which suggested that transfer of learning was much more limited than had been previously believed. As a consequence, they only approved of school subjects that had clear utility in adult life. Nothing was to be learned simply because it was *nice to know*; learning was to take place through the most direct route possible, and nothing extraneous was acceptable.

In this spirit, a curriculum reform movement caught on in the early decades of the 20th century, led by those who have come to be known as the *scientific* curriculum makers, including Franklin Bobbitt and W. W. Charters. These reformers sought to take curriculum-making and school administration away from the amateurs and give them to experts, who could improve them by developing more systematic procedures for them. This movement was somewhat hindered for a time, when the disillusionment of the Great Depression led to a general distrust of corporate practices and a greater interest in community and social reform. Under those circumstances, the child-centered progressivism and social reconstructionism of Dewey and Counts had more appeal. However, by World War II, social criticism was perceived as unpatriotic, and the administrative progressives came back to dominance.

---

[42]Van Schaick, 1941, pp. 65–84

A feature of film that was appealing to administrative progressives was its potential to teach children more efficiently than conventional instruction. They were concerned about how to deliver the ever-expanding curriculum to students; as early as 1918, Bobbitt was concerned that

> New duties lie before us. And these require new methods, new materials, new vision. . . . The new age is more in need of facts than the old; and of more facts; and it must find more effective methods of teaching them.[43]

Many comparison studies were conducted in the 1920s and 1930s to determine the effectiveness of instructional film relative to other methods of instruction. Although the results of those studies varied widely, there was some reason to believe that visual aids, including film, were effective in speeding up student learning.[44] A 1927 ad for Eastman Classroom Films picked up on reformers' concerns about efficiency, arguing that these films "cover their topics in *fifteen minutes*. In that time pupils see more than they could read in fifteen hours."

Administrative progressives advocated sorting students by ability, and instructional film was sometimes promoted for its effectiveness in teaching students of particular ability levels. One popular argument was that films were especially effective in improving the achievement of low-ability students. The belief was that slower students' inadequate literacy skills made it difficult for them to learn through text alone, and that the addition of images provided them another means of access to information—one that was more concrete. In one study of fifth graders in Teaneck, New Jersey, the work of the lowest ability children in the study was almost comparable to that of the high-ability students when films were employed.[45] In another study, a high school in Hammond, Indiana, taught geography by conventional instruction, with films and slides, and with a "modified teaching technique" (no homework and an informal lecture-discussion method). The lowest ability group, which was given modified teaching, films, and slides, did best on a multiple-choice test administered at the end of the unit. The second highest scores were achieved

[43]Bobbitt, 1997, p. 9

[44]Freeman, 1924; Marchant, 1925; Weber, 1928

[45]Hoek, 1934

by the middle ability group, which had received conventional teaching, films, and slides. The highest ability class, who received conventional instruction only, got the lowest scores on the test.[46] One can certainly question the validity and findings of such studies, but the point is that at the time, those studies were used to justify the use of films for low-ability students.

As an additional plus, some people argued that film would lower truancy rates because children would be more interested in attending school if films were shown there. Chicago school superintendent William Bodine was quoted as having said, "the film school will reduce truancy. Less truancy now means less expense to the taxpayers in the maintenance of corrective institutions and prisons."[47] Keeping children in school was of particular interest in the Depression era, when a concerted effort was made to keep teenagers out of the workforce; this era coincided with some of the most popular years for the promotion of instructional films. Besides the benefits to an unstable job market, the interest in using film to reduce truancy also speaks to the idea of schools as civilizers as a mechanism for combating depravity and maintaining social order.

The early decades of the 20th century were ones when huge numbers of immigrants came to the United States—immigrants who were thought to be a danger to social stability and progress. Nickelodeons had sprung up all over the country as a popular new form of entertainment, but were particularly associated with urban, immigrant neighborhoods. Social reformers of the time were concerned about the seemingly low brow entertainment fare of those neighborhoods and sought to regulate (or even close down) those nickelodeons.[48] At the same time, some of the same reformers saw in film the possibility of using the medium to assimilate immigrants, particularly immigrant children. Daniel Czitrom describes the mind set of those reformers:

> The presence of large numbers of "undeveloped minds" in the nickelodeons—immigrants and children—evoked endless assertions about movies as a potential agent of Americanization and moral suasion. . . . The image of ignorant immigrants and incorri-

---

[46]Halsey, 1936

[47]Ellis and Thornborough, 1923, p. 96

[48]Czitrom, 1982, pp. 47–50

gible youth uplifted by movies was a potent and reassuring one
for social workers and civic leaders sympathetic to films.[49]

Czitrom goes on to describe the hope that film could be used to teach
immigrants the virtues of middle-class morality and temperance. He
includes the last stanza of an anonymous poem called "A Newsboy's
Point of View." Written around 1910 in urban Irish slang, the poem
tells the story of the uplifting impact of film on a newsboy, his girl-
friend, and her father:

> All what I see wit' me own eyes I knows an' unnerstan's
> When I see movin pitchers of de far off, furrin' lan's
> Where de Hunks an'Ginnes come from—yer can betcher life I
>   knows
> Dat of all de lan's an' countries, 'taint no matter where yer goes
> Dis here country's got 'em beaten—take my oat dat ain't no kid—
> 'Cause we learned it from de movin'pitchers, me an' Maggie did.[50]

This Americanizing function of film was a good fit with the focus of
the administrative progressives on keeping order and training young
citizens to accept their proper place in the nation's socioeconomic life.

As mentioned in chapter 1, the junior high school had its origins, in part, in a desire to properly channel the energies of adolescents, and some educators believed that film could help in that effort.
This was a time when G. Stanley Hall's ideas about adolescent development and concerns about the deteriorating morality of Jazz Age
youth contributed to a belief that adolescents needed to be *caught*
before they headed down the wrong path. Many educators at this
time believed that they needed to channel the energy of adolescence
toward socially productive ends, and some thought that film could
help. For example, a Chicago social studies teacher reported that her
students found new, productive interests through classroom viewing
of films. One girl followed up on a film about women in industry by
contacting the Women's Bureau; a boy toured local Civilian
Conservation Corps after seeing a film about them.

As is discussed in more detail later in this chapter, concerns
about teenagers were often directed at the popular culture they
enjoyed. Adults were intensely concerned about the effects of
Hollywood films on the attitudes and behaviors of young people,

---

[49]Czitrom, 1982, p. 51

[50]Czitrom, 1982, p. 51

which inspired some interest in using educational films to give children the *right ideas* about theatrical films. A popular belief, expressed here by administrative progressive Charles Hubbard Judd, held that "the reason why the American people have so long put up with weak and often utterly stupid movies is that they have no training in the intelligent appreciation of movies,"[51] and that film appreciation classes would improve Americans' taste in entertainment. Some people believed that schools should be setting aside class time to discuss, analyze, and critique films. Schools across the country initiated motion picture appreciation programs sometimes as part of English classes.

The budget cutbacks of the Depression years created a severe crisis for many American schools. The Public Works Administration (PWA) and the Works Progress Administration (WPA) helped finance the construction and operation of schools, respectively.[52] However, many schools still faced substantial financial difficulties, and embarked on efforts to promote themselves and justify their programs (and the expense of those programs) to their communities. One way to engage in such promotion was through film production. For example, an elementary school in California made newsreels of school events that they showed at public movie screenings at the school. An Indiana high school filmed a variety of activities throughout the year, and then showed the film at their 1934 commencement exercises; they felt the film proved "very successful in showing the public the value of the high school."[53] The Central Needle Trades School of New York City showed several reels of film at their 1935 commencement, showing student activities throughout the year and comparing them to past, less impressive years in the school's history as a way to show how worthy they were of continued funding.[54]

In summary, film was embraced by education reformers with different philosophies and purposes. Each of the two dominant strands of reform saw in film the potential to help them realize their goals, whether those goals centered on changing the nature of the curriculum to be more child centered, or on delivering the existing curriculum more efficiently.

---

[51]Judd, 1923, p. 153

[52]Moreo, 1996

[53]Dale et al., 1937, pp. 282–283

[54]See Dale et al., 1937, for accounts of public relations film making

SOURCES OF EDUCATIONAL FILMS

Educational films came from a variety of sources, ranging from film-makers specifically in the business of producing pedagogical films, commercial filmmakers looking for new outlets for their work, government agencies, public utilities, and companies advertising their products through classroom films. In addition to using these films for classroom viewing, some schools also involved students in filmmaking projects of their own.

The federal government was among the first to produce films for classroom use. The Department of Agriculture, National Parks Service, Bureau of Mines, Army, Navy, and Marine Corps, among others, all produced films in the early years of the 20th century, the first government films being produced by the Bureau of Reclamation in 1911.[55] During World War I, the War and Navy departments had film divisions "for the twofold purpose of supplying informational pictures to the public and of instructing officers and men in the science of war."[56] They were able to cut the training time of officers by using training films describing, for example, the workings of military equipment. The Committee on Public Information, created during World War I to disseminate information about war activities, had a film division. At the close of World War I, many of these films were made available to educational institutions.

The WPA also played a role in the promotion of educational film in the New Deal era. For example, in 1934, it funded a Teachers College project to compile a comprehensive bibliography on motion pictures in education.[57] In the mid-1930s, WPA teachers conducted safety education classes using films and slides.[58]

A number of colleges and universities also took an interest in educational film, sometimes in cooperation with experienced film producers. Some universities were producing educational films as early as the 1910s, including Harvard, Yale, MIT, and the universities of Chicago, Indiana, Iowa, Oklahoma, Michigan, Nebraska, Wisconsin,

---

[55]Ellis and Thornborough, 1923

[56]Ellis and Thornborough, 1923, p. 20

[57]Dale et al., 1937, p. 10

[58]Stack, 1936

and Utah.[59] Extension departments of state universities also played
a role (sometimes more significant than others) in educational film by
serving as the largest non-theatrical distributors of films.[60]

Among the universities actively involved in educational film
was New York University, creating the Educational Film Institute in
the late 1930s. The institute, funded by the Alfred P. Sloan
Foundation (which was involved in economic research), focused on
the use of film to instruct adults and high school students on economic issues. The first film, *The Challenge*, was about technological
unemployment; another, *The Children Must Learn*, dealt with the
economic hardships of rural life. The Educational Film Institute was
widely recognized as "one of the most active documentary film producing groups in the country,"[61] but production halted in the early
1940s because of "economic and cultural changes due to war and
national preparedness" and "dissatisfaction with the critical tenor of
films and scripts on hand in view of changed world conditions."[62] The
Sloan Foundation was unwilling to continue funding the project without evidence of a clear market to justify the expense, and it was concerned that the films would be regarded as unpatriotic as the nation
prepared for war.

Another source of classroom films were production companies
specializing in pedagogical films, which sprung up in the 1920s.
Hollywood film makers sometimes packaged unused entertainment
footage into films for school use, but pedagogical film makers were
critical of the use of Hollywood techniques in films for classroom use.
They specifically avoided the use of Hollywood film styles, eschewing
soundtracks and any techniques that would make the films too entertaining. The staples of these companies were time-lapse nature studies, travelogues, and dramatizations of literature.

A popular series of pedagogical films were the Eastman
Teaching Films produced by George Eastman (of Kodak). These
silent films were actually a blend of the pedagogical and industrial
film to the extent that Eastman's name, company, and industry were
promoted by them, but their content was more like pedagogical films
in that it was carefully aligned to curricular goals. Eastman

[59]Saettler, 1990, p. 108

[60]Ellis and Thornborough, 1923, p. 29

[61]"Film News," 1940

[62]"Film News," 1940

announced his intentions to get involved in educational film in the mid-1920s, first developing a new standard in film, as well as a camera and projector to go with it,[63] then producing a series of silent films for classroom use under the direction of Columbia University's Ben Wood and the University of Chicago's Frank Freeman. All told, some 250 Eastman films were made, much of their content coming from industrial films acquired by Eastman Kodak.[64] These films seem to have been popular with teachers, but the Eastman project ended abruptly with Eastman's death, the advent of sound film, and the Great Depression.

The Eastman Films were kept in circulation by the establishment of Encyclopedia Britannica Films in 1936. William Benton, vice president of the University of Chicago (then a center of progressive education), bought the *Encyclopedia Britannica* with the agreement that the university would buy it back from him at cost. He then purchased the films of Electrical Research Products Inc., who, like Eastman Teaching Films, was a major supplier of educational films to schools. He also persuaded Eastman Kodak to donate their teaching films to the university. Without shooting a single film, he had amassed a library of nearly 500 titles. By 1946, the university had repaid Benton and was averaging more than $300,000 a year in profit from film rentals to schools. Encyclopedia Britannica Films went on to produce hundreds of films from the 1940s through the 1960s.[65]

Finally, many classroom films were what were known as *industrial* or *sponsored films*. These were generally produced by an industry or organization seeking to promote themselves, their product, or free enterprise in general, and they were made available to schools at little or no cost. For example, Borden's Farm products had a film called *Along the Milky Way* about the story of milk, Goodyear provided *The Story of the Airship,* and New York Edison offered films about electricity.[66] A variety of utility companies, government agencies, and the railroad, auto makers, dairy, lumber, rubber, salt, sugar, and tobacco industries (among others) all offered free films to

[63]Ellis and Thornborough, 1923, p. 217

[64]Saettler, 1990, p. 103

[65]Smith, 1999

[66]Brown, 1931

schools. One 1935 estimate indicated that as many as 90% of the
films available to schools were of the sponsored variety.[67]

In some cases, students and teachers produced films of their
own. This use of film was not nearly as common as renting and showing films produced by others because it was relatively expensive and
difficult to do. However, there are many accounts in visual education
journals of student filmmaking. In 1937, Edgar Dale et al. summarized 37 separate articles on school-based film production, most of
which were accounts of projects undertaken in the mid-1930s.[68]
Typically, these projects were dramatizations of works of literature
or newsreels. Teachers involved in these projects described the intensity of student interest and motivation and the degree of cooperation
among students.

The entrance of the United States into World War II brought
the federal government into educational film more intensely than it
had been before. The Armed Forces were faced with a choice: reject
all the potential soldiers who lacked the necessary skills for military
duties or train them. They chose the latter, and they embarked on an
ambitious film project as a major component in their training, enlist-
ing the aid of Frank Capra and others from the Hollywood film
industry. The Armed Forces produced hundreds of films during the
war years; it is estimated that the monthly attendance for Army
films, most of them training films, between July 1, 1944, and June
31, 1945, was over 21 million.[69]

Military training films consisted of several varieties. One
type of film was designed to teach specific skills, like the fundamentals of soldering, artificial respiration, or use of the oxyacetylene
torch. There were also general information films, the function of
which was, in the words of an officer in the U.S. Navy's Training
Film Branch, "to awaken interest and present background material
and factual information which at some future time might be of vital
use to the person using the film,"[70] such as survival tactics if lost at
sea (*Castaways*) or the importance of mastering naval etiquette
(*Proceed and Report*). Then there were films designed to promote vir-

---

[67]Grierson, 1935, p. 8

[68]Dale et al., 1937

[69]Hoban, 1946, p. 43

[70]Hart, 1948, p. 16

tuous attitudes and habits, such as *Keep it Clean*, which emphasized
the importance of sorting one's laundry. Other films encouraged
problem solving by presenting a situation as sailor might find it, then
calling on the viewer to solve some kind of problem while watching.

Military training films had worldwide distribution. A Navy
ship arriving at a port could trade in its films for other ones, and
could even exchange films with other ships at sea. Each port's library
had trained officers to work out an educational program and select
appropriate films. In total, During World War II, 1 million and a half
prints were used and more 16-mm film projectors were purchased
and used by the Armed Forces than by all schools prior to the war.[71]
By 1944, the audience for these films had totaled some 67.5 million.[72]

The use of film had been based on two assumptions: that people would acquire factual knowledge from them, and that people's
opinions would be shaped by them. The Armed Forces hired a staff of
psychologists and social scientists, many of whom became well
known in their fields after the war, to evaluate the effectiveness of
the training films. These researchers used methods that were not
new to social science, but were new to media research. They conducted studies using experimental and control groups, and they matched
pairs by factors such as age, region of birth, and scores on Army
achievement tests. Overall, these studies suggest that the films had a
major effect on the short-term acquisition of factual knowledge, but
not as much effect on changing opinions or motivating soldiers.[73]

At the war's end, advocates of educational film were newly
motivated to promote their cause. They hoped that the apparent success of film in the war effort would increase interest in using films in
schools and that soldiers who had viewed the films would expect
schools in their communities to use this modern teaching aid.
Charles Hoban, a leading educational film advocate who had been
involved in the production of military training films, wrote:

> Now, as never before, educators and the public alike seem to be
> convinced that education must shed its bookish quality, and that
> it must deal vigorously and effectively with social issues and
> moral conduct. Our late enemies have demonstrated the effective-
> ness of organized education in teaching a set of moral principles

[71]Hoban, 1948, p. 23
[72]Smith, 1999, p. 20
[73]Hoban, 1946; Lowery and DeFleur, 1995, chapter 7

(to us, immoral) so effectively as to dominate the thinking, feeling, and acting of an overwhelming proportion of the population.[74]

He tied the use of film to an idea about the purpose of schooling growing in popularity at the time—the idea that schools had to cultivate a population that could maintain American supremacy against foreign competitors, particularly those who used education to cultivate in their own people a sense of their own supremacy. After the war, more than 500 films and filmstrips were released for general use by educational institutions, and the U.S government made their surplus 16-mm sound projectors available to schools. It was not uncommon for students to view pedagogical films in class or in assemblies in the decades following the war.

A particularly interesting category of postwar classroom film was the mental hygiene film, which was related to life-adjustment education. The U.S. Office of Education had commissioned a study on vocational education, which was presented in Washington, DC, in the spring of 1945 by Charles Prosser. The report concluded that high schools were not properly serving America's youth, that some 60% of all students were underserved because they were neither college-bound nor in vocational programs, and there was little in most high school curricula to meet their needs or hold their interest. Prosser recommended what came to be known as *life-adjustment education*, or an expanded curriculum that directly addressed the day-to-day concerns of these students, and the issues and responsibilities they would face as adults. A huge variety of new courses appeared, focusing on issues like dating, marriage, and employment, in an effort to reduce the dropout rate by adapting the curriculum to the needs of American youth.

In the spirit of life-adjustment education, thousands of mental hygiene (or attitude enhancement) films were made from 1945-1970.[75] Their subjects ranged from dating, sex, and marriage to juvenile delinquency, civil defense, patriotism, highway safety, and free enterprise. However, they all shared one common goal: shape the attitudes and behaviors of school-age Americans. Although they strike today's viewers as almost unbearably corny, at the time they reflected real concerns on the part of adults that American children

---

[74]Hoban, 1946, p. ix
[75]Smith, 1999

were abandoning the value systems of their parents and threatening
the social order. This was an era described by mental hygiene film
historian Ken Smith as "traumatized by war, fearful of communist
witch-hunters, terrified of nuclear annihilation, and rocked by fears
of a generational rebellion."[76] Under the circumstances, producers of
these films often thought of themselves as performing an important
service to society.

A major difference between mental hygiene films and other
educational films of the era was that producers of mental hygiene
films deliberately used Hollywood-style film techniques, such as
music soundtracks and dramatic lighting and editing. They had no
qualms about being entertaining as long as they were persuasive.

Although films continued to be used in schools for decades,
they rarely became more than an occasional addition to more conventional methods of instruction. In the 1960s, the availability of 8-mm
sound film reignited some hope that film might be used to transform
education. Louis Forsdale of Columbia's Teachers College expressed
his hope in the proceedings of a conference on education and film
that 8-mm technology (in his words, "the paperback of film"[77]) would
finally make widespread school film production possible. At that
same conference, Marshall McLuhan predicted "a total revolution in
movie content"[78] from this new film technology, whose impact he predicted to be parallel "to the rise of the printed book after 2000 years
of manuscript culture."[79] Although many schools experimented with
film making in this period, their efforts were rarely sustained for
long perhaps because of the 1970s shift back to core academics and
basic skills.

FACTORS PREVENTING THE DEVELOPMENT OF EDUCATIONAL FILM

Using or making films in schools proved far more difficult than many
advocates had imagined. Although film seemed to have the potential
to fit into a wide variety of visions of educational reform, educators
had a difficult time integrating it into classroom practice. One fre-

---

[77]Forsdale, 1962, p. 7

[78]McLuhan, 1962a, p. 16

[79]McLuhan, 1962a, p. 16

quently cited problem was simple hyperbole—that enthusiasts had overstated their expectations in such a way as to make the whole endeavor appear unrealistic or silly. A 1927 article in *Educational Screen* lamented, "the motion picture as an educational adjunct has probably suffered more than any previous innovation through unskillful enthusiasm."[80] Brooklyn teacher George C. Wood expressed the problem in the following way in 1923:

> Five years ago the idea of using motion pictures in the school room was hailed by producers and teachers alike as the beginning of a complete revolution in the methods of teaching. Extravagant claims were made and in some quarters are now made for the film as a more than complete substitute for the teacher and the text-book. Indeed, the imagination of many as to the future of the film in relation to educational processes ran riot and exceeded the bounds of reason.[81]

Besides the disillusionment of hyperbole, a number of more specific issues hindered the integration of film into classroom practice. They can be roughly grouped into several categories, all of which reappear in subsequent chapters about other media: technical problems, incompatibility with teacher needs and interests, and concerns about the medium's effects on children.

Technical Problems

Technical problems should never be presented as the main reason for the failure of an educational technology to take hold because focusing on narrow technical issues tends to obscure some of the deeper reasons that these technical problems prove insurmountable. However, they are not inconsequential problems, either, and deserve to be described in some detail.

A major problem with early educational films was that they were a fire hazard. Nitro-cellulose, or celluloid, film burned easily, making it dangerous to use in classrooms. The danger of fire led to safety laws requiring that films only be projected from fire-safe booths, which were too expensive for many schools to install. Moreover, they limited the use of films to the school auditorium,

[80]Dransfield, 1927, p. 121

[81]Wood, 1923, p. 112

making it more difficult to make them a part of classroom routine. A 1934 survey of 5,000 members of the National Education Association showed that most films were viewed in the auditorium, not the classroom, which was not in keeping with most ideas about how films could best be used for learning.[82] By the early 1920s, acetate of cellulose film, also known as *slow burning* or *safety* film, was available, but most films for school use were still on celluloid film. This further complicated schools' use of film because they had to decide which projectors to purchase or allocate additional funds to accommodate projection of both inflammable and safety-standard films.

Even when safety-standard films became the norm, educational films remained hard to use for another reason: ventilation. Films could only be clearly seen in a dark room, and closing curtains or blinds well enough to permit easy viewing often resulted in a sleepy class. Although daylight screens (which did not require darkening the room) had been developed by the early 1920s, they were unusable in most classrooms because they projected the image from behind the screen, requiring more space than most classrooms had.

The advent of sound film in the late 1920s presented a setback to educational film. Sound projectors were expensive, and the expense was hard to justify to school boards, given that the Great Depression began at approximately the same time as the shift from silent to sound film production. As with the advent of safety film, sound films raised the issue of equipment incompatibility; schools that wanted to use both silent and sound films had to have projectors for both.

The debate over silent versus sound film aside, advocates of educational film were working against the huge financial restraints of the Depression. One cost cutter was to have students serve as projectionists, deliver equipment to classrooms, and maintain equipment. Some schools formed audiovisual clubs to this end, selecting qualified students to participate. It was also expensive to obtain the necessary insurance to use film equipment, particularly in the early years of educational film; one principal estimated that it would cost him $600 a year in insurance to operate a film projector.[83]

---

[82]Dale et al., 1937, p. 50

[83]Ellis and Thornborough, 1923, p. 45

Financial constraints created problems much larger than those of equipment purchases. A major obstacle to the development of educational film was the expense involved in producing such films and the reluctance or inability of producers to produce films without the assurance of a large market for them. Theatrical and industrial films were generally of higher production quality than the more expensive pedagogical films, but their use in schools was problematic because their motives and content were considered questionable by many educators.

Incompatibility with Teachers' Needs and Interests

Certainly there were many teachers who were interested in the classroom use of film. However, they encountered many obstacles when they tried to make films a regular part of their repertoire. For example, teachers often discovered that classroom films from all sources (theatrical, industrial, and pedagogical) treated their subject matter in too general a way to be of much instructional use. Theatrical films released for school use were not made with such use in mind, so they did not particularly fit the curriculum. Generally, these films were useful only to the extent that they dramatized a work of literature being read in English classes or depicted another part of the world or historical period. Industrial films were designed primarily to promote a product or point of view to children, with educational purposes playing a secondary role (although their producers argued otherwise).

Although producers of pedagogical films tried harder than the other producers to design films that fit the curriculum and employed sound teaching techniques, their films were also often considered too general for much classroom application. American school districts were so diverse from one community to another that it was a tough market to predict. Producers could never be sure how a particular subject was taught in different schools or how many schools could be counted on to purchase a film. As a result, they tended to make films that they believed would be of widespread use so they could maximize profits. Meanwhile, many teachers were coming to the conclusion "that the only proper and final solution is the definite outlining and filming of a definite subject designed to teach a particular set of principles or processes and done according to the best pedagogical principles"[84]—just the opposite of how most pedagogical films were designed. By the end of the 1920s, most of these production companies had folded.

Both theatrical and industrial film makers had somewhat hostile relationships with educators. Although there were educators who promoted the use of these free or low-cost films, particularly in the absence of more appropriate films, many educators were doubtful that these film makers would put educational goals over commercial ones. Early on, it appeared that the theatrical motion picture industry would work with educators. Some producers, such as Fox Films, established educational divisions. Fox produced a civics film called *Our Government at Work*, and the *Movietone School Series*, a series of 10 films for junior high classes. However, most of the offerings of these divisions were newsreels and failed theatrical films.

Will Hays, president of the Motion Picture Producers and Distributors of America, addressed the NEA in 1923, when he asked educators to cooperate with him and the MPPDA in improving the movies. The NEA president appointed a committee of educators to work with Hays, chaired by Charles H. Judd of the University of Chicago. However, the relationship between educators and Hollywood was never particularly amicable. Producers wanted educators to confine themselves to pedagogical films, but educators wanted to address problems they attributed to entertainment films, which seemed to be teaching just the opposite of everything school tried to teach.[85] In the early 1930s, educators appealed to the MPPA (the "D" for "distributors" removed due to antitrust action) for permission to excerpt theatrical films for educational use. Despite protests from the film industry, a group of educators was given permission to examine 1,800 film shorts, of which they selected 360 for school distribution. Meanwhile, the educational divisions of theatrical production companies were shut down after failing to make a profit.

Some of the Hollywood films and film shorts made available for educational use were useful for schools. However, there were also many film shorts called educational; but as W. H. George (1935) argued in *The Cinema and School*, "nothing more anaemic could pos-

---

[84]Wood, 1923, p. 112

[85]Judd, 1923, pp. 151–154

sibly be imagined."[86] Educators urged film makers to involve them in production so the films would be more appropriate for school use; in the planning stages of an educational film project at New York University, a memo about the selection of a director emphasized that he "should display a willingness and ability to free himself from the Hollywood state of mind. A dyed-in-the-wool prima-donna production director would educationally be a pain-in-the-neck and a liability to the whole idea."[87] Ellis and Thornborough's handbook on educational film expressed a similar sentiment:

> It is obvious that the production and distribution of instructional films . . . can not apparently be handled properly by theatrical companies. The latter seem to have little sympathy with the school angle, are not possessed of the point of view necessary for success in cooperating with schools and seem to find the profits in the school business not large or rapid enough to suit their investment requirements.[88]

In case it appears that the hostility was one sided, consider the following quote from a theatrical film maker included in Ellis and Thornborough's book:

> The non-theatrical exhibitor is usually a poor business man, he is unreliable, far from a steady customer, he does not know what he wants, yet he is dissatisfied with what has been produced, or else he wants us to produce a film according to his ideas without stopping to consider that such a film might meet the needs of no other user of educational films. In addition, his equipment is often poor, he damages the film far more than does his theatrical neighbor, and yet is willing to pay less than a fifth of the price the theatrical exhibitor expects to pay.[89]

This kind of friction between educational and theatrical film makers was only the beginning of tensions that would reemerge between educational and entertainment media makers for generations to come.

---

[86]George, 1935, p. 45

[87]Dorau, 1939

[88]Ellis and Thornborough, 1923, p. 22

[89]Ellis and Thornborough, 1923, p. 23

Educators had an equally uneasy relationship with industrial film makers, whose profit and publicity motives were highly questionable. Teachers did not categorically reject the idea of industrial films; they were happy to use industrial films that they believed to have real educational value. Despite the perceived problems with using sponsored films, there were also some educators who believed that the only way for film to have a chance in schools was to use what was available at low cost, commercially motivated or otherwise. Producing educational films was such a gamble that unless and until it became clearer to producers that there was a viable market, it seemed unavoidable that sponsored films would have to be used. John Grierson wrote that films could be used for teaching about civics, housing and health, commerce, employment, and unemployment

> for the simple if unromantic reason that they represent the only films that are likely to be properly financed. . . . One may trust the gas and electric and other industries and public services to make a great show of their work in the years to come.[90]

Some educators set about figuring out how to use sponsored films responsibly. A group of educators met in Detroit in 1946 to suggest some guidelines on the use of such films, which included the following:

> Some of these materials do have significant instructional values and do offer experiences not otherwise available. The use of the best of these, however, involves furthering the sponsor's interest in some degree.
> Schools cannot develop adequate audio-visual programs based solely on sponsored materials. . . . The use of a sponsored film can be justified only in terms of bringing to the learner a valuable experience that would otherwise be denied him. . . . Each school system has a responsibility for developing its own criteria and policy with regard to such materials.[91]

As was the case with the relationship between educational and theatrical film makers, the uneasy relationship between educators and industrial film makers set the stage for an ongoing distrust by educators of commercial media and ambivalence or guilt about using such media in schools.

---

[90]Grierson, 1935, p. 7

[91]Hoban, 1946, p. 67

One way to look at the conflict between teachers and film makers is that it represented a larger conflict over who should rightfully control the curriculum of schools—a conflict that has remained a much-debated issue to the present day. Teachers were frustrated by the ways in which the content of these films took the curriculum out of their hands and gave it over to film makers. This issue was evident in debates over the advantages of silent versus sound films. Early educational films, like all early films, were silent. Those in favor of switching to sound films argued that sound made the film experience closer to real experience and the mobilization of hearing along with sight reinforced learning. However, advocates of silent films cited the advantage of flexibility for the teacher, who could choose to narrate silent films in a variety of ways. Silent films gave teachers the freedom to supply their own interpretations of the images depending on their purposes in showing the film and the curricular goals they were trying to achieve.[92]

Another problem that teachers encountered when they tried to use classroom films—one that speaks to the issue of teacher frustration over controlling the conditions of the use of this medium— was that films were difficult to locate and obtain especially if precise timing was needed. There was no centralized system of film distribution, so it took a great deal of time and effort for teachers to make themselves aware of what films were available and how they could be obtained. Films were distributed by museums, government offices, college and university extension divisions, and a variety of national organizations like the YMCA, making the process of locating a particular film somewhat laborious. Films were sometimes distributed on a circuit basis, meaning that schools had to show films whenever they happened to get them, without regard to what they were teaching at that particular time. A number of educational film advocates recognized the threat this complicated system posed to the future of film in classrooms. They argued for state or regional level networks for film distribution, preferably under the direction of professional educators, that would be responsible for informing teachers about films, booking films, and delivering them to schools. Hoban, for example, understood that it did not matter how good the films were unless there was "an almost magic simplicity to their physical use."[93]

---

[92]Hoban, Hoban, and Zisman, 1937, pp. 108–110

[93]Hoban, 1946, p. 110

Some teachers had good equipment and films at their disposal, but lacked the additional administrative support they needed to
make good use of films. As George Fern and Eldon Robbins (1946)
argued in *Teaching with Films*, teachers needed much more from
their administrators than equipment; they needed extensive inservice training, a director of audiovisual aids to maintain equipment
and arrange film loans, and an organized budget for films and film
equipment.[94] W. H. George expressed similar beliefs more than a
decade earlier, arguing that teachers had not had much encourage-
ment to use films, despite that they were an important factor in
school reform. George also argued for changes in teacher education to
prepare teachers to use films suggesting that "young teachers must
know what constitutes a film and really smell celluloid as a part of
their teacher-training."[95] By knowing how films were made, they
could participate more effectively in the production of good educational films. They could also avoid the embarrassment of having technical difficulties during class time and the resulting damage to films or
equipment that could thwart other teachers' efforts to use those
resources.

It seems that some teachers not only resented the ways in
which the use of films compromised their sense of autonomy, but
actually feared that films would be used to replace them. If it was
true that films could be used to teach a variety of subjects with
greater impact and efficiency than a classroom teacher, then it might
also be true that teachers would no longer be necessary if film use
became widespread in schools. This anxiety was probably intensified
by retrenchment moves during the Depression, when the U.S.
Chamber of Commerce was pushing for larger class sizes, shorter
school days, and cutbacks in nonessential offerings, all posing threats
to teachers' jobs. Advocates of educational film insisted that film
posed no such threat. For example, Charles Hoban argued that

> this unholy fear, born of the insecurity which comes from basic
> ignorance of the role of films in an educational program, still
> echoes in current educational literature, often from sources that
> should know better. A more real basis of anxiety is not that
> motion pictures will replace teachers, but that teachers (1) will

[94]Fern and Robbins, 1946, pp. 123–133
[95]George, 1935, p. 38

fail to use educational films, and (2) will not use them to best
advantage when they use them at all.[96]

In retrospect, it is clear that teachers need not have been concerned
about losing their jobs to films. However, it was a real concern to
some of them, and they would not be the last generation of teachers
to fear that a new educational technology would replace them.

Some educators' criticisms of film were related to larger critiques of the entertainment film industry and of mass media and
mass society more generally. As early as 1934, George S. Counts
noted the "powerful trend toward consolidation and centralization"[97]
in the film industry. He expressed his concern that Hollywood films
would cultivate "mass standards for speaking, for gesturing, for travel, for furnishing homes, for choosing and wearing clothes, for making love, for breaking the law, for committing robbery, arson, and
murder."[98] He also feared that the film industry, seeking the largest
possible audiences and profits, would produce films that appealed to
the lowest imaginable taste. Rather than being used to democratize
high culture and uplift all citizens, Counts saw a potentially powerful
medium being taken over by commercial interests and profit motives.

In 1948, media and education scholar Charles Siepmann reit-
erated Counts' concerns. He observed that a mere five companies produced nearly all the films viewed by Americans, resulting in "the creation, if not the imposition, of stereotypes of taste and interest."[99]
Where he saw the teacher's job in a democratic society as cultivating
individuals who could think for themselves, he perceived the goal of
the mass media as being just the opposite—"the creation of a mass
mind readily responsive to mass influences and the imposition of
stereotypes of taste and outlook measured in terms of box-office
receipts."[100]

Counts and Siepmann were expressing views that were at the
core of scholarly thinking and debate about the role of mass media in
society. The early decades of the 20th century were years when mass
media were believed to have powerful, uniform effects on their audi-

[96]Hoban, 1946, pp. 103–104

[97]Counts, 1934, p. 198

[98]Counts, 1934, p. 199

[99]Siepmann, 1948, p. 4

[100]Siepmann, 1948, p. 5

ences and when theories of the mass mind created by industrialized, mass culture were in circulation. Related to these concerns were fears more specifically about children and the effects of films on children. These fears certainly influenced teachers' attitudes about using films in schools.

Fears About Film's Effects on Children

As mentioned earlier in this chapter, the years in which educational film was promoted were also years when adults were deeply concerned about the attitudes of youth. Concerns about the role the movies might be playing in the apparent moral decline of young Americans led to a number of research studies attempting to understand that role. To the extent that what happens with a medium inside schools is affected by children's relationship with that medium outside schools, these studies are worth some detailed attention here. Some teachers were reluctant to use films because they believed films were appropriate only as entertainment, and therefore, were unsuitable for classroom use. A 1921 *New York Times* editorial linked illiteracy to moviegoing, arguing that "children brought up on the movies too often lack patience to read."[101] Ellis and Thornborough quote a librarian who criticized films for failing to exercise children's minds the way reading does; she felt that, "In motion pictures the boy finds nothing that calls for the exercise of the mind. He becomes in a sense the father of the mentally sterile man."[102] These criticisms fit with criticisms of visual education more generally, which sometimes portrayed it as superficial, trivial, or pedagogically unsound in comparison with book learning. The fear was that children's associations of films with fun might lead them to believe that learning is easy, turning them away from the values of hard work and perseverance.

At the same time, however, there were teachers and librarians reporting increases in student reading and gains in literacy skills that they attributed to film viewing—for example, when students would see a film based on a novel and then seek out the novel.[103] In their 1937 literature review, Dale et al. went so far as to claim that "the value of the motion picture in developing *written and oral*

---

[101]Ellis and Thornborough, 1923, p. 37

[102]Ellis and Thornborough, 1923, p. 48

[103]Ellis and Thornborough, 1923, pp. 73–74

expression is so well established that writers take this for granted and pass on to other values."[104] Still the verdict was out among many teachers as to motion pictures' impact on literacy.

There was also growing concern, to the point of outrage, over the film industry's impact on the behaviors and attitudes of American children. Stories of Hollywood scandals frightened parents, leading them to call for regulation of the motion picture industry. The public perception of film was further damaged by the Payne Fund studies, the findings of which suggested that films did indeed have terrible effects on children. The Payne Fund Studies were a dozen research studies conducted in the late 1920s "to secure authoritative and impersonal data which would make possible a more complete evaluation of motion pictures and their social potentialities."[105] At a time when 77,000,000 Americans were going to the movies each week, a third of them children and adolescents, and when the content of films was unrated and relatively uncensored, adults feared that the movies were damaging their children's attitudes, behaviors, knowledge, and health. The Payne Fund studies were meant to find out just how much damage was being done. These studies are described in Lowery and DeFleur's (1995) *Milestones in Mass Communication Research* as "the first major scientific assessment of the effects of a mass medium,"[106] for which the best social scientific research techniques of the time were employed.

One study, conducted by Edgar Dale, surveyed motion pictures of 1920, 1925, and 1930 to determine the typical subject matter. In 1920, 82% of the films viewed for this study were about crime, sex, and/or love; in 1925, the percentage of films on these themes was 79%; and in 1930, 72%. Henry Forman, who wrote a book summarizing all the Payne Fund studies, speculated about the effects of this subject matter on children, concluding that "to give crime and sex so large a representation in the motion picture is surely to threaten the morals and characters of our children and youth."[107] Later in the book, he described films as "a veritable school for crime."[108] Overall he found that the Dale study showed the people who populate motion

---

[104]Dale et al., 1937, p. 175—emphasis in original text

[105]Charters, 1933, p. iv

[106]Lowery and De Fleur, 1995, p. 21

[107]Forman, 1935, p. 35

[108]Forman, 1935, p. 38

pictures as "a tawdry population, often absurdly over-dressed, often shady in character, much given to crime and sex, with little desire or need, apparently, of supporting themselves on this difficult planet."[109]

Concerns about the effects of film on adolescents were very much a part of more general concerns about Jazz Age youth. When the extravagance and frivolity of their lifestyle was shattered by the Depression, some people feared that these young people would not have the capacity or determination to work toward the goal of national recovery, and they believed that the movies were one source of the problem. Henry Forman expressed this concern as follows:

> One of the easiest gateways to blurred and confused conduct is the ready assumption, frequently derived by the young from the movies, that luxury, extravagance, easy money are the inalienable right of everyone. The recent economic depression has shown us one result of an almost universally accepted concept that wealth is easily attainable. The study of the case of various young delinquents shows to what an extent the same concept derived from the movies has played havoc with the youthful lives.[110]

Although in retrospect one might attribute Jazz Age excesses to a variety of factors, at the time the new medium of motion pictures seemed to be a major contributor to a mind set that was believed to have contributed to the economic ruin of the nation.

Another question addressed by the Payne Fund studies was that of the information retained by children from films. Thousands of children were shown films and then tested on the contents. This study found that children remembered more from films, and retained that information longer, than many people had previously believed.[111] Moreover, misinformation in films appeared to actually decrease the acquisition of accurate information in the same films.[112] Where it had previously been believed that children neither understood nor remembered films, now it appeared that "what they see is present in their memories, practically intact, waiting only for a stim

---

[109]Forman, 1935, p. 45

[110]Forman, 1935, p. 184

[111]Charters, 1933, pp. 7–8

[112]Forman, 1935, p. 60

ulus to arouse it."[113] Films were like land mines lurking in the minds of children waiting to be set off.

So children remembered what they saw, but did it affect their attitudes or behaviors? One study compared the attitudes of children who go to the movies four to five times a week to children who go approximately twice a month. The findings?

> We have found that the movie children average lower deportment records, do on the average poorer work in their school subjects, are rated lower in reputation by their teachers on two rating forms, are rated lower by their classmates . . . are less cooperative and less self-controlled as measured both by ratings and conduct tests, are slightly more deceptive in school situations, slightly less skillful in judging what is the most useful and helpful and sensible thing to do, and are somewhat less emotionally stable.[114]

Of particular concern was the effect of sex scenes on adolescents. Autobiographies of teenagers revealed that at least a third of them consciously imitated what they saw in love scenes, with one teen describing films as "a liberal education in the art of lovemaking."[115] A college freshman wrote that, "almost all of my knowledge of sex came from the movies."[116] Another wrote, "I think the movies have a great deal to do with the present-day so-called wildness. If we did not see such examples in the movies, where would we get the idea of being 'hot'? We wouldn't."[117] Of particular concern was the possible contribution of films to sexual delinquency. A 16-year-old inmate in a women's prison wrote, "a movie would get me so passionate after it was over that I just had to have relief. You know what I mean."[118] Approximately 25% of the female inmates in this study acknowledged "engaging in sexual relations after being aroused at a movie,"[119] and male inmates told stories of bringing girls to movies to sexually arouse them, then taking them to secluded spots to rape them.

[113]Holaday and Stoddard, 1933, p. 42
[114]Forman, 1935, p. 132
[115]Forman, 1935, p. 150
[116]Forman, 1935, p. 166
[117]Forman, 1935, p. 167
[118]Forman, 1935, p. 222
[119]Forman, 1935, p. 224

"The road to delinquency, in a few words, is heavily dotted with movie addicts"[120]—not only sexual delinquency, but all sorts of criminal activities seemed to be encouraged by the movies. Prison inmates generated lists of the tips they picked up from movies, including the importance of establishing an alibi, carrying a machine gun in a violin case, not leaving fingerprints, looking for secret panels hiding wall safes, renting an apartment to use as a gang hangout, and eluding police by turning up an alley, turning off the lights, and speeding in the opposite direction. Some 32 aspects of crime technique could allegedly be learned from the movies.

Many adults also feared that children's health was adversely affected by movies. A study was designed to see whether children's sleep patterns were disrupted by movie viewing. A hypnograph—an electronic sensor that detected movement in the bed—was attached to the cross-bars of 20 beds in the Ohio State Bureau of Juvenile Research. One hundread and seventy children each spent 50 consecutive nights in the hypnograph beds, during which time they were taken shopping on some nights, taken to the movies on other nights, and given a few cups of coffee before bed some nights. The findings of this study showed that children varied greatly in the extent to which their sleep was affected, but that a movie appeared to be "about as disturbing to sleep patterns as sitting up till midnight or . . . as the drinking of two cups of coffee in the evening."[121]

Another study designed to measure health effects attempted to measure the intensity of emotional responses to films. Children's fingertips were placed in liquid electrodes while they watched movies and their heart rates were monitored. Adolescents appeared to be twice as excited by films as adults and children three times as excited as adults—except in the case of erotic scenes, when adolescents were the most excited of all.[122]

Although the Payne Fund researchers tended to emphasize the inconclusive nature of their findings, those findings were suggestive enough of harmful effects to lead W. W. Charters, a prominent administrative progressive and author of a summary of the Payne Fund Studies, to write that, "the conclusion is inevitable that from the point of view of children's welfare the commercial movies are an

---

[120]Forman, 1935, p. 232

[121]Charters, 1933, p. 55

[122]Forman, 1935, p. 100

unsavory mess."[123] Despite that the researchers involved in these projects rejected the conclusion that movies caused negative attitudes and behaviors, the findings of these studies were commonly interpreted as proving such causal effects, reinforcing what Lowery and DeFleur described as "the *legacy of fear* that had been kept alive by strident denunciations of the evils of propaganda during the same decade."[124] These concerns, combined with some of the other problems and frustrations involved in using educational films, hindered the widespread integration of film into classroom practice.

CONCLUSION

Despite the beliefs held by a variety of education reformers that film had a place in their plans, potential and effort alone were not enough to secure a prominent place for film in American public education. Educational film may have gotten caught in the rising and ebbing tides of different strands of progressivism—in particular, in the backlash against child-centered progressivism in the 1940s and 1950s. The anticommunist backlash of the McCarthy era was felt both in Hollywood and in American public education, both of which were targets in the witch hunt. In particular, the child-centered progressivism with which film was so often associated was linked to communism, and efforts were made to purge schools of its influence. Life-adjustment education, regarded as a strand of child-centered progressivism, was blasted by critics who blamed it for the lower than acceptable academic achievement of American students and the anti-intellectualism of American education and American society. These same critics tended to look down on audio-visual educational materials, regarding them as inferior to books. In a similar spirit, Hollywood films were regarded by critics as lowbrow and anti-intellectual.

Educational film's appeal to the administrative progressives, who were coming back to dominance after World War II, kept it alive in military research laboratories. It also played a role in some of the curriculum revision projects sponsored by the federal government in the 1950s. However, it no longer monopolized the attention of promot-

[123]Charters, 1933, p. 55

[124]Lowery and DeFleur, p. 1995, p. 41

ers of educational technology. By that time, a variety of other media were the new focus of attention and research, and film never regained the degree of interest it had received in the 1920s and 1930s. Although many an American adult can remember being herded into his or her school auditorium to see a film, few had an educational experience that was fundamentally transformed by the medium.

3

RADIO

*The radio is a magic link of common experience in education. . . .
Who can vision the significance of the fact that distance for the ear
has been annihilated; that by voice the world becomes one neighborhood; that no matter what the size of the school or where it is
located, the great of all the earth may visit the pupil in his own
classroom . . . the roof of the classroom has been blown off and the
walls have been set on the circumference of the globe.*

—Ben Darrow, *Radio: The Assistant Teacher* (1932)

By the time radio broadcasting had been organized into a formal,
commercial enterprise in the late 1920s, educators had been experimenting with it for a number of years. Many colleges and universities
had been transmitting code signals in the previous decade and then
applied in the 1920s for licenses to operate radio stations. According
to a survey conducted by the U.S. Commissioner of Education in
1922, there were already 60 educational institutions experimenting
with radio by that time.[1]

---

[1]Perry, 1929, p. 38

Although the most often cited beginning of broadcasting into American classrooms is a February 1924 experiment conducted in Haaren High School in New York City, it was actually preceded by an experiment of RCA and the New York City Board of Education in DeWitt Clinton High School, where seniors received a radio broadcast on American history on June 24, 1923.[2] Although these appear to be the first broadcasts to K–12 schools, neither was the very first broadcast of an instructional program into a classroom; that honor appears to go to Nebraska Wesleyan University, where a physics professor gave a lecture via radio on December 20, 1921.[3]

Early reactions to radio echoed early sentiments about the telegraph. Radio was described in a 1933 League of Nations report as "a force, the nature of which would seem to be beyond human understanding."[4] According to radio education pioneer Ben Darrow, it was a "new giant of communication. . . . No one can estimate the full power of this new device which science has placed in the hands of civilization."[5] A New York City high school teacher delivered an address in 1924 in which he marveled at how "the world is so small today, that even perchance beyond the seas some may be listening even now to my words," and how radio is "one of many compelling factors that are obliterating, especially for America, national boundaries."[6] Ben Darrow believed that radio

> has almost unlimited possibilities. No one can estimate the full
> power of this new device which science has placed in the hands of
> civilization. Even the very civilization of the future may depend
> largely upon the control and the direction of this power.[7]

His sentiments might seem a bit exaggerated today, but he was expressing a popular view of his day.

The hopes for educational radio were high enough that, in May 1929, Secretary of the Interior Ray Lyman Wilbur called a conference, bringing together members of the Bureau of Education and

---

[2]Atkinson, 1942c, p. 12

[3]Atkinson, 1942a, p. 13

[4]*School Broadcasting*, 1933, p. 5

[5]Darrow, 1932, p. 64

[6]Wilkins, 1924, p. 158

[7]Darrow, 1932, p. 64

the Federal Radio Commission, NBC president M. H. Aylesworth, CBS president William S. Paley, representatives of the American Council on Education and the National Education Association, and other interested parties. The purpose of the conference, financed by the Payne Fund, was to begin examining the work done so far in educational radio. In his opening remarks, Wilbur expressed his belief that "it seems inevitable that great use must be found for the radio in our public education system."[8]

Out of this conference came the Preliminary Committee on Educational Broadcasting, which distributed questionnaires to thousands of teachers, principals, and superintendents. These questionnaires indicated that many teachers were excited about the potential of radio to bridge the classroom and world outside the school, and either had used radio to that end or looked forward to doing so. Secretary Wilbur hoped to see radio used in this way, writing in 1930 that "the thing I would particularly like to see would be to have the Government officials in the States and counties brought into immediate contact with the school room so that the children would see a live government instead of a dead government."[9]

However, a number of impediments to the use of radio were identified in this survey, which would be echoed for decades. For one, educators felt that the curriculum was already too full, precluding the addition of radio lessons. They were concerned that radio instruction would be unsatisfactory by making children into passive listeners or lacking the feedback mechanisms of live instruction. They identified technical problems, like static and weak reception during school hours. They cited lack of funds in their schools' budgets for radio equipment. They preferred the phonograph, which permitted playback. Finally, they wondered if radio was just a fad that would quickly fade, and whether they would be wasting their time expending the energy that effective use of radio lessons required.

Many public schools, colleges, universities, and commercial stations were involved in educational radio from the late 1920s to the early 1940s. A variety of projects were undertaken, some more successful and widespread than others. Although some were meant as temporary projects to address some short-term need, others were envisioned as permanent transformations of schools. The height of

[8]in Perry, 1929, p. 65

[9]Advisory Committee on Education by Radio, 1930, p. 13

interest and use was in the mid- to late 1930s, when as many as half of all American schools experimented, however briefly in some cases, with radio. Interest dropped off during World War II and never fully recovered, particularly once radio had been eclipsed by television.

HOPES AND PLANS FOR EDUCATIONAL RADIO

Even more so than film, educational radio developed and peaked during a period when child-centered progressive pedagogy was at its height. It is no wonder, then, that most of the popular arguments in favor of educational radio were a close fit with ideas about this style of progressive education.

Americans were well aware in the early 20th century that they lived in a world in flux, attributable largely to technological change. Like film, radio was believed to be helpful in addressing the challenges of a rapidly changing world. Some progressive education reformers argued that schools had to change to meet the needs of a changing society, and that radio could be used to help schools make the appropriate changes. E. George Payne, a radio education scholar, expressed this sentiment as follows:

> In an age of momentous changes, such as characterize events taking place in the twentieth century, appear new institutions and agencies that require a readjustment of our educational institutions, our curriculums, our programs of instruction, and our methods. Perhaps no new inventions and subsequent developments have had a more far-reaching effect than the motion picture and the radio.[10]

Educational broadcasting advocate W. Levenson argued that, "the teacher must be provided with the latest devices to prepare the children to live happily in a complex society."[11] Ben Darrow further believed that through radio, "the human mind will rise to an entirely new level of precision and efficiency and there will be such an enlargement of consciousness that the common man will be familiar with matters which today only a few can understand."[12]

---

[10]Payne, in Harrison, 1938, p. xv

[11]Levenson, 1945, p. 4

[12]Darrow, 1932, p. ix

Like film, radio was promoted as compatible with many aspects of child-centered progressivism. First, advocates celebrated the democratizing potential of the medium, which was seen as a way of bringing important social, political, and cultural events to the masses. Federal Radio Commission member Ira Robinson wrote, "[Radio is] the greatest implement of democracy yet given to mankind. It is the voice of the people, indeed, the expression of the soul of the people unto themselves and unto the other nations of the earth."[13] Some people argued that the ability of radio to put a voice to a political leader's words would improve the political process; as Assistant Secretary of Commerce John Dickinson wrote, "we at last find realized the conditions of a true democracy, for the people of the country are actually within sound of the voice of their leader and in a position to consider and reflect upon the program which he brings before them."[14] Wisconsin radio program director H.B. McCarty expressed a similar sentiment, writing, "Confidence will be renewed—or at least, misunderstanding will be removed. There will be no mistaking the President's meaning. . . . The people will know exactly where the President stands and what he aims to do."[15] This connection to political leaders was used to promote school radio use. After many classes listened to the live broadcast of the 1929 inauguration of President Hoover, hundreds of schools invested in radio equipment.[16]

Another popular argument in favor of using radio in schools was that it would help democratize education by equalizing opportunity, particularly for children in rural schools. Teachers in remote rural schools often lacked an extensive education, or were not well versed in all subject areas. Radio had the potential to bring the rural teacher, "isolated from the academic and social centres of the country . . . a knowledge of new educational methods, and a wealth of information and illustrating material which can bring life to his class and immensely stimulate his own teaching."[17] Educational radio advocate Max Bildersee wrote:

---

[13]Robinson, 1930, p. 3

[14]Dickenson, 1934, p. 39

[15]McCarty, 1934, p. 19

[16]Harrison, 1938, p. 3

[17]Clausse, 1949, p. 13

In annihilating distance, and in passing effortlessly through
physical classroom barriers, in making exceptional and unusual
events, materials, and personalities available to school children
everywhere, radio has contributed immeasurably to the equalization of opportunities for education throughout the nation.[18]

Like film, radio was also promoted in the spirit of progressive
education for its ability to connect schoolchildren with the world outside their classrooms. Radio seemed well suited to make school
lessons seem more relevant, more a part of actual happenings in the
world, particularly because it could bring an event to children as it
happened. It could bring "to the necessarily narrow confines of the
school an echo of the concerns and activities of daily social life. . . . In
current affairs and culture alike, it offers the teacher an invaluable
auxiliary instrument."[19]

Another way in which radio was promoted in keeping with
progressive pedagogy was in its sensory appeal. In much the same
way that film was promoted for its appeal to the eye, radio was promoted for its appeal to the ear. A 1927 article in *Eye and Ear
Instruction* made the following prediction:

It has been commonly remarked that children are losing their
ability to use their ears readily, this possibly resulting from too
much emphasis on speech on the part of teachers and parents. It
is now predicted that radio may restore keenness to the auditory
sense.[20]

The idea was that children would develop more sophisticated listening skills if they listened to radio lessons.

Educators also hoped to stimulate children's interest in
learning through radio, and to encourage further inquiry inspired by
radio broadcasts. In *Radio in the Classroom: Objectives, Principles,
and Practices*, Margaret Harrison (1938) believed that radio could
"increase the number, variety, and intensity of children's interests.
This probably is radio's greatest contribution to school life."[21] Carroll
Atkinson, arguably the most thorough documentarian of radio educa-

---

[18]Bildersee, 1954, pp. 33–34

[19]Clausse, 1949, p. 6

[20]"Eye and ear instruction," 1927

[21]Harrison, 1938, p. 13

tion, quoted in one of his books a 1926 *Kansas Farmer* article, which claimed that "Radio beats sulfur and molasses for taking the accumulated lethargy out of American rural youth of school age."[22] The article went on to report that student tardiness had been eliminated in schools with radio.

Some educators believed that children would become more active learners when radio broadcasts were employed. For example, a foreign language teacher argued in 1930 that "the only valid theory on which to base educational school broadcasting is the activity theory; namely, that the object of teaching scholars by radio is to encourage them to ask questions."[23] A 1933 League of Nations report on radio education argued that radio had the potential to "stimulate a desire for self-instruction and to induce children to visualize the happenings of every day life, to ask questions, and to raise rather than to solve problems—in short, to arouse their intellectual curiosity."[24] Another piece to this argument was that teachers would lecture less, becoming learners along with students. H. M. Buckley, of the Cleveland public schools, argued that "the teacher receives constant stimulus from the radio lesson. She joins the pupils as an inquirer and a learner. Her emphasis is upon learning rather than teaching. She becomes a guide and a stimulator in a learning situation."[25] These hopes were similar to those expressed, just slightly earlier, for classroom use of films.

Like film, radio was sometimes advocated in the context of the project method, where students engaged in learning projects through which a variety of subject areas were addressed (as opposed to being lectured in discrete subject areas). Dr. William John Cooper, U.S. Commissioner of Education, wrote a 1932 article in *School and Society* where he described the use of something like the project method in Russian schools and suggested that radio be used to advance project teaching in the United States.[26] In 1937, the Lewiston, Idaho, schools began to use radio as a central part of their

---

[22]Atkinson, 1942a, p. 16

[23]Mercer, 1930, p. 370

[24]*School Broadcasting*, 1933, p. 7

[25]Buckley, 1934, p. 81

[26]Cooper, 1932

experiment with a workshop approach to school, described next in
Radio Development in a Small City School System (1943):

> The classroom, it was believed, could be transformed into a
> Workshop . . . and the community could become the laboratory in
> which students gained experience for the living done both in and
> out of school. . . . In the Workshop, it was reasoned, the student
> would be allowed to choose his own project along the lines of his
> personal interests. But students in the Workshop would have to
> assume far more *responsibility* for the results of their work than
> was the custom where there were classroom contacts only. . . .
> Thus a workshop was created. It was designed to combine speech
> and radio work with school and community needs where the
> experience would be real, not synthetic . . . and not merely the
> presentation of work before a room full of classmates.[27]

Lewiston students researched, wrote, and produced radio programs
related to areas of interest to them or importance to their community.

Given the interest at the time on project-based learning and
student activity, it was not uncommon for public school systems, colleges, or universities involved in broadcasting to put students on the
air. In some cases, the use of student talent was necessitated by lack of
funds for more experienced performers; in other cases, teachers
thought it would be a good way to help children learn. Students were
on the air in musical and dramatic performances, discussion groups,
spelling bees, and storytelling sessions, among other things. In some
cases, individual programs in a series were prepared by different
schools or classes in a district, taking turns throughout the school year.

A key aspect of child-centered progressivism was an emphasis on community and collaboration. One of the most frequently and
fervently cited advantages of radio in the 1920s and 1930s was its
power to unify people and foster understanding and appreciation of
people of different backgrounds—an issue of particular concern to
Americans (unknowingly) between the world wars. Radio was argued
to be "peculiarly fitted to create international friendship through real
familiarity between peoples, and so to produce that common spiritual
and intellectual foundation which is the only safeguard of permanent
peace."[28] Radio education advocate Dorothy Gordon believed strongly
in the potential of radio to unite diverse people:

[27]Berry, 1943, pp. 33–34
[28]Forman, 1935, pp. 123–131

> Radio can dramatize the backgrounds of the various ethnic
> groups that compose our population and teach effectively that
> each of these groups, each race and each religion, through their
> diversified cultures, have made rich contributions to our national
> life. . . . American radio must be a factor in teaching our children
> the acceptance, not tolerance, of each other's differences and a
> recognition of the enrichment that these very differences con-
> tribute to the mosaic pattern, which is America.[29]

Again these hopes for radio were similar to those expressed for film.

As World War II approached, faith in American public
schools was shaken as Americans wondered whether their children
would fall prey to the influence of totalitarian leaders in Europe.
Americans watched Hitler and Mussolini using radio to promote
their causes and feared the apparent power of radio propaganda.
This was a time when Americans were increasingly aware of the
power of mass media persuasion and when theories of media effects
suggested that those effects were extremely powerful. The effect of
radio, according to the League of Nations report, seemed to be "far
more direct, far more violent, and one that retains a remarkably
more human aspect—and consequently of a nature to engender bit-
terness and hatred—than that exercised by gramophone records or
even the cinematograph."[30] One of the arguments explaining the success of Hitler and Mussolini to gain the support of their nations' citizens was that schools in those nations had failed to create free thinking individuals, resulting in a mass mind of undifferentiated, uncriti-
cal people who were easily swayed by film and radio propaganda.
Charles Siepmann pointed out that "Fascism is not dead. Modern
technology alone has made it possible."[31] Radio, it was believed, could
be used in schools to train children to be critical thinkers so they
could resist anti-American media propaganda should they be exposed
to it. In an age when mass media were believed to have dramatic
effects on their audiences, this purpose of radio education seemed
particularly critical. The irony should not be lost, however, that the
same people who advocated radio education to protect children from
anti-American radio propaganda tended also to promote the use of
radio for pro-American propaganda.

---

[29]Gordon, 1942, p. 115

[30]*School Broadcasting*, 1933, p. 7

[31]Siepmann, 1948, p. 6

Some people hoped that the apparent power of radio to sway public opinion for the worse was proof that they could harness the persuasive power of radio for good. Hitler equipped German schools with loudspeakers in 1935, and Mussolini followed suit in 1937.[32] Some Americans thought ahead, realizing that many of these fully indoctrinated youth would survive the war. It would not be enough for the United States to simply win the war; in *All Children Listen,* Dorothy Gordon (1942) argued that American children would have to be "as eager and as fanatic about Democracy as the young Nazis are about their way of life"[33] to ensure the future of democracy in the world. American schools took up the cause of cultivating patriotism in young citizens sometimes through the use of radio. Gordon continued:

> The war that America is fighting is a war for survival. Ports, sea-lanes, oil fields, markets, these things are only markers, counters in this game Democracy is playing with Death. . . . unless we fight for this freedom in the minds of tomorrow as well as on the battlefields of today, we fight with arms but no armor. . . . In short, while the fight on the battlefield is with men, there is an important fight on the homefront for children, those men of tomorrow, and tomorrow. And radio is the blitz-weapon of that fight.[34]

Just as film was enlisted to the cause of patriotism and national security, radio education was seen as an essential tool for protecting the nation.

Although most ideas about educational radio were in keeping either with child-centered progressivism or patriotism building, some arguments in favor of radio education were more in tune with the priorities of the administrative progressives. These arguments promised that radio would teach more material, more effectively, and more rapidly than traditional instruction. Although it was rarely explicitly stated, some of these arguments implied that radio could be used to cut costs by providing specialized instruction through radio teachers instead of by hiring teachers who were skilled in those subjects. Education Commissioner Cooper remarked in 1932 that besides making teachers more expert in their subjects, "I can also see where there

---

[32]Gordon, 1942, p. 85

[33]Gordon, 1942, p. 112

[34]Gordon, 1942, pp. 13–14

can be one individual in each city to teach the history and another to teach the geography and another the arithmetic, etc."[35] As might be expected, ideas like these tended to come from administrators, not teachers; many teachers felt some anxiety over the prospect of being rendered obsolete by new technology. However, despite the anxiety felt by some teachers, many took an interest in radio and participated in radio education projects in their schools.

EDUCATIONAL RADIO PROJECTS

The growth of radio stations triggered a flurry of educational radio activity from a variety of sources, including elementary and secondary schools, colleges and universities, and commercial broadcasters. Their purposes for broadcasting also varied, often involving some commercial or publicity motive in addition to—or instead of—an academic goal. The earliest school broadcasting, in the 1920s, was typically for the purpose of public relations. The expense of the expanding offerings of the public schools, particularly at the secondary level, needed to be justified to school communities, and many districts used radio to promote their plans and involve parents in supporting those plans. Ben Darrow referred to radio as "a magic link of common experience in education, bringing together again the home and the school, which were separated with the advent of the present system . . . [the teacher's] classroom work will be still more resultful and the Magic Link will draw into the educative process many groups not hitherto active and some not even friendly."[36]

The New York City public schools experimented with radio from February to May 1924, primarily in an effort, according to a 1924 report by the New York City Board of Education, to "acquaint the general public and especially the citizens of our city with the workings of our vast school system upon which such enormous sums of money are so generously expended."[37] The broadcasts were primarily information segments presented by school administrators, describing their educational programs, and, in many cases, adding a

---

[35]Cooper, 1932

[36]Darrow, 1932, p. 265

[37]New York City Board of Education, 1924, pp. 13–14

big sales pitch to convince people of the value of those programs. An address about teacher recruitment described the school system as:

> an organization reaching into every part of the life of a great city or a great state; stimulating and advancing its industry, inspiring its workers, uplifting the morale of all its people; visiting not merely the broad and well-lighted highways of the people's days but penetrating their homes from its proud mansions to its dingy homes in the slums; reaching at once the blest and the unfortunate, the lame, the blind, the deaf; uplifting, so far as education can uplift, the mentally defective.[38]

As in all eras, although citizens generally supported the idea of universal, free public education, they needed to be persuaded that public schools were worth the public funds spent on them.

Some of the New York City radio addresses echoed the sentiments of Horace Mann and the common school advocates, urging citizens to support school expenditures for the good of society if not for one's own children. These addresses emphasized the importance of spending money on special programs and facilities to educate polio victims, tubercular children, children with heart disease, and malnourished children. These children were provided with such things as home schooling, open air schools, and school lunches. Even if your child is not one of these, the arguments went, the programs deserved your support because these programs would turn New York's liabilities into assets. As one address emphasized, "the happiness and gratitude of those children and their parents is evidence of public money well invested."[39] An address by a representative of the State Federation of Labor promoted *continuation schools* or schools required by law for teenagers under age 18 who left school to go to work, arguing that these children "become submerged in blind-alley occupations only to reappear at intervals in the ranks of unskilled, discontented labor or in the courts of juvenile delinquency."[40] Much as Mann and others had argued a century earlier, the expense of public school programs was justified for its indirect benefit to all and its potential to reduce crime and pauperism.

---

[38]New York City Board of Education, 1924, p. 50

[39]New York City Board of Education, 1924, p. 76

[40]New York City Board of Education, 1924, p. 136

New York was certainly not alone in its use of radio for public relations. After discontinuing their efforts during the worst years of the Depression, the Indianapolis schools went back on the air in 1935 to inform the public about school activities. The Akron, Ohio, public schools began broadcasting public relations programs in 1935, and then added programs for classroom use. One of the original purposes of the broadcasting activities of the Denver schools in 1935 was "to interpret the schools to the community."[41] The Providence, Rhode Island, schools also began broadcasting in 1935, with public relations as one of their main objectives. Their programs included a series of evening programs for adults describing school activities. Atlanta, Detroit, Indianapolis, Olympia (Washington), Kalispell (Montana), Minneapolis, and San Francisco were among the other cities to use radio for the purpose of public relations.[42]

More indirectly, colleges and universities used radio for public relations by producing educational programs for high school use. Carroll Atkinson suggested that the reason universities made many more good programs for high school students than younger children was they most wanted "to encourage future attendance (and incidentally tuition fees) on the broadcasting institution's campus."[43] In much the same way that colleges and universities today offer educational programs to high school students in the hope of someday enrolling those students as undergraduates, universities in the early days of radio believed they could boost enrollments by advertising themselves through high school radio broadcasts.

The use of radio for promoting public education intensified during the Depression, when public schools faced severe cutbacks while they were trying to argue that education could rebuild and restore a great America. The National Education Association broadcast a weekly program called "Our American Schools" in the early 1930s on Sunday evenings, the purpose of which was "to increase popular determination to maintain educational opportunities for children in the present emergency."[44] Some other plans for radio education were also a product of the Depression. For example, radio was seen as a way to educate Americans about the workings of their gov-

---

[41]Atkinson, 1942b, p. 95

[42]See Atkinson, 1942b, for accounts of school use of radio for public relations

[43]Atkinson, 1942a, p. 12

[44]"N.E.A. broadcasts weekly radio programs on 'Our American Schools'," 1933

ernment and economy. The National Advisory Council on Radio in Education and the American Political Science Association developed the "You and Your Government" series in the spirit of helping to restore American prosperity. In his preface to *Government in a Depression: Constructive Economy in State and Local Government,* radio education advocate Levering Tyson (1933) argued:

> As a result of unprecedented governmental changes the United States today is committed to a series of gigantic experiments. . . . Upon the outcome of these experiments may largely depend the happiness and prosperity of every man, woman, and child for years to come. Understanding of backgrounds and of the reasons for the measures that are projected is a matter of immediate and vital concern to all.[45]

The "You and Your Government" broadcasts were designed to educate listeners about the nature of economic problems and their solutions, including government's role in solving those problems.

Some school districts ventured into radio instruction because of crises. For example, a polio epidemic delayed the opening of the Chicago elementary schools in September 1937, at which time the Chicago Board of Education prepared emergency radio programs to provide instruction in math, English, science, social studies, and physical education for Grades 3 to 8 until the schools could be opened. Seven local radio stations donated time in 15-minute periods, and five newspapers carried digests of each lesson, including assignments for students.[46] Some 315,000 students received instruction in this manner, and the Board of Education began to take a greater interest in radio education.

A similar crisis presented itself in Milwaukee in the same year, when the school year began with a mild epidemic of scarlet fever. The Health Department closed the kindergarten and first grade, at which time a daily series of broadcasts in storytelling, music, and art was initiated. In this case, the district did not continue its use of radio after the emergency was over. (Incidentally, it appeared that the broadcasts may have actually defeated the purpose

---

[45]Tyson, 1933, p. vi

[46]See Atkinson, 1942b, for accounts of the Chicago, Milwaukee, Long Beach, and Dayton projects.

of keeping the children at home because some of them went to each other's houses to hear the programs, thus spreading the disease.)[47]

In Long Beach, California, it was not an illness, but an earthquake, that resulted in a series of emergency broadcasts intended to supplement the work of schools, which were often open only for half-day sessions. These broadcasts began on April 1, 1935, on two commercial stations that donated air time; as in Chicago, local newspapers helped out by printing the lectures.

In Dayton, Ohio, the crisis was financial. In the fall of 1938, the Board of Education ran out of money and closed the schools, which served approximately 34,000 students.[48] WHIO, a CBS station, offered its facilities to the schools. Teachers and students presented lessons in subjects like English, Latin, history, math, and science during four periods each day, and network educational programs were used to supplement the local programs. The programs were discontinued later that fall when the schools reopened. Although the district tried to continue experimenting with radio, their efforts only lasted a few months.

Then there were many cases where radio was used for regular classroom use unrelated to any particular crisis. In much the same way that educational films were made by commercial film makers, colleges, universities, and (to some extent) public schools, educational radio programs came from a variety of sources. A major difference between film and radio was that there was much more radio production activity in public schools than film production. That is not to say that it was the norm for American schoolchildren to be involved in radio broadcasting—more that many school systems had broadcasting licenses and aired a combination of locally produced shows and offerings from commercial networks and colleges and universities.

As mentioned earlier, the New York City public schools are credited with the first radio broadcast to a K–12 classroom. The second experiment, in Haaren High School, was a much larger and better documented project than the first in DeWitt Clinton High.[49] In the Haaren High experiment, RCA offered free air time each school day from 2:00 p.m. to 2:30 p.m. for the broadcasting of talks on such topics as music, history, civics, geography, nature study, and arith-

---

[47]Atkinson, 1942b, p. 115

[48]Atkinson, 1942b, p. 118

[49]Atkinson, 1942b, p. 12

metic.[50] This project, like many early educational radio projects, served the dual purpose of education and public relations intended to make the public more aware of the work of the public schools.[51] Students took part in some of the broadcasts, such as glee club, orchestra concerts, and spelling bees. The project lasted until May 1924, and a lapse in educational radio ensued.

In 1936, the City of New York offered air time to the Board of Education over municipally owned WNYC, along with $5,000 for the development of classroom radio lessons, which were to be written by New York City teachers. Twenty schools were chosen to receive the lessons and to be studied for the effectiveness of the radio programs. Teachers had been somewhat prepared for the idea of radio by a 1935 series of talks over WNYC designed as inservice training for them, and in 1936 some of them were chosen to write programs "intended specifically to fit the curriculum of the city schools."[52] A studio was built at Brooklyn Technical High School, and the staff at the Board of Education studio was expanded. Schools formed committees of faculty members to evaluate the programs, which were often written and performed by teachers and students. High school, junior high school, and elementary principals each had a Radio Committee, the central administrative office housed a Radio Coordinator, and a radio bulletin was distributed to all schools to inform principals and teachers about programs. As the programming expanded, it took up more and more air time on WNYC, crowding out other branches of city government that wanted to use the station. As a result, New York City was granted a short-wave allocation by the FCC in October 1938. Three years later, in June 1941, the Board of Education was also given permission to build an FM transmitter.

The Board of Education-sponsored programs included series in art, foreign languages, guidance, history, literature, and physics; some schools also used programs broadcast over commercial networks, such as the NBC Music Appreciation Hour and the CBS School of the Air. At the same time, the Board of Education was sensitive to concerns about the appropriateness of commercial messages in schools. In May 1941, they adopted a resolution establishing some new regulations to govern the use of radio in schools. It acknowl-

[50]Atkinson, 1942b, for an account of the educational radio projects in New York, Cleveland, Oakland, Atlanta, Indianapolis, and Rochester.

[51]Atkinson, 1942b, p. 13

[52]Atkinson, 1942b, p. 15

edged that radio "can be used so readily as a means of propaganda,"[53] and called on teachers to protect children "either by excluding all programs of a propaganda nature or by teaching pupils to evaluate radio programs properly."[54]

The Cleveland, Ohio, schools were also considered to be pioneers in radio education, beginning in 1925 with a music appreciation program. The Cleveland Board of Education had a unique philosophy of radio education, which was modeled by other school districts. They adopted the idea of the radio instructor as master teacher who would not only motivate students, but serve as a model for classroom teachers as well. The district carefully evaluated their radio efforts, conducting experiments to compare the instructional effectiveness of the radio lessons to traditional lessons and finding a slight advantage to radio instruction. They developed a standard method of preparation of radio lessons, including the following six steps as summarized by Carroll Atkinson (1942) in *Public School Broadcasting to the Classroom:*

(1) Lesson is prepared by a specialist with cooperation of the curriculum center for the subject concerned.
(2) Lesson is tested in one of the radio experimental centers that are equipped with public address systems, including all rooms in the buildings.
(3) Lesson then is revised for general broadcast in light of observed pupil and teacher reactions.
(4) All classrooms receiving lessons are provided in advance with teacher's outline, pupil worksheets, slides, reference books, pictures, maps, lanterns, victrola records, and other materials to make the lesson effective.
(5) Lesson is broadcast by one who knows the subject, has practiced the specific lesson, and has an acceptable radio voice.
(6) Provision is made for a follow-up by teacher and class at close of broadcast.[55]

The Cleveland schools developed curriculum centers or laboratory schools from which radio lessons were broadcast. At the elementary level, most programs were of the master teacher variety, meant as much to serve as inservice training for teachers as they

[53]Atkinson, 1942b, p. 16

[54]Atkinson, 1942b, p. 16

[55]Atkinson, 1942b, pp. 27–28

were meant to instruct children. These programs were broadcast by master teachers so that novice teachers could improve their skills by modeling their more experienced colleagues. At the secondary level, programs tended to be dramatizations produced by the high school radio workshop.

The Cleveland schools were able to build a station of their own in the late 1930s through funding from the Rockefeller Foundation. They obtained a license from the FCC for a short-wave channel and purchased 150 radios to supply their schools. The station, WBOE, was on the air every school day from 8:30 a.m. to 4:30 p.m., offering lessons for all grade levels as well as programs for teachers and parents. In addition to their own programming, they also included some of the offerings of NBC, CBS, the Mutual Broadcasting System, and the Blue Network. Network offerings included CBS' "Frontiers of Democracy," NBC's "Gallant American Women," Mutual's "Good Health and Training," and news broadcasts.

Another city school system that was an early experimenter in radio instruction was Oakland, California. They began in May 1924 with two 20-minute periods each week in subjects like English, guidance, geography, literature, and history; each lesson began with 4 or 5 minutes of music to give teachers a chance to tune into the station. Radio committee members would observe in classrooms to monitor students' attitudes toward the programs, and then they would meet together to compare notes and make improvements to the radio lessons. Oakland's radio activities only lasted 2 years.

The Atlanta, Georgia, schools got their start in radio education in 1926, when a radio manufacturer gave each of their schools a battery-operated radio. Unfortunately, the hot summer weather ruined the batteries, and the Atlanta schools did not resume their radio experiments until the 1930s. In the spring of 1938, they experimented briefly with a fairly ambitious plan, installing equipment in every school and using half-hour broadcasts, 5 days a week, as part of the regular curriculum work. Monday programs were about art and music, Tuesday and Wednesday "for and by elementary schools" (e.g., airing a school spelling bee), and Thursday was reserved for junior and senior high programs. Friday was kept open for national network programs, like the "NBC Music Appreciation Hour" or programs from the American School of the Air. During the 1938–1939 school year, broadcasting was cut back to 3 days a week; at the end of the year, Atlanta discontinued its radio activities.

The Indianapolis schools began using radio in classrooms in 1931. A year later, Depression budget restraints required them to discontinue their radio programs. In subsequent years, however, radio use resumed as schools bought equipment and began receiving programs from the Ohio School of the Air and the American School of the Air. A particularly successful program that they developed was an art show, where instruction sheets were sent to teachers for use as a follow-up to the broadcast. Requests for instruction sheets quickly grew to more than 10,000. Throughout the 1930s, Indianapolis added to its radio offerings, including a social studies program written and presented by students, music appreciation shows, and junior high guidance programs.

The Rochester, New York, schools were also known as active radio educators. The Rochester School of the Air began broadcasting in 1933, when a shortage of seating at the secondary level kept many seventh graders in elementary schools, and a science teacher started to broadcast lessons to them. In subsequent years, sixth and eighth grades were added as were high school chemistry and physics. Rochester offerings also expanded beyond science, including story hours, current events, geography, music, and art. An estimated 50,000 students were enrolled in these programs.

These are but a few examples of the radio activities of public schools. Dozens of school systems in all regions of the country were involved in radio education in the 1930s, although most of these activities did not last more than a few years. Although some schools produced their own programs, it was easier, less expensive, and more popular to use the programs provided by colleges and universities, as well as those offered on commercial stations.

Colleges and universities were involved in radio education from the start. In many cases, they had been experimenting with wireless telegraphy and then applied for licenses to operate radio stations in the early 1920s. For example, the University of Iowa had been broadcasting code transmissions since 1911, and then received its radio license in 1922.[56] In 1942, Carroll Atkinson estimated that "there have been thirty-eight American universities and colleges that more or less successfully have broadcast programs intended for classroom use,"[57] about a half dozen of them being "genuinely successful."

---

[56]Atkinson, 1942a, p. 19

[57]Atkinson, 1942a, p. 12

Colleges and universities varied greatly in the type of educational programming they provided and in the way in which they aired their programs. Some universities owned and operated their own stations; others used donated time on commercial stations. In some cases, programs produced locally by universities were picked up by a network and aired nationally. Some institutions offered programs to schools in an informal sense, in that they aired programs that were potentially appropriate for use in schools, and some schools used those programs. Other colleges and universities worked in close conjunction with schools to develop programming that was planned with the state or school curriculum in mind. For example, the State University of Iowa designed programs in 1934 that were aligned to the Iowa State High School Course of Study.[58] In 1925, the Kansas State College of Agriculture and Applied Science broadcast programs for country schools every weekday at 9:00 a.m.; a scarcity of radio receivers led to the discontinuation of the programs in 1927. The Colorado State College of Education created the Rocky Mountain School of the Air to provide programming to high schools. Other universities providing radio lessons to schools included Baylor, Cornell, Miami, Purdue, and the universities of Kansas, Kentucky, Michigan, Minnesota, Nebraska, New Mexico, North Dakota, Oklahoma, and Texas.

One of the most famous and extensive efforts of a university to broadcast to schools was the Ohio School of the Air, first organized in 1928 as a collaborative effort among Ohio teachers, the Payne Fund, Ohio State University, and a Crosley radio station.[59] They went on the air in January 1929, building an audience of over 100,000 students in 22 states by April of that year.[60] Besides offering lessons in such areas as history, literature, health, and art, the Ohio School of the Air broadcast live proceedings in the state Senate and House of Representatives, the inauguration of a new Ohio governor, and Herbert Hoover's presidential inauguration.[61]

As well received as the Ohio School of the Air was, it struggled to stay in existence. It lost its state funding in 1936 and had to cease operations for a year. The Crosley Radio Corporation then

[58]Atkinson, 1942a, p. 21
[59]Perry, 1929, p. 7
[60]Perry, 1929, p. 7
[61]Perry, 1929, p. 22

picked it up for 2 years, and then it switched hands again, becoming a sustaining feature of the Mutual Broadcasting System. However, when that station became an NBC affiliate, the project ended. After that, Ohio State University resumed its support, but the project was shut down again in 1939 due to lack of funds.[62]

Institutions of elementary, secondary, and higher education were not the only ones interested in radio education; commercial broadcasters took an interest as well. One of the greatest success stories of instructional radio was a commercially produced music appreciation program. In 1928, NBC launched its "Music Appreciation Hour," hosted by NBC Symphony Orchestra conductor Walter Damrosch. Within 3 years of its inception, this program had an estimated listening audience of 6 million children in schools across the country.[63] Districts with schools of the air often refrained from broadcasting their own programs on Fridays at 11 a.m., Eastern Standard Time, "in deference to the splendid R.C.A. Educational Hour conducted by Walter Damrosch."[64] This program went a long way toward convincing many educators to use radio in schools.

CBS was not to be outdone by its competitor; it launched the American School of the Air on February 4, 1930,[65] broadcasting a variety of programs coast to coast. CBS expanded its offerings the next fall, offering programs for nearly all grade levels in such subjects as American history, music appreciation, storytelling, and current events.[66] The name was changed to "School of the Air of the Americas" in 1940 when CBS expanded its reach to cover 22 countries in the Western Hemisphere.[67] Educational programming by these major national networks helped cultivate educators' interest in using radio, as well as their confidence that there would be enough programming available to make the investment worthwhile.[68]

As popular as some of the commercial offerings were, conflicts between educational and commercial broadcasters grew in

---

[62]Atkinson, 1942a, pp. 30–31

[63]"Dr. Damrosch has audience of six millions," 1932

[64]Perry, 1929, p. 18

[65]"The American School of the Air," 1930

[66]"American School of the Air enlarges program," 1930

[67]Atkinson, 1942c, p. 96

[68]Harrison, 1938, p. 4

intensity. In much the same way that educators doubted the motives of theatrical and industrial film makers in providing films to schools, they questioned the propriety and educational value of using commercial broadcasts in schools. This conflict had much to do with the direction radio education took, and it is discussed in some detail later in this chapter.

The U.S. military also took an interest in education by radio having been involved in radio since its invention. With the declaration of war in 1917, President Wilson had seized all amateur radio apparatus and commercial radio facilities, putting them under Navy control. Although the Navy did not retain its monopoly control over radio at the war's end, as some Navy and government leaders had hoped it would, the military remained involved in radio in a variety of ways. When the United States entered World War II, the War Department engaged social scientists in radio experiments to develop programs for morale building. Expecting a long war in the Pacific, the War Department recognized the need to make soldiers understand that they would be there for several difficult years. To that end, the Armed Forces Radio Service prepared and tested programs designed to convince soldiers that the war would be long, and that it was important for them to remain committed to the cause. However, it turned out that the programs were not needed because the use of atomic weapons brought the war to an accelerated conclusion.[69] Still it is worth noting that the military conducted research on the effectiveness of radio as a training and motivational medium, as they did with film and as they would with later media.

FACTORS PREVENTING THE DEVELOPMENT OF EDUCATIONAL RADIO

As excited as many advocates were about radio education, they faced huge obstacles. Some argued that the advocates were an obstacle for having exaggerated the potential of radio beyond reason. Where some schools hesitated to use radio at all, others erred in the other direction, jumping in too quickly. In 1938, Margaret Harrison wrote:

---

[69]Lowery & DeFleur, 1995, ch. 7

So quickly were the potential educational possibilities of radio recognized that equipment was purchased for hundreds of schools long before supervisors, principals, and teachers were ready to adapt it to school situations. Use, misuse, and abuse of the classroom radio resulted.[70]

Levering Tyson, director of the National Advisory Council on Radio in Education, cautioned educational radio advocates in 1930 against letting their idealism run wild, fearing that "one of the grave dangers connected with radio broadcasting in education is that it will not be taken seriously"[71] and would be dismissed due to the excessive idealism of some of its promoters.

Part of the problem of moving so fast was that it was difficult to keep track of the big picture of where educational radio should go and how it could get there. George F. Zook, U.S. Commissioner of Education, opened a 1934 conference by saying:

I think that the mechanical developments in the field of radio and motion pictures are so rapid as to make it very difficult for those of us who are engaged in educational work to develop the basis on which those processes may be used in the classroom and in other ways for educational purposes.[72]

A number of issues complicated the process of integrating radio into classroom life, and they were rarely given adequate consideration in the heat of aggressive implementation of the new technology.

Equipment Problems

A common problem was the scarcity of receiving sets in schools, especially in rural schools, where some felt radio had its greatest potential. In some districts, such as one in rural Kansas, children learned to build receivers as a way to furnish the schools with radio equipment. In this district, as in others, the size of the listening audience was limited, according to Carroll Atkinson, "not by lack of interest so much as by lack of radio sets with which pupils might listen."[73]

---

[70]Harrison, 1938, p. 3

[71]Tyson, 1930, p. 136

[72]Zook, 1934, p. 1

[73]Atkinson, 1942a, p. 18

Technical problems created obstacles as well. Poor reception made it difficult or impossible to tune into programs in many schools. Some schools, particularly rural schools without electricity, used battery-powered sets, which required more upkeep than sets that were plugged in. As mentioned earlier, this was particularly problematic in southern schools, where heat sometimes damaged the batteries. The 1933 League of Nations report on radio education pointed out that often, if radio was not being used to good advantage in schools, the reason was poor equipment.[74]

Incompatibility with Teachers' Needs and Interests

A number of problems with educational radio had to do with its incompatibility with the day-to-day professional experiences of teachers. For example, the way radio programs had to be used compromised teachers' autonomy in deciding how to structure the school day. Programs had to be listened to at whatever time they aired, except in those rare cases where schools had recording and playback equipment. Sometimes programs of local origin were planned in consultation with school principals, in which case class schedules and broadcast schedules were brought in line with one another. However, it seems that more typically schools simply had to change their plans if they were going to use radio programs. In this respect, radio was even more difficult than film to incorporate into the school day. As described in chapter 2, teachers could not always predict when a particular film would be available to their school, and they were usually unable to preview the film before using it in class. Although the schedule of radio programs was easier to predict, the time of day when those programs had to be used was more rigid than the time a film could be used. Moreover, like film, the programs could not be previewed.

Programs intended for wider geographic areas (often spanning more than one time zone) or programs that could not be (or simply were not) scheduled with particular schools' class schedules in mind were even more difficult to use. As a 1929 study in Connecticut showed, one of the greatest difficulties in using radio was "lack of

---

[74]*School Broadcasting*, 1933, p. 39

time for programs. It is pointed out that the prescribed courses of study do not permit elasticity."[75] To some extent, transcription services helped by providing recordings, but many educators had to use programs when they aired or not use them at all.

Teachers also had trouble using radio lessons because the lessons were frequently incompatible with the local curriculum. Sometimes programs would cover an appropriate topic, but at the wrong time of year. In other cases, the topic was appropriate, but the vocabulary or syntax did not match the intended grade level. Some programs developed for classroom use were tailored to the curriculum of a particular school system, but most were more general in an effort to be relevant to as large an audience as possible. Teachers were frequently frustrated by programs produced without the participation of experienced teachers, who might have been able to point out these kinds of problems. This problem echoed criticisms of classroom films, many of which were produced with mass distribution in mind, and which, therefore, were not closely aligned to any particular curriculum.

When teachers were actively involved in educational broadcasting, they often lacked the training they needed to produce quality programming. Many educational programs had announcers who were teachers with no training in broadcasting. Professional broadcasters urged teachers to improve their showmanship, NBC vice president John Elwood argued:

> Radio is a show business. If the educator is going to educate by radio, he must grasp the essential fact, and very few educators have yet been able to do so, that he must use showmanship to do the job effectively.[76]

Although it may have been a valid point that teachers needed to learn how to adapt their performances for the new medium, the point was often made in a way that insulted, rather than inspired, teachers.

Besides being called on to become broadcasters without adequate training, teachers were often expected to use radio broadcasts in their classrooms without any training. Using radio lessons was by no means easier than other methods of instruction. To use a broad-

---

[75]"School radio users win prize trips," 1930

[76]Elwood, 1930, p. 21

cast well, teachers needed to preview the material as best they could. This was difficult with live broadcasts although teacher's manuals sometimes gave helpful overviews of programs. Teachers then had to prepare their classes for the broadcasts, and follow up the broadcast with some meaningful discussion or activity. This generally required them to listen to the broadcast carefully, and be able to think on their feet for the follow-up activity, because they could not know ahead of time precisely what would be heard during the program. As described in chapter 2 with respect to film, it was extremely frustrating for teachers to have to fit their professional practices to someone else's radio product, which they had no part in creating and could not even preview before using.

Some teachers preferred phonograph records to radio broadcasts because of the difficulty of using an unpredictable, live radio program. Phonograph records could be previewed, they could be played over and over again, and they could be used at the teachers convenience.

Another problem for teachers was that they felt some anxiety about being replaced by radio. Although most promotions of radio education stressed that the classroom teacher remained the central, key figure in any educational experience, some teachers feared that radio could be used in place of them. Teacher anxiety about replacement by radio also might have been fueled by Depression-era cutbacks in school budgets and calls for schools to operate more efficiently. In the same way that teachers were wary of educational films, out of concern that films might be used to replace them in a time of tight budgets, they were also anxious about the possibility that radio could be used to that end.

The Depression made it difficult not only for schools to purchase radio equipment, but for educational broadcasters to carry on their activities. As Secretary of the Interior Ray Lyman Wilbur remarked in 1930, "There is a desire on the part of a great many teachers to bring the radio into the schoolroom. The question first is that of expense."[77] In some cases, such as the station of the University of Florida, the state cut its funding of the radio station, forcing the station to go commercial to continue to exist. The University of Alabama had to sell its station to a commercial company when it could no longer afford to sustain it. The Michigan State College of

---

[77]Lowery & DeFleur, 1995, ch. 7

Agriculture and Applied Science produced a biology class for 7 years, but had to stop because the cost of making and distributing its teacher's guides was too high. The University of Oklahoma felt it was able to initiate some interesting projects, but lacked the funding to follow up on them.[78] The producers of the "You and Your Government" series struggled with maintaining adequate funding and fell short of their goals because of lack of funds.[79] The Ohio School of the Air was popular, reaching thousands of students in many states; still it struggled terribly to keep its funding and ultimately lost it.

One solution to the funding problem was to work with commercial broadcasters, but effective collaboration between broadcasters and teachers was often lacking. It was not uncommon for teachers and broadcasters each to believe that the other did not understand their needs or concerns. Broadcasters criticized teachers for not being radiogenic—that is, for lacking the talent or flair for performing on the air. Teachers criticized broadcasters for putting entertainment over pedagogy, giving children the fun of a radio program, but not giving adequate thought to pedagogical value or curricular fit.

Some radio education advocates emphasized the importance of cooperation, urging broadcasters to consult with teachers and inform themselves about matters of classroom practice and curriculum. Some universities who experimented with radio discovered that their most successful K–12 ventures were responses to educators' requests, such as Iowa State College of Agriculture's vocational series for high school students and the State College of Washington's shifting of programs into time slots identified by teachers as most convenient.[80] UNESCO's Roger Clausse suggested that broadcasters think not so much of making programs for students as making them for teachers; that is, programs needed to be designed in such a way that teachers perceived them to be meaningful and useful.[81] The League of Nations' report on radio education also emphasized that producing radio lessons required the "closest and constant co-operation" between teachers and broadcasters.[82]

---

[78]See Atkinson, 1942a, for many accounts of problems encountered by college and university stations

[79]*Four Years of Network Broadcasting*, 1936, p. 27

[80]Atkinson, 1942a, pp. 33 and 88

[81]Clausse, 1949, p. 30

[82]*School Broadcasting*, 1933, p. 39

In short, some teachers had a strong desire to use radio with their students, but found it too difficult to orchestrate particularly given their lack of control over the conditions of its use. Others had trouble finding programming that was appropriate for their curriculum and lacked the expertise to produce their own programs. Finally, teachers sometimes questioned the motives for introducing radio into schools because it represented to them either a threat to their profession or an intrusion of commercialism into their classrooms. Each of these problems or concerns had been raised slightly earlier with respect to film and would subsequently reemerge with those media that came after radio.

Commercial Broadcasters and Educational Radio

From the start, there was strong disagreement about the role commercial broadcasters should play in educational radio. At a time when the industry was new and when commercial funding was a relatively new idea, many people questioned the integrity of such a system and the chances that it would serve schools well. This issue was prominent at the 1929 Radio Education Conference convened by Secretary of the Interior Ray Lyman Wilbur, which was attended by educators and commercial broadcasters. NBC and CBS representatives claimed to have the best interests of schools at heart. NBC representative John Elwood was quoted as saying that NBC had "all the place for education that education wants,"[83] but some people had doubts. FRC member Ira Robinson argued that "radio was born a crippled child, birthmarked by advertising and commercialism, and it behooves every one of us to get it out of that deformity."[84] The 1930 report of the Advisory Committee on Education by Radio, a committee formed as a result of this conference, stated:

> Commercial stations show a tendency to reduce educational programs to shorter and poorer periods as their time becomes more salable, and when they do offer educational programs it is usually in the endeavor to cultivate general good will and create publici-

---

[83]in Hill, 1942, p. 9

[84]Robinson, 1930, p. 9

ty, rather than to build up a sound educational method and research with the help and guidance of educational experts.[85]

In *Radio in Education: The Ohio School of the Air and Other Experiments*, Armstrong Perry (1929) also described the quick encroachment of commercial interests on educational ventures:

> While educators are making progress in the use of radio, and in some cases rapid progress, business concerns are moving still more swiftly. Daylight hours, once so little sought by advertisers that it seemed as though they might always be available for school programs, are now being filled rapidly with programs advertising department stores and other business concerns. In some cases educational programs that were well established after years of effort have been crowded out by advertising programs.[86]

Commercial broadcasters tended to defend themselves by arguing that teachers had too poor an understanding of radio to utilize it to its best educational advantages. NBC's John Elwood insisted that educators had to accept that radio programs must involve the elements of entertainment and showmanship if they are to be effective, saying, "perhaps it is a blow to the pride of the educator to feel that his product is not in universal demand; nevertheless, there is no use dodging the fact, because it is true."[87] There were also those who argued that free competition among commercial broadcasters improved the quality of their educational broadcasting because broadcasters feared losing private control of radio. For example, Carroll Atkinson argued, "This fear has been a powerful incentive for the creation of the splendid educational services the American public today receives, at no cost, from commercial stations."[88] In other words, some people had faith that public demand for quality programming would make it good business for commercial broadcasters to live up to their educational responsibilities, and that if broadcasters failed to live up to that obligation the government would intervene.

In a few cases, commercially sponsored programs were widely respected. The RCA Music Appreciation Hour and the CBS School of

---

[85]Advisory Committee on Radio in Education, 1930, p. 36

[86]Perry, 1929, p. 75

[87]Elwood, 1930, p. 9

[88]Atkinson, 1942c, p. 14

the Air were launched, at least in part, to boost sales of radio sets, but these programs seem to have been generally well liked by teachers. As Carroll Atkinson described:

> [The CBS School of the Air] originally was a commercial program sponsored by the Grigsby-Grunow Company for the purpose of boosting sales of Majestic radios in competition with the sets manufactured by the Radio Corporation of America, which in its turn had sponsored Dr. Walter Damrosch's music appreciation program as a sales incentive for RCA radios.[89]

Grigsby-Grunow also sponsored a contest where teachers who wrote winning essays on "How the Radio Can Be Used in Education" won trips to Europe and Alaska.[90]

In the case of these programs, there were no commercials. The programs were, in effect, the ads; they promoted the sale of radios and projected a positive image of NBC and CBS. (Initially, the American School of the Air included a plug for its sponsor, the Grigsby-Grunow Company, but that ended when the sponsor abandoned the project and CBS took it on as a "sustaining feature"—i.e., a program that is not supported by advertising.) As stated earlier, these programs played a major role in winning the favor of teachers toward radio. According to Atkinson, "the NBC Music Appreciation Hour . . . unquestionably was responsible, more than any other program, for the introduction of radios into the American classroom."[91] The School of the Air of the Americas was officially adopted by at least 12 state education departments and was officially endorsed by the National Catholic Education Association, representing over 10,000 schools.

Ohio School of the Air's Ben Darrow did not particularly object to the involvement of commercial broadcasters, arguing that it is no worse to allow a program sponsor to identify itself than it is to endow chairs, permit publishers to identify themselves in their books, or name a building after its donor.[92] Others objected not to the involvement of commercial broadcasters, but to the potential monopoly they were building for themselves, which threatened to squeeze out educa-

---

[89]Atkinson, 1942c, p. 14

[90]"School radio users win prize trips," 1930

[91]Atkinson, 1942c, p. 78

[92]Darrow, 1932, p. 257

tional broadcasters. Still others offered the notion that objecting to commercial involvement was anti-American. National Association of Broadcasters president William S. Hedges argued that, "Perhaps you could remove all idea of a commercial world under a communistic system, but it is impossible in the United States."[93] He also referred to commercial sponsorship of educational programs as "pure philanthropy, since it assists in relieving the tax burden of the people."[94]

Ultimately, however, the philanthropy of the major networks ended or educators found their purposes to be too much at odds with those of the commercial broadcasters. For example, Columbia University had a Home Study program in the 1920s that relied on donated time from NBC. However, the university decided, according to Armstrong Perry, that "the industry was conducting its activities in such a superficial way from the educational point of view that the University did not wish to lend its name to anything done at that time,"[95] so the project was discontinued. The University of Nebraska broadcast programs to schools, including a music program for rural schoolchildren, but had to cancel its programming because the CBS affiliate that aired its programs repeatedly cut back on the time it donated to the university.[96] NBC and CBS had both formed education departments in 1930, but gradually shifted away from their commitment to schools to a more vague focus on public service.

In 1930, two major radio education associations were formed, each representing a different position on the relationship between educators and commercial broadcasters. The National Advisory Council on Education by Radio (NACRE) was formed in November 1929, with Levering Tyson as its director, funded by the Carnegie and Rockefeller foundations.[97] Some believed it was in the pocket of commercial interests, formed at the behest of RCA and GE executives and used by them to promote their own ends. Whatever the case, this group included both educators and commercial broadcasters and advocated their working together.[98]

---

[93]Hedges, 1930, p. 49

[94]Hedges, 1930, p. 53

[95]Perry, 1929, p. 44

[96]Atkinson, 1942a, p. 66

[97]Hill, 1942, p. 12

[98]Tyler, 1934, pp. 97–115

The NACRE began to produce programs in collaboration with commercial broadcasters. In 1931, NBC gave air time to the National Advisory Council on Radio in Education who, in collaboration with the American Political Science Association, produced the "You and Your Government" series.[99] Although this series was originally aired in the evenings, it was also recorded by the Rocky Mountain Radio Council and used in schools. The Listener's Handbook described the programs as follows:

> This series of civic broadcasts is intended to give you accurate and impartial information concerning your government, its problems, and your part in their solution. . . . What we hope to bring about through these broadcasts is a greater interest in and a more intelligent approach to the problems of government by presenting informally and interestingly the facts as seen by sound scholars and well-informed public men.[100]

NBC's original offer was one 30-minute slot one evening a week. Later that offer was reduced to 15 minutes, and then the program was moved to a less desirable time slot. All told, 210 programs were produced—107 half-hour programs and 103 of the 15-minute variety. Program topics included things like "Issues Between the Parties," "Constructive Economy in the National Government," and "Redrawing the Boundaries of Local Government."

Although the series producers felt a certain gratitude to NBC, they also concluded in *Four Years of Network Broadcasting* (1936) that the interests of commercial broadcasting were simply incompatible with those of education:

> Our experience has demonstrated a conflict between the commercial interests of the Broadcasting Company and the educational uses of the radio which threatens to become almost fatal to the latter. Educational broadcasting has become the poor relation of commercial broadcasting, and the pauperization of the latter has increased in direct proportion to the growing affluence of the former.[101]

---

[99]Reed, 1922

[100]*Four Years of Network Broadcasting*, 1936, p. 4

[101]*Four Years of Network Broadcasting*, 1936, p. 49

More specifically, they had trouble maintaining national airing of their programs. NBC affiliates were not required in any way to
air the program, so it often lost out to local competition. Neither the
series producers nor NBC had accurate lists of which stations were
using the program, so it was difficult to know who was using the
series, or how: "The situation became more and more aggravated as
time went on and as the commercial possibilities and ambitions of
the stations and the NBC increased, and in some cases conflicted."[102]
When the program first went into production, NBC's educational programming was under the direction of a vice president, but the status
of educational programming was diminished during the life of the
series, making it more difficult to keep the program alive. Without
any consistent participation of stations and without genuine support
from NBC, it was impossible to sustain a successful educational radio
venture. Still the NACRE retained its belief that educators and commercial broadcasters could work together.

The second organization formed in 1930 was the National
Committee on Education by Radio (NCER), financed by the Payne
Fund and including representatives of nine education organizations:
the American Council on Education, the National Catholic
Educational Association, the National Education Association, the
Jesuit Educational Association, the National Association of State
Universities, the National University Extension Association, the
National Council of State Superintendents, the Association of Land-
Grant Colleges and Universities, and the Association of College and
University Broadcasting Stations.[103] It came into being when
Commissioner of Education Cooper called a conference in Chicago in
1930 as a response to some educators' criticisms of working with com-
mercial broadcasters. He appointed the committee, with National
Education Association's Joy Elmer Morgan as temporary chair; the
Payne Fund provided a small grant to support the committee's
work.[104]

Joy Elmer Morgan was particularly vehement in her condem-
nation of the increasing commercialization of radio and its consequences for education. In 1934, she pointed out the danger to free
speech that private radio monopolies posed:

---

[102]*Four Years of Network Broadcasting*, 1936, p. 4

[103]Tyler, 1934, p. v

[104]Hill, 1942, p. 16

> Genuine freedom of thought is impossible when the machinery
> through which thought must flow on a national scale is in the
> hands of monopoly groups supported by competitive business
> enterprises who have an immediate interest in keeping the facts
> from the people. The very points at which facts are most needed if
> the people are to govern themselves wisely are the points at
> which freedom of speech is most certain to be denied.[105]

Morgan went on to stress the harm done to children by commercialization:

> I can conceive of no greater violation of trusteeship than the way
> the radio groups have exposed the child mind to commercialism.
> ... For the first time in human history we have turned over this
> tender child mind to men who would make a profit from exploiting it—to men who have no real understanding of the consequences of their acts for if they had, they would hang their heads
> in shame and make their apologies to generations yet unborn.[106]

The NACRE and NCER went to battle in the years after their
creation, particularly as Congress moved toward its Communications
Act of 1934. Educational broadcasters had been disheartened by the
1927 Radio Act and the Federal Radio Commission it established,
which tended to side with commercial broadcasters. Although
President Hoover stressed the importance of educational radio, the
FRC was not particularly friendly toward it, requiring a quality of
equipment and regularity of broadcast schedule that many educational stations could not meet. These requirements forced many educational broadcasters to surrender their licenses, the number of educational stations dropped from 121 in 1925 to 58 in 1931.[107] It
became a primary mission of the NCER to watch out for the interests
of educational stations, staying on the alert for any license applications that might pose a threat to them. In 1931, they found that 45 of
160 applications to the FRC threatened educational stations; the stations in jeopardy were notified by the NCER, and some requested
their help.[108]

---

[105]Morgan, 1934, p. 28

[106]Morgan, 1934, pp. 28–29

[107]Hill, 1942, p. 22

[108]Hill, 1942, p. 25

The NCER did a number of other things to promote educational broadcasting. They helped educational stations meet FRC airtime requirements by providing radio scripts to stations. The Committee also had a regular publication, *Education by Radio*, and they held conferences. They also promoted the idea of community listening groups and radio councils, which would serve as advocates for more responsible behavior on the part of commercial broadcasters, and support educational broadcasting. Although their funding for research was limited, they conducted several studies in the United States and abroad to find out about the radio activities of various educational institutions.[109]

The NCER promoted teacher training, which they felt had not been receiving adequate attention. A few universities, such as the University of Iowa, Columbia University, Northwestern University, and the University of Wisconsin, offered courses for teachers in radio education, but there had not been enough training to make much of a difference in schools. Around the time that the NCER focused its attention to teacher training, the Federal Radio Project established workshops in Washington, DC, and New York, which also helped promote the cause. In *Tune in for Education*, Frank E. Hill (1942) praised these initiatives:

> The effect of these two projects was that of turning on an electric light in a partially darkened room. Overnight educators everywhere began to see that if they wanted to use radio effectively, they must understand it as a technical instrument.[110]

The NCER also advocated Congressional legislation to allocate 15% of channels for educational broadcasting. This was in keeping with the recommendations of the Advisory Committee on Education by Radio, which had called for "an adequate number" of radio channels to be reserved for educational stations owned and operated by educational organizations and for them to be granted "the use of such amounts of power and hours of operation as are needed to enable such stations to perform the service for which they are intended."[111] They went on to recommend that it be a condition of the granting of a commercial license that the station "be placed at the

---

[109]See Hill, 1942, for a detailed account of the activities of the NCER.

[110]Hill, 1942, p. 90

[111]Advisory Committee on Radio in Education, 1930, p. 65

disposal of the officials of public education for certain reasonable periods each day and evening, during the life of the license, for use by officials in broadcasting educational programs without interference or control from the owners of the station or their agents."[112] These actions were necessary, the Committee argued, because educational broadcasters who depended on commercial stations "were in much the same position as a public school housed in a privately-owned building from which pupils and teachers might be excluded at the will of the owner."[113]

The NCER understood that their request was controversial. At that point, educational stations had not produced much high-quality programming. In many cases, they were not using as much air time as the commercial broadcasters were offering them. The NCER's defense was that these stations had not been afforded the facilities, funding, or time slots that would enable them to provide better programming, and that when they were adequately provided for they would do better work.[114]

In 1931, Senator Fess of Ohio introduced a bill requesting that 15% of broadcasting channels be reserved for educational use. This "Fess Bill" was not passed. Although many educational organizations supported it, it was vehemently opposed by commercial broadcasters. In 1932, a Congressional resolution called for the FRC to survey the commercial and educational activities of radio and report their findings to the Senate. To many educators, the report was not an objective document, but a defense of commercial radio. The Fess Bill was reintroduced in 1933; although it was not passed, it prompted a new Congressional resolution for the investigation of radio activities. Then came the Communications Act of 1934, which included the provision that the newly formed Federal Communications Commission would look into the feasibility of allocating some fixed percentage to nonprofit organizations and submit its report and recommendations to Congress by February 1935.

The FCC held hearings, during which most testimony was against fixed percentages. In January 1935, the FCC recommended to Congress that it would be best not to set fixed percentages for nonprofit organizations, but to call for the good-faith cooperation of com-

---

[112]Advisory Committee on Radio in Education, 1930, pp. 65–66

[113]Advisory Committee on Radio in Education, 1930, p. 66

[114]Hill, 1942, p. 90

mercial broadcasters in promoting educational broadcasting. The FCC established the Federal Radio Education Committee chaired by U.S. Commissioner of Education John W. Studebaker. This committee was friendlier to education than the FRC had been. Frank Hill pointed out that the FREC helped to advance research in radio education. He also believed that commercial networks began to act more responsibly with regard to commercialism and public service after the FREC was established.[115]

Still educational broadcasting did not fare nearly as well as it could have in these hearings. Educators had presented a divided front against the more powerful commercial broadcasters, appearing not to know themselves how best to develop educational radio. Levering Tyson put it in the following way:

> We have wasted time in fruitless and unwarranted disagreement, in a destructive attack upon the American broadcasting system and its supporters without proposing constructive measures to inspire confidence that we know what we are talking about . . . because we have failed to set our own house in order, we have not convinced anyone, including ourselves, how radio can be used in education, nor have we solved basic problems in program production.[116]

Although the debate that split radio educators was arguably a legitimate one where both sides had some valid arguments, the fact that these educators could not reconcile their differences made them an easy target for commercial broadcasters.

Apart from the loss of air time to commercial interests, educational broadcasters had another competitor for time: World War II. In cases where educational programs were presented as "sustaining" programs on commercial stations (i.e., programs offered by the stations with no advertising), programming related to defense activities often squeezed out the educational broadcasters. Although concerns about national security were used to promote the use of radio in schools, the war did more harm than good to educational radio. Children's entertainment programming also dropped off during the war, from 40 shows in 1940 to 27 in 1945. In *Program Patterns for Young Radio Listeners in the Field of Children's Radio*

---

[115]Hill, 1942, pp. 73–76

[116]Tyson, 1934, p. 15

Entertainment, Dorothy Lewis and Dorothy McFadden (1945) argued that this drop was "undoubtably caused to some extent by the increase in news and other types of wartime broadcasts."[117]

Within a decade of the creation of the first national broadcasting networks, it was clear that commercial interests would dominate radio. In 1933, progressive education reformer William Heard Kilpatrick expressed his dismay at the path radio was taking:

> The radio seems to demand a special word, since its public status in this country is still in the making. Unrestrained competition in broadcasting is of course impossible. Public control is essential. The question not yet settled with us is whether this control shall subordinate public service as now to the private gain of advertising or whether the radio shall be run for public service. In the opinion of many, including these authors, the waste in our present regime of broadcasting, based as it is on advertising, is nothing less than a tragic disgrace.[118]

George S. Counts was similarly concerned, arguing that radio's "primary concern today certainly is neither the educational nor the cultural elevation of the masses. It is operated in the interest of commercial sponsors, engaged in the sale of almost every conceivable commodity."[119] Educational broadcaster H. B. McCarty was more optimistic, insisting that "surely the weaknesses of the present system will not be perpetuated."[120] However, looking back now, several generations later, it is clear that not only were those weaknesses perpetuated, but they were carried over into the structure of the media industries that came after radio.

Fears About Radio's Effects on Children

Another damaging blow to radio education, and one that paralleled the story of educational film, was the belief that radio was bad for children. Radio was so popular as a home amusement for children that it was hard for some people to imagine it had a place in serious academic study particularly because so many educators and parents

---

[117]Lewis and McFadden, 1945, p. 53

[118]Kilpatrick, 1969, p. 140

[119]Counts, 1934, p. 204

[120]McCarty, 1934, p. 23

objected to the programs children listened to. While they feared that radio might breed passivity in school, they also feared children would be overstimulated emotionally from listening to adventure shows and serial thrillers at home. Dorothy Gordon (1942) described the problem in *All Children Listen*:

> Enthralled by the new emotional stimulus they were lured away from almost every other form of leisure-time activity. . . . They gobbled their food; they neglected outdoor recreation, they threw off all responsibilities . . . parents were startled to find their children awakening at night, screaming with terror in nightmares.[121]

The stimulating nature of radio programming led some educators to strongly caution against exploiting this particular feature of the medium in its classroom use out of the fear that "over-excitement of the pupils' imagination results in a state of mental tension that disturbs the normal functioning of their faculties. Instead of awakening ideas, they are given but fleeting and superficial impressions."[122]

Adults had a variety of concerns about radio's impact on children. Herta Herzog of the Office of Radio Research of Columbia University conducted an extensive survey of literature on children and radio. One issue she found in that literature was the fear that radio might create a kind of emotional starvation in children:

> What does it mean for the emotional development of a personality if, in their early youth, children are conditioned to live on borrowed experiences? To what extent will they be trained this way, later on always to look for somebody else to provide excitement for them and thus fall easy prey to any kind of propaganda which makes use of their emotional starvation?[123]

She also found concerns that children were imitating the language styles of radio programs, particularly slang expressions. The concern here was that,

> mechanized phrases tend to become a substitute for the full and creative use of language as a means to express one's feelings and thoughts. The mutilated and mechanized use of language might,

---

[121]Gordon, 1942, p. 42

[122]*School Broadcasting*, 1933, p. 19

[123]Herzog, 1941, p. 44

in the long run, make for a mutilation of the total personality. Cliché-words might finally make for and express a cliché-soul.[124]

Some critics objected to the kind of music that radio most often played. In his remarks at a 1934 conference on educational radio, one speaker quoted radio pioneer Lee DeForest as saying that, "Nine-tenths of what one can hear [on the radio] is the continual drivel of second-rate jazz, [and] sickening crooning by degenerate sax players."[125] He went on to lament that "jazz of a debased sort with 'crooning' which recently received the well-merited rebuke of Cardinal O'Connell are given almost unlimited time, while the more valuable educational broadcasts are debarred or restricted to unimportant hours."[126] Disdain for the musical selections of radio stations was a common sentiment of educators and adults more generally at the time. As was the case with film, adults attributed the loose morality of Jazz Age youth on the media enjoyed by them.

Objections were also raised to the commercialism of children's programming, which often invited children to send in boxtops or bottle caps to receive prizes. Besides costing parents money in products they would not otherwise buy, it meant, according to Lewis and McFadden, "that the child often goes to undesirable places to add to the collection, bothers the neighbors, and has to handle germ-laden material."[127] In other cases, the commercialism was less overt and deemed less objectionable. For example, a program called "Children and Charm School" involved "enrolling" children listeners for small weekly fee, which meant that the children would receive a kit of play materials with which to participate in art projects related to this program, which was sponsored by a crayon company.[128] Another program interviewed children on the street, who received free ice cream if they answered questions correctly; this one was sponsored by a dairy company.[129]

Outrage inspired action. A group of mothers in Scarsdale, New York, initiated a wave of protest that spread across the nation

---

[124]Herzog, 1941, p. 56

[125]Davis, 1934, p. 3

[126]Davis, 1934, p. 6

[127]Lewis and McFadden, 1945, p. 68

[128]Lewis and McFadden, 1945, p. 20

[129]Lewis and McFadden, 1945, p. 22

in the early 1930s, contributing to a 1933 promise from the National Association of Broadcasters that they would clean up their programming.[130] In 1934, the Women's National Radio Committee was formed to press broadcasters to improve the quality of their programming. In 1936, CBS adopted a new policy on children's programming, NBC followed in 1938, and the NAB released a code for children's programs in 1939. Some of the newly established policies were that no children's programs would include torture or its suggestion, horror, profanity, kidnapping, or sound effects meant to simulate death or torture. In 1939, the Radio Council on Children's Programs was formed, with representatives from the radio industry, women's groups, schools, advertising agencies, and other interested groups. They worked with the NAB to promote quality children's programming, then disbanded in 1942 because of the wartime emergency.[131]

CONCLUSION

"School broadcasting has come to stay!" proclaimed Ben Darrow in 1932.[132] However, he appears to have spoken too soon. In 1934, NBC's Judith Waller expressed her disappointment in the state of instructional radio. She wrote:

> Educators are not, as a whole, radio-minded in any sense of the word. . . . The majority of them sit back and growl and grumble at the radio without making the slightest attempt to do anything constructive to change what, they believe, is a lamentable situation. . . . Radio has decidedly not become a part of the consciousness of the average educators.[133]

At the same time, she still hoped for future developments: "Surely, somewhere there must be educators with enough interest and imagination to bring something real out of all the efforts of the various educational and regular commercial radio stations alike."[134]

---

[130]See Gordon, 1942, for more information on 1930s children's radio policies

[131]Lewis and McFadden, 1945, p. 1

[132]Darrow, 1932, p. 237

[133]Waller, 1934, pp. 31–32

[134]Waller, 1934, p. 36

Near the end of the 1940s, Charles Siepmann acknowledged that radio education had not developed as some had hoped, but believed that "in this age of technological improvements, and here in America, the center of such enterprise, growth and development of classroom uses of these media is assured."[135] He, too, was mistaken; educational radio was pretty well finished in the United States after World War II. Although some people tried to revive instructional radio when peace was restored, there were too many obstacles preventing it from becoming a key element in classroom practice. Its ties to progressive pedagogy were of no use because the postwar years were a time of vicious attacks on progressive education. Although radio was potentially compatible with the newly emerging educational priorities of the era, it did not stand a chance against the new medium—television—that eclipsed it.

---

[135]Siepmann, 1948, p. 1

4

TELEVISION

Television not only has a part in modern education—it may become the greatest vital force in modern education. To ignore it is to bury one's head in the sand.

—Madeline S. Long, *Educational Leadership*
(April, 1952)

Although the explosion of television onto the American landscape took place in the 1950s, early experiments in instructional television began much earlier, when the State University of Iowa was given an experimental visual broadcasting license in 1931. However, wartime activities delayed television's development and popularization, and it was not until the 1950s that television was heavily promoted for its educational possibilities.

The 1950s ITV experiments took place under what some considered to be near-ideal circumstances for guaranteeing success. Advocates claimed that television would be a fantastic tool to address the huge crisis of teacher shortages and school overcrowding, and huge sums of federal and foundation money were poured into ITV experiments. A number of impressive projects were undertaken at this time, some involving statewide or even national broadcasts that reached hundreds of thousands of students. The U.S. military also conducted extensive experiments with television as a training medium.

For clarity's sake, it is important to distinguish between *educational* and *instructional* television, both of which began to develop at mid-century. Educational television (ETV) refers to programs of an educational nature that are broadcast to the general public and are generally noncommercial. Instructional television (ITV) refers to programming used in classrooms regardless of whether available to a wider audience, and this is the primary focus of this chapter. Some ITV was made available through commercial and noncommercial broadcast stations, and some school districts used closed-circuit TV systems that sent programming only to those schools and classrooms wired for such reception.

Whatever the means through which television was broadcast into classrooms, most ITV experiments ended when foundation funding ended. ITV was expensive, so it was difficult for schools to fund it themselves. It was often regarded with "negative resignation"[1] by teachers, who perceived it as being imposed on them by administrators and outsiders as a solution to a problem for which they imagined other solutions. It lives on to the extent that teachers today sometimes use TV broadcasts or videotapes in class and in certain forms of distance learning. However, ITV was conceived primarily as a way to solve a 1950s crisis in public education; when that crisis eased, the momentum behind ITV slowed as well.

ORIGINS OF EDUCATIONAL AND INSTRUCTIONAL TELEVISION

After World War II, the number of TV stations on the air had ballooned, leading the FCC to impose a freeze on new station construction. At that point, there had not been, nor were there any plans to establish, channel reservations for educational stations. Until late in 1950, educators had not shown much interest in securing reservations of channels for educational stations when licensing resumed. However, toward the end of that year, the Joint Committee on Educational Television (JCET) was formed, with representation from

---

[1]Cassirer, 1960, p. 58

the American Council on Education, the Association for Education by Radio-Television, the National Association of Educational Broadcasters, the National Association of State Universities, the National Council of Chief State School Officers, and the National Education Association. 1950 was also the year that WOI-TV, the station owned by Iowa State College, became the first nonexperimental educational TV station in operation, having applied for its license before the freeze.[2]

The JCET, with funding from the Ford Foundation, went to work preparing testimony for hearings in 1951 on the question of reservations. Unlike the 1934 hearings on reservations for educational radio stations, the 1951 hearings were a victory for educational broadcasters. By 1952, the year the FCC lifted its ban on the construction of new TV stations, the FCC had reserved 242 out of 2,053 new stations for non-commercial use. The first educational stations on these reserved channels began operation in 1953, primarily providing programming to the general public (as opposed to classroom programming). These stations had to struggle to say afloat. Viewers were often unaware of the existence of their local educational station, station staffs tended to be too small and untrained, and there was no educational or public TV network permitting stations to pool programming resources. Still, the fact that these stations came into being at all represented a notable victory for educational broadcasters.

Educational television received a boost from the Ford Foundation, whose Fund for Adult Education (FAE), established in 1951, provided financial assistance for various aspects of educational broadcasting. The FAE established the Educational Television and Radio Center, a central program center to produce, acquire, and distribute programs. The ETRC became the National ETRC (NETRC) in 1959, which became NET in 1963. Still there was no formal ETV network; the NET served as a clearinghouse by providing 10 hours of videotaped programming per week to ETV stations. Meanwhile the Communications Act of 1962 had provided $32 million for the construction of ETV stations.[3]

In the mid-1960s, President Johnson asked the Carnegie Corporation to study ETV, resulting in the creation of the Carnegie

---

[2]See Blakely, 1979, for more detailed information on early efforts to secure channel reservations for educational TV.

[3]Blakely, 1979

Commission on Educational television. In their 1967 report, they recommended the creation of a nonprofit Corporation for Public Television that would be partially federally funded and would distribute money to ETV stations. In November 1967, the Public Broadcasting Act was signed into law, authorizing $38 million for ETV and radio over the following 3 years, establishing the Corporation for Public Broadcasting, and authorizing $500,000 for a study of ITV and radio.

The Ford Foundation was not only a huge contributor to ETV; it also provided substantial funding for ITV through its Fund for the Advancement of Education (TFAE), also established in 1951. TFAE was created primarily to help recruit and train teachers, to extend equal educational opportunity to all children, and improve school curriculum, management, and financing.[4] According to TFAE, they funded projects involving the use of television "not to replace teachers, but to carry the works of the best teacher to a much wider body of students"[5] and reorganize the utilization of school staff and space. Also, $30 million for ITV was made available through Title VII of the National Defense Education Act of 1958, which provided funding for research on open and closed circuit ITV. By 1960, 81 NDEA grants had been made for ITV research.[6] It was also an NDEA grant that was used in 1962 to create the National Instructional Television Library, which duplicated and distributed ITV programming.

Earlier funding for audiovisual education had come from sources like the Payne Fund and the Rockefeller Foundation—organizations that had no particular program or agenda in mind for school reform. Rather, they simply funded projects they thought were interesting. ITV funding marked a significant shift. The Ford Foundation had a clear reform agenda that they sought to fund, and they funded it heavily. Their purpose was to bring liberal education to all students and restore serious intellectual work to schools, while finding more efficient ways to conduct public education. By the early 1960s, the Ford Foundation had invested $80.7 million in educational television, more than $20 million of which was specifically for ITV.[7]

[4]The Fund for the Advancement of Education, 1961, p. 19

[5]The Fund for the Advancement of Education, 1961, p. 53

[6]Smith, 1961, p. 9

[7]Blakely, 1979, p. 169; Finn, 1972, p. 130

ITV took a variety of forms. Much of the earliest ITV programming, before the FCC reservations for educational stations, was broadcast over commercial channels. Even after the FCC decision, some of the most successful ITV ventures involved commercial broadcasters. Meanwhile ETV stations sometimes chose to broadcast programming intended for classroom use. Besides commercial and educational TV outlets, ITV could be transmitted to classrooms through closed circuit systems, as well as via Instructional Television Fixed Service (ITFS). Closed circuit did not require FCC licensing; ITFS licenses were first issued in 1963, permitting a single licensee to broadcast on four channels.

Many school districts across the nation were involved in some kind of ITV project. Educational technology historian Paul Saettler documents that, "by the 1960s almost every course in the public school, college, or university curriculum was being taught somewhere by either open- or closed-circuit television, on educational or commercial stations or in educational institutions."[8] To understand the motivation behind these projects, it is important to look more closely at the tone of educational policy at the time and the ways in which television fit some of the reform priorities of the day.

HOPES AND PLANS FOR ITV

Early hopes for instructional television were enormous. In 1951, a public relations director for the Philadelphia schools wrote, "Let's face it. Television is here. It is a powerful educational medium. We dare not ignore it."[9] In 1953, Association for Education by Radio-Television executive Leon Hood argued that "television has progressed to the point where we can no longer doubt our right to take it into the family of audio-visual aids."[10] In 1955, ITV advocate Hubert Morehead described ITV as "the most exciting educational voyage since our nation embarked on the universal education of its citizens."[11] In 1954, ITV advocate Lawrence Conrad wrote:

---

[8]Saettler, 1990, p. 367

[9]Gable, 1951, p. 46

[10]Hood, 1953, p. 33

[11]Morehead, 1955, p. 179

> Television may well prove to be the power tool of education. Even
> if it brought no new learning experiences into the schools, televi-
> sion could certainly increase the effectiveness of the teaching,
> and it might well expand the size of the classroom to include vast
> numbers of people to whom the lessons are not now available.
> Such is the speculation in which we are now indulging as we
> make ready what may be the greatest of all experiments in edu-
> cational method.[12]

To some reformers, television seemed to be a wonderful fit with educational priorities of the time. The postwar years were a time of
intense crisis in American public education, summarized well by
audiovisual education advocate James Finn:

> The educational system . . . is ill with an inflaming manpower
> problem consisting of a rapidly growing student population, a
> shortage of qualified teachers, increasing demands for space, rising
> costs, potential ceilings on funds, and accelerating demands from
> teachers and from the culture, and, in addition, suffers increasing-
> ly from an indigestion problem brought on by the exponential
> growth of knowledge and the variety of demands from the society
> for educated manpower and a decrease in the uneducated.[13]

These conditions seemed to call for new educational methods that
would cut costs and maximize the capabilities of an undersized workforce of teachers.

As described in chapter 1, public schools in this era were
attacked to an unprecedented degree. The deficiencies of World War
II military recruits had raised concerns about the quality of
American education. In the postwar years, these deficiencies were
seen as a serious threat to national security, and a severe assault on
public education ensued. A string of bestsellers detailed the criticisms. For example, Arthur Bestor (1953), author of *Educational
Wastelands*, and Albert Lynd (1950), author of *Quackery in the Public
Schools*, lamented that progressive educationists (referred to as
regressive by Bestor) had relinquished curricular control to pedagogy
experts, leading to a decline in the degree to which the liberal arts
and sciences were valued and a tide of anti-intellectualism in
American society and its public schools. They blasted life-adjustment

---

[12]Conrad, 1954, p. 373

[13]Finn, 1972, p. 84 (originally published 1964)

education for purporting to address the real needs of students while actually failing miserably to prepare students with the rigorous academic training they would need for the complex world they faced.

In the midst of this assault on public education came the launch of Sputnik in 1957, which intensified American anxieties about national security and the future of democracy. Comparisons between American and Russian schools led to intensified criticism of American public education. In *The Troubled Crusade: American Education 1945–1980*, education historian Diane Ravitch (1983) described how "Sputnik came to be a symbol of the consequences of indifference to high standards. In popular parlance, Sputnik had happened not because of what the Russians had done but because of what American schools had failed to do."[14]

Out of these concerns came a renewed interest in new technologies as possible solutions to educational problems. Some of the reform ideas—particularly an increased focus on math, science, and foreign languages and an interest in separating and paying special attention to gifted students—coalesced around tasks that technologies of automated instruction could be used to address and are discussed further in chapter 5.

The hands-down, prime hope for ITV was that it could be used to solve the pressing problems of school overcrowding and teacher shortages by providing mass instruction. Enrollment in elementary schools increased by 8 million between 1945 and 1955; American public schools were short an estimated 135,000 teachers and 132,000 classrooms at the end of the 1950s. Nearly 100,000 teachers were not fully certified, and schools were 1,850,000 students in excess of capacity.[15]

In this climate of shortages, coupled with fears about national security, the efficiency experts once again stepped to the forefront of educational policy, attempting to eliminate waste by identifying talent and sorting students so they could be educated for their place in the social order, quickly and cost-effectively. Under the circumstances, television seemed an ideal solution. Harry Skornia, Executive Director of the National Association of Educational Broadcasters, believed that television was "the one new instrument we have which is likely to be able to contribute significantly to the

---

[14]Ravitch, 1983, p. 229

[15]The National Program in the Use of Television in the Public Schools, 1960, p. 1

solution of the present crisis"[16]—that "in television, society has a force capable of shaping the mass mind more effectively and economically than any other instrument now available."[17]

Communications scholar and ITV advocate Charles Siepmann warned in 1958 that "we shall not long remain the richest country or the happiest (if we claim to be such) or the proudest if we fail to develop the mental resources of our people,"[18] arguing that television "is one indispensable tool that we can and must use to extricate ourselves from the grave trouble we are in, but of which all too few still seem to be aware."[19]

Military research with ITV sought to develop efficient, cost-effective training methods. Faced with constant shortages of instructors and focused on standardizing and streamlining training procedures, in 1950 military researchers began to conduct extensive ITV experiments.[20] One goal of these experiments was to determine whether ITV could be used to reduce the training time of instructors—that is, if a TV instructor could be trained more quickly than a classroom instructor. In one study, the instructional time was reduced from 3 to 4 months to 1 week, with no loss of teaching effectiveness.[21] In 1958, military researchers Kanner et al. described the advantage of using TV instructors in the following way:

> By means of television and prompting equipment, it is possible to take a person with no knowledge of a given course's material, with none of the special skills required of a good instructor, give that person about one or two hours of rehearsal per hour of television instruction, and present this instruction to trainees with no loss in training efficiency.

One can certainly challenge the assumptions that these researchers were making about the irrelevance of the teacher, but their research seemed to prove (at least to them) that ITV instruction did not even require a qualified teacher to serve as the TV instructor.

---

[16]Skornia, 1955, p. 84

[17]Skornia, 1955, p. 85

[18]Sipmann, 1958, p. 162

[19]Siepmann, 1958, p. 2

[20]For detailed accounts of these experiments, see Kanner, 1958; Kanner, Katz, Mindak, and Goldsmith, 1958; Kanner and Marshall, 1963; Kanner, Runyon, and Desiderato, 1955; Rock, Duvak, and Murray, undated

[21]Kanner, Katz, Mindak, and Goldsmith, 1958, p. 283

Televised instruction also appealed to the military because it could be standardized to a degree impossible with conventional instruction. Classroom instructors were perceived by military researchers to be something of a hindrance to change because "after the materials have been rewritten, it is necessary to train the instructor to present them as prepared and without change with succeeding teaching presentations."[23] However, it was common for individual instructors to deviate from the curriculum as presented to them, and researchers sought to develop ways to stop such deviations. One report described the administrative advantages of using television when trying to modify instruction:

> It is possible to make complete daily changes in instruction with little or no effort required to memorize or learn these changes by the instructor since he can read them from the prompter. The prompter also insures standardization of the presentation no matter how many times it is given.[24]

Military research also suggested, on a whole, that televised instruction was as and sometimes more effective than conventional instruction. Moreover, television had advantages that other forms of instruction did not, such as closeups, split screens, animation, and superimposition of images.[25] Researchers recognized the possibility that students' inability to ask questions of a TV teacher might reduce student achievement. However, one 1955 report argued that "examination indicated that the majority of questions did not materially add to the teaching effectiveness of the instruction."[26] To a large extent, researchers believed they could revise TV scripts to address the questions that students would be likely to ask if provided the opportunity to do so.

In summary, military ITV research was undertaken to reduce training time—both of students and instructors, thus cutting training costs. It was also meant to help streamline the process of modifying training by giving the instructional role to TV teachers, who only needed to be good script readers. Finally, it seemed a good medium for standardizing instruction within and among military installations

---

[23]Kanner, Katz, Mindak, and Goldsmith, 1958, p. 285

[24]Kanner, Katz, Mindak, and Goldsmith, 1958, p. 285

[25]Kanner, Runyon, and Desiderato, 1955, p. 165

[26]Kanner, Runyon, and Desiderato, 1955, p. 165

because everyone would receive the same training through the same broadcasts. Those who developed these military applications of ITV assumed it would be appropriate to apply their approach to K–12 classroom ITV, roughly equating children with military trainees and K–12 instruction with military training procedures. This assumption would later come under fire, particularly with the 1960s resurgence of child-centered progressive approaches to K–12 education, but for a time the military focus on efficiency and cost-effectiveness was perceived to be a legitimate focus for K–12 educators as well.

In civilian life, many of the projects funded by the Fund for the Advancement of Education centered on efficiency issues. In particular, TFAE took an interest in the ideas of Alexander J. Stoddard, who promoted the automation of certain aspects of instruction and the use of teacher aides to perform subprofessional tasks that are typically expected of teachers. He believed that the systematic aspects of transmitting content to students should be left to audiovisual methods of instruction, and teachers should concern themselves more with social and developmental issues, working with students individually and in small groups.[27] Stoddard envisioned an educational system where students would spend parts of the school day in extremely large classes, some of which would be TV-taught. As a result, schools would achieve substantial cost savings by requiring fewer conventional classrooms and fewer trained teachers.[28]

Beyond matters of efficiency, ITV advocates promoted television's potential in line with other trends in curriculum reform of the 1950s and 1960s. Curriculum reform of the time, funded largely by the federal government, focused in part on increasing student motivation and activity. In that spirit, television was promoted for its ability to "bring the students most effectively to the very edge of learning"[29] by grabbing and holding students' interest. It could make experiences and events seem more real than other media could, as well as provide experiences that traditional instruction could not. It could dramatize and visualize issues, making them more engaging to students.[30]

Another characteristic of curriculum reform at the time was its emphasis on increasing the involvement of scholars and experts in

[27]Murphy and Gross, 1966, p. 36

[28]Finn, 1972, pp. 135–136

[29]Smith, 1961, p. 18

[30]National Education Association, 1958, p. 12; Cassirer, 1960, p. 41

K–12 education. Critics were concerned that teachers—both the fully certified and the uncertified—were inadequately prepared in their disciplines. The solution they offered was to have university-level scholars participate in curriculum development and produce teacher-proof curricula. Television was advocated by some of these reformers as a way to bring experts into the classroom, both to enrich and enliven the experience of students and bring teachers up to date in their fields. A 1961 Ford Foundation report argued that "in addition to superior teachers, television makes available to students the nation's top scientists, writers, poets, and other stimulating personalities, thus offering educational experiences far beyond anything possible in the conventional classroom."[31] As for the benefit to teachers, the report claimed that the classroom teacher would be "relieved by the studio teacher of the necessity for extensive preparation," leaving "more time to devote to other phases of the subject, to total class planning, and to working with individual students."[32] It could also provide "a splendid opportunity for cross-fertilization of ideas"[33] between classroom and studio teachers, not to mention a common base of experience for the classroom teachers of a particular school, who could then have more meaningful meetings and discussions about their teaching.

Television was also believed to have excellent public relations potential for school districts. Some educators tried to use it to explain the activities of schools to parents. ITV consultant Madeline Long recommended that schools purchase TV sets as a public relations device.[34] In the UNESCO report *Television Teaching Today*, Henry Cassirer (1960) described how, "realizing that the work of schools is being evaluated every day at the dinner table in the light of accounts brought home by the children, schools feel that they should tell their own story so parents may better appreciate their efforts."[35] He then described some of the ways in which schools used television for that purpose, airing classroom activities and school board meetings. Committee on Television in Education chair Lawrence Conrad wrote the following in 1954 about the public relations potential of television:

---

[31]The Fund for the Advancement of Education, 1961, p. 62

[32]Smith, 1961, p. 21

[33]Smith, 1961, p. 23

[34]Long, 1952, p. 417

[35]Cassirer, 1960, p. 61

> Through television, the school has gone out to visit the parents;
> and it reaches not simply the mothers who happen to have leisure,
> but all the working parents as well, and almost all those great
> numbers of people who think they have no direct interest in the
> schools, but whose votes control the destiny of public education.[36]

Conrad went on to argue that television was a wonderful means "to
put before the whole public a knowledge of the schools and thus to
create a sympathetic understanding of their aims."[37] In an age when
funds were stretched, schools needed every possible way to justify
their expenditures to their communities, and television was offered
as a possible component of their public relations work.

ITV PROJECTS

The first regular use of in-school telecasting began in the 1948 to
1949 school year on three commercial stations in Philadelphia.[38]
Lessons were broadcast in music, art, civil defense, science, fitness,
and social studies. Program schedules were sent to schools 1 month
in advance, and the board of education conducted inservice training
for teachers. By 1959, over 200,000 students in Philadelphia's public
and private schools were watching ITV programs on a weekly basis.
When the success of commercial television led to the cutback of air
time for educational broadcasting on commercial stations, ITV programs were aired on the newly established WHYY-TV, an educational television station.[39]

Meanwhile the Ford Foundation's Fund for the Advancement
of Education began to fund a variety of ITV projects. Their first ITV
grant went to the New Jersey State Teachers College in Montclair to
help teachers prepare TV lessons in fifth-grade American history for
presentation over a closed-circuit system in nearby schools.

The first statewide ITV project, also TFAE funded, began in
1952 in the Alabama public schools. According to historian Paul
Saettler, the purpose of the project was "to raise the standard of

---

[36]Conrad, 1954, p. 373

[37]Conrad, 1954, p. 373

[38]Smith, 1961, p. 6

[39]Cassirer, 1960, pp. 38–39

instruction throughout the state, a goal most observers agree was successfully achieved."[40] They used the state ETV network to provide courses for elementary, secondary, and college classes as well as for teacher training. One hundred schools participated in first year, reaching a height of about 600 in 1960 to 1961. According to the TFAE book, *Decade of Experiment: The Fund for the Advancement of Education 1951-1961*, by 1961 an estimated 300,000 students were receiving instruction in music, art, languages, and science, "for which their schools previously had poorly qualified teachers or none."[41]

The Pittsburgh schools received TFAE funding in 1955 and cooperated with a local educational station to offer courses in reading, French, and arithmetic for fifth-grade students, "this being the first public school attempt anywhere to teach basic subjects via open-circuit TV."[42] Over the next 4 years they added 29 courses, and most of the schools (including parochial schools) in the metropolitan area joined the program as well as many schools in other parts of western Pennsylvania. By 1961, 125,000 students in 437 schools were involved.

One of the most famous ITV experiments took place in Hagerstown, in Washington County, Maryland. The Electronic Industries Association and the Fund for the Advancement of Education formed a joint committee to discuss the possibility of conducting a large-scale project exploring the uses of television for instruction, and they chose Washington County as the site for their experiment, where nearly a third of the elementary school teachers did not have bachelor's degrees, and 75 out of 352 elementary teachers had only emergency teaching certificates. ELA provided all the equipment, TFAE underwrote other project expenses, and the Chesapeake and Potomac Telephone Co. developed the closed-circuit system required to provide programming to the participating schools.

The project began in fall of 1956, with 25 telecasts being aired each day across a wide range of subjects. By the end of the decade, 122 lessons a week in all major subjects were being transmitted live, plus another 19 filmed or taped lessons. Ultimately, more than 50 courses were offered via closed-circuit television. Although TFAE funding ended in 1961, the project continued after that time. By 1963, all of the county's schools were wired.

---

[40]Saettler, 1990, p. 366

[41]The Fund for the Advancement of Education, 1961, p. 56

[42]The Fund for the Advancement of Education, 1961, p. 56

Television appeared to improve student achievement. Fifth graders in the district, using television and regular instruction, made almost two years' progress in math in nine months. Generally, achievement on standardized tests was raised in a variety of areas, with students performing above national norms.[43] Television enabled the county to offer subjects like sequential science from first grade on by offering them via television. The Board of Education argued that television brought greater equality of educational opportunity because underprivileged, rural, and small high schools could all provide improved education through television.[44]

Although the Board of Education claimed it was seeking improvement of education, not savings in staff or budget, it certainly seemed to find and celebrate those savings. A 1961 report by the Fund for the Advancement of Education, claimed that "to handle its present student and teaching load by purely conventional methods, Washington County would have to hire no fewer than 135 additional teachers."[45] A report by the Washington County Board of Education made reference to the potential cost effectiveness of ITV, pointing out that after only a few years, the cost of the ITV classes was almost down to the cost of conventional instruction. The reorganization of course loads could make one "pre-tv teacher" into one and three-fifths teachers with television. Additionally, a district could hire only a few specialized teachers whose classes could be broadcast to the entire district, rather than having to hire as many of those teachers as would be necessary to reach all students by conventional means.[46] In the end, the Hagerstown project is a classic example of an attempt to use television to spread out thin resources and improve instruction in subjects believed to be related to national security.

Another interesting ITV project was Purdue University's Midwest Program on Airborne Television Instruction (MPATI), which received $4.5 million from the Ford Foundation. This program broadcast educational programs on videotape from an airplane flying at a high enough altitude over part of Indiana to reach schools in six states. Beginning in the summer of 1960, 20 colleges and universities

---

[43]See Washington County Board of Education, 1964, for more information about the Hagerstown project.

[44]Washington County Board of Education, 1964

[45]The Fund for the Advancement of Education, 1961, p. 56

[46]Washington County, Maryland, Board of Education, 1964

sponsored ITV workshops to train teachers in its use. Nineteen universities served as resource institutions, offering workshops, professional consultation, and program evaluation. The first telecasts aired in April 1961; five programs were broadcast simultaneously 4 days a week. Unfortunately, this project was expensive; the Ford Foundation had hoped that the increased audience achieved by airborne television would reduce costs enough to make ITV more viable, but this was not the case, and their grant ended in 1966. MPATI stopped broadcasting in 1968, but continued for several more years as an ITV library.

Although the results of the early ITV experiments were somewhat mixed, the Ford Foundation believed that the projects had been successful enough to warrant a more ambitious national undertaking. The National Program in the Use of Television in the Public Schools was created in 1957 with money from the Fund for the Advancement of Education to explore the viability of the Stoddard Plan, which (as described earlier) involved the use of television to instruct extra-large classes for part of the school day. In the first year, nearly 40,000 students in more than 200 schools of all varieties across the nation received some kind of daily televised instruction in large classes, typically 5 to 10 times the size of conventional classes. By the 1960 to 1961 school year, 300,000 students were being instructed in this manner in approximately 1,000 schools.[47] The plan was for participants to receive funding from the Ford Foundation that would be phased out over time.

The schools of Dade County, Florida, serve as a good example of a district that participated in the National Program. Half of the students in a particular grade worked in small classes for half a day, studying fundamentals like reading and math, while the other students were in large classes. The large TV classes were for subjects like science, social studies, and conversational Spanish. Students also had large (non-TV) classes for art, music, and physical education. Class sizes were as big as 600, averaging around 300. They were typically held in the school auditorium or cafeteria.

The Ford Foundation expressed satisfaction in 1961 with the National Program, which it claimed "has achieved two objectives: first, it showed that television could be used to teach very large classes, with resultant savings in teaching time and classroom space; second, it gave preliminary confirmation to the belief that the use of TV

[47]The Fund for the Advancement of Education, 1961, p. 58

could improve the quality of teaching without an increase in cost."[48] Studies of participating schools found that many schools in the National Program had discovered that large-class TV lessons freed teachers to give more time to small classes and individualized instruction. The program appeared to be cost-effective as well. For example, in Dade County, there were 30,000 students in TV courses, and, according to TFAE (1961), "the school system has been able to handle nearly a third more students than it was designed for, and to save the equivalent cost of twenty-seven additional teaching positions and twenty-nine more classrooms."[49]

Generally, it seemed that students learned as well or better through these methods, provided that studio and classroom teachers and curriculum specialists and principals worked well together. Still it was not easy to provide the necessary TV instruction. To return to Dade County, for example, ITV seemed to be effective in helping ease the teacher shortage, but enrollments continued to grow. As a result, according to J. Murphy and R. Gross (1966) in *Learning by Television*, "TV programs were ground out in great volume without sufficient preparation or careful choice of studio teachers,"[50] and the program deteriorated.

A particularly interesting ITV/ETV project took place in New York City from 1957 to 1961. According to the New York City Board of Education, the Chelsea Closed-Circuit Television Project was, "a pilot project to explore the values of closed-circuit TV as a service to a low-income, poly-lingual, urban neighborhood and its public school."[51] Conducted by the Board of Education, the Hudson Guild Neighborhood House, and Language Research, Inc. (of Harvard University), and funded by the Fund for the Advancement of Education, this project established a closed-circuit TV system linking PS 33 (the local elementary school), the Hudson Guild (a neighborhood house established in 1895), the Lower West Side District Health Center, and the four low-rent housing units of the John Lovejoy Elliott Houses. In short, its objective was "to raise the sights of a neighborhood and its public school,"[52] and is interesting both for its

---

[48]The Fund for the Advancement of Education, 1961, p. 58

[49]The Fund for the Advancement of Education, 1961, p. 58

[50]Murphy and Gross, 1966, p. 45

[51]New York City Board of Education, 1962, p. 1

[52]New York City Board of Education, 1962, p. 5

efforts to link schools with other community resources, and for its fairly unique goals, which deviated from the standard issues of cost-cutting and teacher shortages.

For 2 years, "CCCTV" (Chelsea Closed Circuit Television) aired every weekday from 9 a.m. to 9 p.m. They began in 1958 with language programs, quickly adding programs on health, information, entertainment, and language. Programs presented as part of the school curriculum were usually broadcast to the community as well. Inservice courses and demonstration lessons were aired for teachers. Some programs featured local students discussing issues or high-lighted activities in PS 33. Overall, this was a project providing pro-grams of local interest, made locally, and featuring local people.

By the fall of 1959, viewing had dropped off. Many viewers had disconnected the cable from their TV sets at home, feeling that CCCTV was controlled not by them, but by outside authorities. Some residents did not distinguish clearly between CCCTV and the Housing Authority and so were suspicious of this free gift that had been given to them. A report on CCCTV by the New York City Board of Education pointed out a fundamental flaw of the project:

> a grass-roots conflict between the fundamental purpose of the community effort and the proposed medium, television. There is in the very nature of television, as in other mass media, the dan-ger of a certain authoritarianism, an imposition from without upon a passive receptor. But community growth comes from with-in and involves participation on the part of the people.[53]

This issue of *who* initiates educational reform had been problematic with film and radio and would later be problematic with technologies that came after television. The conflict usually centers on the ques-tion of whether the initiative comes from teachers or administrators, the argument being that reform cannot be successfully imposed from the top down. The case of CCCTV was a little different from this standard teachers versus administrators framing of the conflict, but represented essentially the same problem—the suspicion felt by a group when they feel something is being imposed on them for their own improvement.

There were also conflicts between the English- and Spanish-speaking residents. About half the residents were of Puerto Rican

---

[53]New York City Board of Education, 1962, pp. 139–140

origin. Many of the English-speaking residents believed that all of the CCCTV programming was for the Puerto Rican residents. Meanwhile some of the Spanish-speaking residents were offended by the language instruction courses, perceiving them as evidence of the contempt felt by the English-speaking residents toward the Puerto Ricans. Additionally, CCCTV was trying to heighten residents' sense of identity with their community, which many residents were reluctant to do. The Board of Education's report pointed out this conflict:

> Some of the Elliott Houses residents seemed to find their ego satisfaction in the conviction that they were different from the other residents. "The housing project is fine for those other people, but for me it is a stopgap measure". . . . With such persons it became a virtue to reject their neighbors, sight unseen. People of this view were not readily reachable by a television program designed to unite.[54]

Again, it was evident that a project aiming to improve a community required a sophisticated understanding of that community—that understanding preferably cultivated through participation of community members.

Although it was a short-lived project, CCCTV represents an interesting attempt to address the educational needs of a particular community in a somewhat holistic fashion. It also demonstrates the complexity of issues involved in the use of educational media, issues that go far beyond matters of hardware, installation, and technical training. Incidentally, this project was also unusual in that it involved putting students on the air, which was not at all the focus of most ITV projects.

Some ITV experiments involved the use of television for teacher training. The most elaborate project took place in the Texas schools, where every teacher-training college and university in the state participated in a broadcast TV program that aired on 18 local commercial TV stations. Recent college graduates could enroll in this 1-year TV course at 1 of the 18 schools, and upon completion of the course, they would receive a temporary teaching permit. Permanent certification could come after adding 12 semester hours in residence at a participating institution as well as another year of teaching experience. Between 1956 and 1969, 1,007 people enrolled in the pro-

---

[54]New York City Board of Education, 1962, p. 144

gram; 604 of them continued on to receive permanent certification. This was a project financed by the Fund for the Advancement of Education, which withdrew its funding after being disappointed by enrollments lower than they had hoped for, dropout rates higher than they had hoped for, and a resulting per capita cost that proved prohibitive.[55] When grant funding ended, so did the program.

Although the existence of ETV (i.e., noncommercial, public TV) stations after 1952 made for a different relationship between educators and commercial broadcasters than had existed with radio, commercial broadcasters were sometimes involved in ITV projects. For example, the Fund for the Advancement of Education financed a show called "Continental Classroom," which first aired on NBC on October 6, 1958, and was designed so that any college or university could offer credit for the course. The first "Continental Classroom" course was a physics course, offered five days a week at 6:30 a.m. to keep high school science teachers up to date in their field by exposing them to the latest work of scientists and scholars. During the first week it was on the air, approximately 5,000 students registered in over 250 colleges and universities, and the daily viewing audience was estimated at 270,000. In 1959, the physics course was repeated, and a chemistry course was added, gaining an audience of 525,000, with approximately 3,000 viewers receiving course credit. This success led to the addition of courses in math and American government. "Continental Classroom" aired on more than 150 NBC stations, with local instructors holding on-campus meetings for discussions, tests, and experiments.[56] After TFAE funding ended, the program was supported for a time by several corporate sponsors.[57] "Continental Classroom" was cancelled in 1961 despite what Murphy and Gross describe as "an impressive record of participating colleges and active viewers."[58]

NBC was not the only network with an early morning ITV program. CBS had "Sunrise Semester," which was produced by New York University, distributed by CBS, and broadcast by many CBS affiliates in the same 6:30 a.m. time slot as "Continental Classroom." "Sunrise Semester" went on the air in New York in September 1957, with a course in comparative literature. The response to the show far

---

[55]The Fund for the Advancement of Education, 1961, p. 61

[56]Smith, 1961, pp. 114–115

[57]The Fund for the Advancement of Education, 1961, p. 61

[58]Murphy and Gross, 1966, p. 10

exceeded the expectations of its producers; publishers were flooded with requests for the books being discussed on the program.[59] Subsequent courses were offered on topics including classics, government, mathematics, Western civilization, physical science, and sociology. These programs generally had audiences of approximately 150 viewers enrolled for credit and another 90,000 viewers watching for their own enjoyment or enrichment.[60] In September 1963, the programs were made a network offering to CBS affiliates, enlarging the audience to an estimated 1.5 to 2 million.[61] By September 1963, "Sunrise Semester" was a national program, aired by 111 CBS stations, and it was the only educational program on commercial stations. It stayed on the air until the 1980s, when the networks discovered that those early morning hours could be profitable. In much the same way that educational radio programs lost their time slots to more lucrative ventures, "Sunrise Semester" only stayed on the air until CBS figured out how to turn a profit during that time slot.

In short, the 1950s and early 1960s were a time of ambitious experimentation in ITV, primarily toward goals of efficiency and economy, but occasionally with other purposes in mind. However, even those projects deemed successes tended to be short lived. Although one might explain away the relative failure of ITV as the inability to maintain funding, there are a number of other factors worth taking into consideration as well.

FACTORS PREVENTING THE DEVELOPMENT OF ITV

Despite some high hopes for ITV and conditions that (in some ways at least) were conducive to its development, even some advocates were willing to admit in the 1970s that ITV "has not fulfilled its sometimes too boisterously pronounced promise and potential."[62] One obvious problem was funding. As noted earlier in this chapter, ITV was expensive and only developed to the point that it did through external funding—particularly from the Ford Foundation. In 1963, the Ford Foundation discontinued support for ITV, because, accord-

---

[59]Cassirer, 1960, p. 78
[60]Cassirer, 1960, p. 79
[61]Blakely, 1979, p. 249
[62]McBride, 1977, p. 65

ing to ETV historian R. J. Blakely, "there was a need for a national noncommercial service, to strengthen National Educational Television and to help broaden the financial resources of community-corporation stations."[63] The Ford Foundation had also come to the conclusion in 1966 that, "as it has been used to date, TV cannot upgrade the quality of American education; it can only alleviate the problems created by having too few teachers, too many students, and swelling curriculums."[64] After abandoning ITV, the Ford Foundation committed itself more deeply to ETV instead.

Another problem for ITV was that it was somewhat in competition with ETV. ITV advocates needed stations to air their programs, and they often turned to educational TV stations for air time. However, ETV stations did not want to use their air time for narrow instructional purposes because they conceived of their mission as serving their entire communities. They believed that commercial broadcasters were not serving the general public well and saw their primary goal as meeting the needs of the general public, not of providing classroom instruction.[65]

Other problems with ITV had to do with teacher resistance and difficulty matching the goals and requirements of ITV with teachers' goals and practices. Teachers were critical not only of ITV, but of television in general, and those larger concerns about the medium certainly affected how teachers felt about using it with their students, much as it affected teachers' attitudes toward film and radio.

Incompatibility with Teachers' Needs and Interests

Administrators tended to think of ITV more as an alternative to teachers than as an aid to teachers. Given the bulging enrollments and teacher shortages of that time, administrators were attracted by the possibility that television could teach in place of teachers or reduce the necessary qualifications of the classroom teacher by transferring instructional responsibilities onto the televised master teacher. It should not be surprising, then, that teachers often responded to ITV with hostility.

---

[63]Blakely, 1979, p. 169

[64]Murphy and Gross, 1966, p. 10

[65]Blakely, 1979, p. 137

ITV was an educational reform that, like many others before and after it, did not originate with teachers. Instead it emerged from the administrative problem of arranging the instruction of large numbers of students with inadequate numbers of well-prepared teachers. It was almost exclusively concerned with the transmission of curricular content to students, not with the cultivation of relationships between teachers and students or among students. To be fair, ITV advocates rarely dismissed the importance of interpersonal relationships and a sense of community in schools; it was not uncommon for them to emphasize that this arena was the one for which classroom teachers were most qualified and needed. However, in relegating teachers to the function of bringing an element of humanity to the classroom, these reformers were stripping teachers of their academic function and removing teachers from their role as curriculum designers. Teachers were left with the job of previewing and following up on televised lessons prepared by someone else, often outside of the district or region, whom they had never met and with whom they had never discussed their professional needs or goals. They found themselves in much the same position that their predecessors had been in with respect to film and radio, where classroom media had been produced by strangers without sufficient regard for local curricula or teachers' goals.

Rarely did ITV broadcasters and teachers work closely together; hence, most ITV programs did not fit the curriculum of the teachers who were expected to use them. As audiovisual coordinator William King argued in 1954, "educational TV programs must be planned by and for teachers. Programs must be a part of the regular school curriculum in order to be successful."[66] The report of a 1959 seminar at NEA headquarters argued that, because programmers did not pay much attention "to the problems of fitting the programs to the needs of classroom teachers and learners, educational TV has remained up to now chiefly a transmitter of information, a teacher talking to students in front of a camera."[67] The report later stressed that "TV program planning must be an integral part of the total curriculum picture and contribute to the instructional goals and objectives of the organization of which it is a part," particularly "if a pro-

[66]King, 1954, p. 20
[67]Foshay, 1959, p. 9

gram maker wishes to use his medium for genuinely improved learning, not just to cope with shortages."[68]

ITV was promoted to teachers as a way to professionalize
their work, by leaving them primarily to one-on-one and small-group
instruction while television handled their routine tasks. However,
teachers did not always share that view. The following is a 1960
quote from *The American Teacher Magazine*, a publication of the
American Federation of Teachers:

> It seems clear that the purpose of educational television is not at
> all that of improving education, but rather that of cutting educa-
> tion costs by downgrading teachers financially through creating a
> kind of caste system in which the actual student contacts will be
> in the hands of second class teachers, receiving, of course second
> class pay, and through an enormous increase in classroom size.[69]

Dr. Harold E. Wigren, TV consultant to the National Education
Association, emphasized that teachers did not oppose the use of television when it could help with a teaching goal they believed was
important. What they resented were unwarranted claims about television's educational potential made by people with little or no classroom experience. He described the rightful indignation expressed by
teachers "over some of the things they hear proponents of total teaching by television say about teaching and about teachers."[70]

Following is a good example of the kinds of things said by
ITV proponents about teachers taken from a 1956 article co-authored
by several prominent ITV researchers for the U.S. Army:

> close scrutiny of the behavior of instructors standing before a
> class revealed much irrelevant ad-libbing, reliance upon home-
> brewed analogies which often broke down even in the course of
> their presentation, and lengthy answers to student questions of
> frequently dubious cogency.[71]

Military ITV research reports tended to be more blatant in
their expression of the unimportance of classroom teachers. Their
narrow focus on training, as opposed to education, meant they had

---

[68]Foshay, 1959, p. 36

[69]Walter C. Varnum, in Cassirer, 1960, p. 56

[70]Harold E. Wigren, in Cassirer, 1960, p. 56

[71]Desiderato, Kanner, and Runyon, 1956, p. 59

little interest in the student–teacher relationship except in terms of
its possible importance in the effective transmission of information.
Meanwhile teachers resented the equation of "great teaching" merely
with "great transmission." Teachers College President Hollis L.
Caswell pointed out this distinction:

> Often it is argued that television can extend the influence of
> great teachers from a few students to many hundreds or even
> thousands. What is overlooked is the extent to which teachers are
> great because of their direct, personal influence on students.[72]

Contemporary theories of mass communication processes reinforced
the transmission metaphor for teaching and learning. Shannon and
Weaver's information theory model for the communication process—
still found in many introductory communication theory textbooks—
described that process as one where a message is encoded for transmission through some channel and then decoded by a receiver at the
intended destination. Information theory did not concern itself with
the significance of the message or its impact on the recipient. Rather,
it described communication as a rather mechanical process whose
purpose was to move messages accurately, not to consider the meaning of the message or its impact on the people involved in the communication process. This way of thinking about the mass communication process was clearly reflected in much of the thinking about ITV,
where the focus was on moving curricular content into children's
minds as efficiently and accurately as possible, not on considering the
significance of the relationship between classroom inhabitants or the
meaning of the curriculum to students.

    Some of the tension between classroom teachers and ITV pro-
ducers seems to have been a product of "a really incredible misread-
ing of who teachers are, why they teach and, therefore, where they
perceive their interests to reside."[73] Teachers did not necessarily
want to be part of a teaching team with a studio teacher, relinquish-
ing some of their authority to that teacher. Some questioned the
claim that both teachers were equals, believing instead that students
would believe that the TV teachers were superior (hence, selected as
TV teachers) and taking offense at not being chosen. For example,
some teachers in the Chelsea Closed Circuit project were resentful,

[72]Cassirer, 1960, p. 61
[73]Berkman, 1977, p. 99

believing they should have been chosen to be TV teachers.[74] Rarely
did plans for implementing ITV take into account the issue of teacher
autonomy and how to preserve for teachers a sense of professional
pride and control over the conditions of their work.

ITV required teachers to adapt themselves to television in
terms of accepting the curriculum as offered by the broadcasts.
Additionally, if teachers wanted to use ITV, they were hostages of the
broadcast schedule. Television programs were timely in ways that
films were not, but films could be used more flexibly in that they
could potentially be shown at any time of day that suited the teacher's
needs. Moreover, films could be previewed by the teacher, and segments could be shown more than once in class if need be; these were
features that ITV did not possess. Although some ITV libraries were
in operation and some schools had the capacity to record programs,
teachers were mainly dependent on broadcast schedules (as they had
been with radio), which did not always suit their needs—particularly
at the secondary level, where, according to Henry Cassirer, "individual high schools find it more difficult to fit their 'bell schedules' to the
programme schedules of television stations."[75]

ITV programs were often of relatively poor quality, a problem
cited in a 1966 Fund for the Advancement of Education report as one
of the "prime causes for instructional television's limited
acceptance."[76] Many programs were simply classroom lectures
unadapted for television. Others were paced inappropriately due to
the lack of feedback from a class/audience. At a 1959 meeting at the
NEA headquarters, a group of teachers evaluated a selection of ITV
programs submitted by schools and ETV stations in response to a
request for examples of the best programs available. They concluded
that, "all in all . . . the evaluation of the present product of educational television as represented by the kinescopes available for study was
strongly negative."[77] They found too much talking head teaching, too
much answer giving, not enough question-asking, too little attention
to making students active learners, and an overemphasis on showmanship. A 1963 to 1964 survey by the National Instructional
Television Library produced similar findings; they deemed only 9.2%

---

[74]New York City Board of Education, 1962, pp. 206–207

[75]Cassirer, 1960, p. 61

[76]Murphy and Gross, 1966, p. 6

[77]Frazier and Wigren, 1960, p. 12

of the available ITV series to be fit for distribution, ruling out 70%
entirely for lack of instructional effectiveness.[78]

Despite that demand far exceeded supply of teachers in the
years in which ITV was most heavily promoted, it appears that many
teachers feared that television would be used to replace them. In
1959, Finette Foshay's report on a seminar sponsored by the
National Education Associaiton described how "classroom teachers
felt threatened by the specter of their jobs being swallowed up by the
mechanical monster."[79] Although this was a time of teacher shortages, it was also a time of increased mechanization of many aspects
of life, which fueled concerns that education, too, would become
mechanized. The report on the Chelsea Closed Circuit project
acknowledged such teacher resistance and fears:

> These teachers (and teachers as a profession) tend to regard edu-
> cational TV as an inadequate replacement for an essential and
> time-honored profession (and in some instances as a threat to
> their jobs). They are reacting, partly, to today's climate of increas-
> ing automation with the machine displacing the human worker.[80]

Where teachers of the film and radio years feared that those media
would be used to stretch Depression-era budgets and eliminate their
jobs, teachers of the early years of television feared that the fascination with streamlining and automation would lead to their replacement by television.

Although most of the policy talk promoting ITV stressed that
it would be absolutely inappropriate to use television to replace
teachers, it is hard to argue that the use of ITV had nothing to do
with cost-effectiveness (and, therefore, with staffing decisions). In
Hagerstown, for example, effective use of ITV made it possible for
three elementary art and music teachers to do the work of 33 teachers.[81] Although the district did not dismiss any teachers as a result of
the use of ITV, it is no wonder that teachers were alarmed, particularly if they were thinking far enough into the future to imagine
what might happen to their job security when overcrowding eased.

---

[78]Murphy and Gross, 1966, p. 62

[79]Foshay, 1959, p. 9

[80]New York City Board of Education, 1962, pp. 206–207

[81]Cassirer, 1960, pp. 36–37

Along with criticisms that schools were substituting television for teachers came the feeling that ITV promoters traded quality for economy. Communications professor and ITV scholar George Gordon wrote that ITV producers "define teaching in both superficial and totally non-professional ways. They quantify what is qualitative by nature, and like good pitchmen, they are interested in profits (or objectives) without noticing that means (or processes) is what the big game is all about."[82] In 1959, Finette Foshay argued that one of the primary factors limiting the realization of ITV's potential was "the idea, uncritically accepted, that educational television's reason for being is to cope with shortages of teachers and classrooms. This idea has led too frequently to an abandonment of educational goals in favor of serving administrative necessities."[83]

It would not be fair to claim that all teachers were opposed to ITV. Certainly there were teachers who found the broadcasts to be useful and did not feel that their job security or sense of professionalism was compromised by television. Still it appears that many teachers were guarded in their acceptance of television, because it was not entirely clear that it was brought into schools with teachers' or students' best interests at heart.

Concerns About Television's Effects on Children

Many teachers were critical not only of ITV, but of all television. Teachers were often the last on the block to buy a TV set; because they "disdained to receive Milton Berle in their own living rooms, they also excluded the 'idiot box' from their classrooms."[84] Some teachers echoed the concerns their predecessors had expressed about film and radio by fearing that children would not take ITV seriously, believing that children perceived television as an entertainment medium. Teachers were also concerned that children would come to expect all learning to be as easy and fun as television, or they would expect school to imitate the entertaining qualities of television.

---

[82]Gordon, 1977, p. 150

[83]Foshay, 1959, p. 46

[84]Murphy and Gross, 1966, p. 11

Overall teachers seemed more concerned about countering the potentially negative effects of television on children than on welcoming the medium into classrooms. Teachers, and adults more generally, were concerned that television fostered unrealistic expectations in children and that it made children violent, less discriminating in their sense of culture and good taste, antisocial, illiterate, and passive.

There has been perhaps no more researched mass media question than that of the effect of televised violence on children. Studies attempting to pin down the relationship between TV violence and violent behavior range from small student papers to huge projects, the latter including such works as *Television in the Lives of Our Children* (1961) and the 1971 report to the Surgeon General, entitled *Television and Growing Up: The Impact of Televised Violence*. Researchers were typically unable to identify a causal connection between violent imagery and violent action, producing noncommittal findings like the following passage, now well known to media scholars:

> For *some* children, under *some* conditions, *some* television is harmful. For *other* children under the same conditions, or for the same children under *other* conditions, it may be beneficial. For *most* children, under *most* conditions, *most* television is probably neither particularly harmful nor particularly beneficial.[85]

The prior quote came from *Television in the Lives of Our Children*, the summary of a series of studies conducted in the late 1950s. The findings of these studies suggest that aggression was somewhat higher in high TV viewers, and that in some cases "television may both suggest the tool of violence and help build up the aggression drive that needs such a tool. Then, when aggression in a real-life situation is at a sufficient height, the child remembers how aggressive acts were done on television."[86] Overall, however, the report's authors stressed the absence of clearly causal or widespread relationships between television content and children's behavior, calling instead for an emphasis on what children do with television, rather than on what television does to children.

[85]Schramm, Lyle, and Parker, 1961, p. 1

[86]Schramm, Lyle, and Parker, 1961, p. 161 (emphasis in original text)

Ten years later, another large study produced similar results. In 1969, Senator John O. Pastore requested that a committee be formed to study the impact of TV violence. The Office of the Surgeon General assembled the Advisory Committee on Television and Social Behavior, which consisted of 11 experts in the behavioral sciences and in mental health.[87] They conducted 23 separate projects and summarized their findings in a summary report and five additional volumes. These studies ranged from interviews with parents—suggesting that many adults believed their children's sleep to be disturbed by violent television—to controlled experiments, where groups of children were shown violent, prosocial, or neutral programming, and their aggressiveness was monitored. Some of these experimental studies showed no significant differences with regard to aggression, although others suggested that children who viewed violence were more likely to act aggressively.[88] Furthermore, some children demonstrated an increase in prosocial behavior after viewing prosocial programming, contributing to the sense that television *did* influence behavior. Still the committee concluded that television had no adverse effect on most children.

The report to the Surgeon General was controversial in that commercial broadcasters had been given the power to edit the list of possible committee members. They removed seven social scientists from that list, all researchers with strong backgrounds in the type of work to be done. Meanwhile all three of the sociologists on the committee were affiliated with CBS, and two of the psychologists had network affiliations. As a result, the report received a hostile reaction from social scientists and was accused of being "an apologist for, and defender of, the broadcast industry."[89]

It seems that reports like *Television in the Lives of Our Children* and the Surgeon General's report did little to assuage teachers' fears. It became more and more common to call for combating the potentially negative effects of television (however flimsy the proof that they existed) than to use television for instruction. Television-related articles in education journals often focused on television's dangers and on arming children against those dangers,

---

[87]U.S. Surgeon General's Advisory Committee on Television and Social Behavior, 1971, p. 15

[88]U.S. Surgeon General's Advisory Committee on Television and Social Behavior, 1971, p. 15

[89]Lowery and DeFleur, 1995, p. 330

rather than on the medium's instructional potential. In that spirit, as early as the early 1950s, calls were made to incorporate critical viewing into the K–12 curriculum.[90] The authors of *Television in the Lives of Our Children* argued that "anything to which children devote one-sixth of their waking hours has obvious importance for schools. If children are helped to know good books from poor ones, good music from poor music, good art from bad art, there is no reason why they should not be helped to develop some standards for TV."[91] The call for *TV literacy* (or *media literacy* or *visual literacy*) intensified, as various organizations were formed to take up the cause—not only because of concerns about violence, but also in the spirit of arming children against the assault of lowbrow, *mass culture*.

On the issue of social interaction, the concern was that children, particularly those without siblings or with working mothers, were spending too much time alone with television and not enough time with other children. Some studies suggest that it was insecure children, those "who felt rejected by their peer groups, who expressed more worries and more fears, and more anxiety about growing up,"[92] who were most at risk of being isolated by their TV habits. Overall, it appeared that "a child goes to television to escape from pressing social problems, to leave the field of frustration, and to obtain vicariously some of the satisfactions he is unable to obtain from real interpersonal relationships."[93] This era, like many others, was one when adults were concerned that young people were increasingly alienated from mainstream society. Therefore, it should not be surprising that adults were afraid that children were acquiring antisocial habits and attitudes from television.

Concerns about the relationship between TV viewing and literacy generally fell into one of two categories. Many teachers were concerned—as their predecessors had been about film and radio—that children were spending so much time watching television that they were spending less time reading or were coming to prefer the pleasures of television to those of reading. The other fear was that the conditions of TV viewing worked against literacy—that reading required concentration and focused attention, whereas TV viewing appeared to require

---

[90]Hood, 1953; Long, 1952; Roy, 1954

[91]Schramm, Lyle, and Parker, 1961, p. 184

[92]Schramm, Lyle, and Parker, 1961, p. 119

[93]Schramm, Lyle, and Parker, 1961, p. 121

nothing whatsoever. The possibility that television was lowering literacy rates was a popular subject in education journals of the time.

Fears about television's potential contribution to declining literacy rates were related to fears that television was breeding a passive generation. In 1953, American Psychological Association representative F. J. Van Bortel argued that educational TV stations had to "be instrumental in making *doers* out of the present host of *viewers*."[94] California teacher Arnold Leslie Lazarus reported in 1956 on a Ford Foundation-funded study he conducted, in which he found a displacement of hobbies and creative pursuits as children watched more television.[95] *Television in the Lives of Our Children* ultimately emphasized that a normal child "is not in danger of being made abnormally passive by television,"[96] but not before painting a more disturbing picture of those few who are affected:

> All of us have seen the television set used as baby sitter, the child sucking his thumb as he watches, completely absorbed in the program. Many of us have seen a television addict, a child who is uncomfortable at home until he can turn on the set, and then buries himself in the program, shutting out all the outside world.[97]

Concerns about passivity and literacy, in particular, were particularly influential in teachers' attitudes toward ITV because it sometimes appeared that children's use of the medium was having effects on them that worked directly against what was expected of them in schools. Although television seemed an ideal solution to one educational problem of the time—too many students and too few teachers—it did not seem to have much to offer the other problems of the day, such as the alleged anti-intellectualism in schools and the neglect of core academics and traditional literacy skills. The potentially negative effects of television, coupled with teachers' resistance to a reform that was not their idea and did not seem to have their best interests at heart, may have been as influential in stopping the development of ITV as funding problems were.

---

[94]Willey and Van Bortel, 1953, p. 253

[95]Lazarus, 1956, pp. 241–242

[96]Schramm, Lyle, and Parker, 1961, p. 160

[97]Schramm, Lyle, and Parker, 1961, p. 159

CONCLUSION

ITV had some moments in the limelight in some well-funded projects. However, even those projects produced uncertain results. A 1961 book funded by the Fund for the Advancement of Education conceded that,

> The medium can take credit for helping understaffed schools to cope with ever increasing enrollments. But television has not transformed education, nor has it significantly improved the learning of most students. In short, TV is still far from fulfilling its obvious promise.[98]

Later in the book, the authors point out that, "by and large, the really innovating schools are doing little with television."[99] In a similar spirit, Henry Cassirer observed that "television is used in the United States more to compensate for deficiencies than to provide new resources for education which make a contribution to the best of schools."[100] Toward the end of the 1960s, curriculum and methods were changing, with a reemerging emphasis on inquiry, discovery, collaboration, and opening back up beyond traditional academic subjects, and television was not as appropriate for those goals as it had been for goals of economy and efficiency in delivery of content.

Even before the neoprogressive shift and its impact on the ITV agenda, the changing focus of educational psychology was already undermining ITV to some extent. Although some psychological research in the 1950s and 1960s was compatible with ITV, that research increasingly focused on individualizing instruction through automated systems that allowed each user to follow a different path at a different pace than that of his or her peers. These systems moved away from image-based forms of audiovisual instruction to text-based forms and offered what appeared to be a preferable, more active experience for students. Unlike film and radio, television did not have the monopoly on the interest of educational technology researchers, only some of whom remained interested in developing a mass medium for instruction as new forms and systems of automated instruction attracted the attention of education reformers and appeared to discredit the foundations on which ITV was based.

---

[98]Murphy and Gross, 1966, p. 9

[99]Murphy and Gross, 1966, p. 9

[100]Cassirer, 1960, p. 61

5

AUTOMATED INSTRUCTION

CAI is here to stay. It's an essential part of a just-beginning revolution in education that will hopefully endure longer than the last one . . .

—Carl E. Helm, *Audio-Visual Communication Review*
(Fall, 1969)

In the period during and after World War II, audiovisual education generally took one of two major forms: mass instruction, such as ITV, or individualized automated instruction, in the form of teaching machines, programmed learning, and, slightly later, computer-assisted instruction (CAI). Both forms of audiovisual instruction were, at least in large part, products of military research and development and efforts to systematize and standardize instruction. What was unique to automated instruction was that it marked the first time that educational technologies were integral components in learning research, having been developed as means of formulating and testing new learning theories. The 1950s and 1960s were a period in which educational technologies and learning theories fused in such a way as to legitimize one another, and when technology was first used as a link between learning research and classroom instruction. Postwar interest in applying new technologies to public school instruction also came from the unprecedented sums of federal funds made available for research and development in this area, which offered a much-needed source of funding to psychological research that had previously been funded by the military.

Like ITV, methods of automated instruction were applied to or justified by school reform movements or educational crises of the time. They were advocated by those who sought to align school reform with cold war foreign policy issues, as well as reformers focused on educational equity in the era following the 1954 *Brown vs. The Board of Education* decision. Federal funding for educational technology tended to focus on one of these two areas of concern, and private foundations increasingly had specific reform agendas toward which they directed their funding, generally similar to those targeted by federal funds. Major publishing and information technology industries, perceiving a potentially lucrative new market, provided the means of distribution for these new instructional machines and materials.

Application of methods of automated instruction to schools was most active from the late 1950s to the early 1970s, with teaching machines and programmed instruction attracting, then losing, attention slightly ahead of CAI. As the focus both of educational policy and educational psychology shifted, interest in these audiovisual materials waned. The theoretical underpinnings of automated instruction do live on in certain contemporary educational practices, but the intensity of early interest in automated instruction can hardly be said to have radically transformed the character of American public education.

ORIGINS OF AUTOMATED INSTRUCTION

World War II brought together psychologists and audiovisual specialists in military research laboratories to develop training programs to efficiently and effectively prepare new recruits for their roles in the armed services. When the war ended, research continued due both to the spirit of cold war preparedness and an interest in extending this work out beyond military applications. If the military origin of these instructional methods is not widely known, it is probably because they entered schools "by the side door"[1] of educational psychology, many of whose researchers conducted their work under military contract.

Those involved in developing automated, individualized military training took a great interest in behaviorism, which derives from theories formed by Edward Thorndike, an educational psychologist of the early 20th century who believed that learning was affected by such things as rewards and punishments received by the learner and the learner's sense of satisfaction or failure. He argued that learning involved the establishment of neural bonds between a stimulus and response when that stimulus produced a satisfying response for the learner, leading, ultimately, to some desired pattern of behavior in the learner. Learning of this sort could be strengthened through repetition and reinforcement; that is, through cementing the bond between stimulus and response, and by encouraging the response by following it with pleasurable feedback while accompanying other responses with unpleasant feedback. With this conception of learning, the teacher's role was to connect appropriate stimulus–response pairs and provide the appropriate positive and negative feedback to students' responses.

Thorndike is also known for his work on transfer of learning, which dramatically challenged the prevailing beliefs about transfer. He lived at a time when *mental discipline* was promoted—that is, when it was believed that rigorous study in one discipline would improve a student's ability to think effectively in other disciplines as well. For example, many students were required to study Latin at the time out of the belief that the work of learning Latin would cultivate the mental discipline required to learn difficult material in other domains. However, Thorndike's research, according to educational psychology scholar Roy Pea, "devastated the discipline hypothesis and helped open up a period of vocationalism in American schooling."[2] The possibility that learning was domain specific led many social efficiency education reformers of the time to promote narrow education for students, specifically tailored to their probable future occupations.

Equally important to the later development of automated instruction were the machines often associated with it. Although pro-

---

[1]Edgar Dale, in Noble, 1991, p. 24

[2]Pea, 1988, p. 193

grammed instruction did not require the use of machines, often taking the form of textbooks, workbooks, or other printed materials, it
developed out of the idea of the teaching machine and often did
involve one or another type of machine. Prototypes of teaching
machines were developed by Sidney Pressey in the 1920s. He developed what were primarily meant as grading machines, although he
also believed they could be used for some drill work and that immediate scoring made testing into a form of self-instruction. One of his
machines consisted of a box with a revolving drum with questions
printed on the drum. The box would expose one question at a time,
and students would answer by pressing one of four buttons. A correct
answer released the drum and exposed another question. One of
these machines even dispensed a candy wafer for some determined
number of right answers.[3] Another of Pressey's inventions was a
punchboard system of grading, where a sheet of paper was placed
between two sheets of 3" X 5" pressboard. Students pressed their
pencil tips into columns of holes to answer multiple-choice questions;
a right answer pushed the pencil through the paper, whereas a
wrong answer did not.[4]

In 1932, Pressey predicted that his machines would be part of
"the coming 'industrial revolution' in education,"[5] a particularly good
selling point, he believed, in the Depression era:

> Education is the one major activity in this country which is still
> in a crude handicraft stage. But the economic depression may
> here work beneficently in that it may force the consideration of
> efficiency and the need for conveniences and labor-saving devices
> in education.[6]

Pressey emphasized that industrialization did not have to mean
mechanization. Rather, he believed that his machines would free the
teacher "for those inspirational and thought-stimulating activities,
which are, presumably, the real function of the teacher."[7] He also
believed that his machines could generate enthusiasm for learning
better than traditional methods:

---

[3]Fry, 1963, p. 25

[4]Pressey, 1960, pp. 69–88

[5]Pressey, 1932, p. 668

[6]Pressey, 1932, p. 672

[7]Pressey, 1926, p. 374

there are at present many things now done in our schools and colleges in very unnecessarily labored and enthusiasm-killing fashion. The writer is convinced that mechanical aids are possible which would do much to relieve the situation.[8]

Pressey was unable to popularize his ideas or inventions among educators in the 1920s and 1930s perhaps because the dominance of child-centered progressivism kept such mechanized methods and materials in check.[9] However, the convergence of audiovisual education, behaviorism, and the postwar educational crisis sparked an intense interest in teaching machines in the 1950s. The military had discovered behavioral psychologist B.F. Skinner and took great interest in applying his theories of instruction to military training. Funding for experiments with teaching machines came largely from such military sources as the Army, the Office of Naval Research, and the Air Research and Development Command of the U.S. Air Force.[10]

Skinner, probably the best known of behavioral psychologists, described learning in terms of stimulus–response pairs and the arrangement of "contingencies of reinforcement," stressing the importance of immediate and appropriate feedback in the conditioning of behavior. "A student is 'taught,'" according to Skinner, "in the sense that he is induced to engage in new forms of behavior and in specific forms upon specific occasions."[11] He believed that the traditional classroom setting did not provide enough reinforcement or reward to promote effective, efficient learning, but that his teaching machines could solve that problem by providing immediate feedback. He also argued that human behavior was too complex to be changed without "rather elaborate apparatus," that "the human organism requires . . . subtle instrumentation."[12]

Skinner's work was also characterized by the careful breaking down of material to be learned into the smallest possible steps so that students would, in theory, master the material bit by bit. Skinner believed that this system would minimize student error, thus ensuring frequent enough success (and, therefore, positive rein-

---

[8]Pressey, 1926, p. 376

[9]Noble, 1991, p. 28

[10]Lumsdaine and Glaser, 1960, p. vii

[11]Skinner, 1960, p. 140

[12]Skinner, 1960, p. 140

forcement) to motivate the learner to master the material. His machines controlled the dispensation of new information so that learners would only be exposed to something new when their chance of understanding it was high.

Skinner built *vanishing,* or *fading,* into his programs, where learners were initially provided with clues to the correct answer to keep the error rate as low as possible, but where those clues were gradually withdrawn. He also used *shaping,* where students were first rewarded for approximations of the desired behavior and then for more closely demonstrating that behavior and then only for the specific behavior desired.

Skinner worked primarily with *constructed-response* programs, where students were called on to write in an answer to a question. Students would be shown a question in one window of the teaching machine and then called on to compose an answer in another window. Once committed to that answer, it would be covered by a clear window so the student could no longer change it, and the correct answer would appear in yet another window.

Skinner's programs were linear programs, meaning that there was only one sequence by which a learner could proceed through them. Most teaching machines used linear programs because they were the easiest to adapt to mechanical devices. Other researchers worked with multiple-choice formats, often opting for a branching sequence, where students moved through the program in different ways depending on their responses. One of the best-known types of branching programs were those of Norman Crowder of the U.S. Air Force. His *scrambled books* were programmed texts where students would read a question on one page and turn to a different page depending on the answer they chose. From there, they would be directed to further questions. A problem with scrambled books, however, was that it was easy to cheat with them because there was no way to conceal material until a student answered correctly, the way one could do with a machine.

The U.S. Armed Forces used a variety of automated training aids and devices to promote rapid, individualized learning. For example, the Navy used multiple-choice machines during World War II, placing them in recreation rooms where, according to E. B. Fry (1963) in *Teaching Machines and Programmed Instruction: An Introduction,* "students tried to 'beat the machine' by answering all the questions correctly."[13] In 1955, the Air Research and Development Command of the Air Force developed a multiple choice machine that could be used in three different modes: coaching (where the student was told the right answer), single error permitted (where the student was allowed one wrong answer), and practice (where an unlimited number of errors was allowed).[14] The "Tab Item" was developed for training Air Force maintenance personnel in the early 1950s; programmed information was presented on a page with answers concealed behind tabs.[15] Another device developed initially for military training was the Subject-Matter Trainer, which presented items in a window on the left and answers for selection in a window on the right; a green light signified a correct response, whereas a buzzer went off for wrong answers.[16] Yet another was the Card-Sort Device, which presented questions on cards in a window; those answered correctly were dropped into one bin, while incorrectly answered cards were recycled and presented again.[17]

The "Videosonic," developed by the Hughes Aircraft Company, combined a 35-mm slide projector and a tape-recorded narration. Students responded by pressing buttons on a panel attached to the machine. According to E. B. Fry, the Videosonic was used by the armed forces "as a controlled-performance training device to teach men how to work with complex equipment by introducing the equipment one small step at a time."[18] A modified version of the Videosonic removed the response panel and had learners working on assembly line units set up in front of them. Another machine paired a multiple-choice recording device with television, showing questions on the screen; it could be used with open or closed circuit television systems. Yet another used a computer, slide projector, and electric typewriter; the program was presented on the slides, with branching controlled by the computer.[19]

The introduction of the computer to automated instruction came more out of research interests than the intention to make wide-

---

[13]Fry, 1963, p. 25

[14]Fry, 1963, p. 26

[15]Glaser, Damrin, and Gardner, 1960, pp. 275–285

[16]Briggs, 1960, pp. 229–304

[17]Briggs, 1960, pp. 229–304

[18]Fry, 1963, p. 26

[19]For descriptions of all these machines, see Fry, 1963

spread use of computers for instruction. Computers were prohibitive-ly expensive, so it was not feasible to think in terms of extensive introduction into schools. Essentially, the research interests in com-puter-based instruction fell into one of two categories: systematizing, standardizing, and streamlining training; and simulating teaching machines as a way to understand thinking processes.

Training researchers took an interest in the branching style of programmed instruction. Linear programs brought each learner through the material in the same sequence, which was inefficient in that it did not permit learners to bypass material they had already mastered. Branching programs permitted more individualized train-ing, zeroing in on the learner's weak points and sequencing instruc-tion in such a way as to address those weaknesses. However, branch-ing programs were more complicated, and the computer was well suited to manage the branching feature.

The preparation of instructional lessons came to be conceived of as analogous to programming a computer. In *The Classroom Arsenal: Military Research, Information Technology, and Public Education* (1991), Douglas Noble describes how

> Such a view of instruction and of human beings lay at the heart
> of programmed instruction and of military training at that time.
> Instruction was a process of control, achieved through carefully
> sequenced presentations and immediate feedback to student
> responses. The computer, a technology perfectly suited to the con-
> trol of information, was the quintessential technology for the
> delivery of such instruction.[20]

Researchers saw the computer as a tool for streamlining and econo-mizing instruction by providing branching programs that addressed only those curricular areas that a particular student had not yet mastered.

There were also military training researchers who were interested in developing computer simulations of teaching machines as a form of learning research.[21] A research advantage of computeriz-ing programmed instruction was that many experimental variables could be controlled and manipulated through the use of the comput-er, which could then monitor the effects of such manipulations. These researchers were not focused on improving K–12 education through

---

[20]Noble, 1991, p. 85

[21]Noble, 1991, ch. 3

computers. Rather, according to Noble, they "came to view the computer-based teaching machine more as a laboratory for scientific experimentation in instructional programming than as a device for instructional delivery."[22]

Research of the 1960s went beyond behaviorist teaching machines to the idea of systems thinking, prompting an expansion of the idea of educational technology from technologies *for* instruction to technologies *of* instruction. That is, systems thinking centered on the idea of the human–machine system, where the goal was to streamline and standardize the functioning of the system by adapting both people and technologies to the goals of the system. It borrowed from military lessons in World War II training and behaviorism, particularly in terms of its focus on minimizing waste through efficient instruction and the development of specific, behaviorally stated performance objectives on which training was built. Such specific goals made evaluation easier and more objective, in that they clearly defined mastery of tasks and identified the overt behavior that would demonstrate mastery. These goals also served as limiting factors in training, specifying as much what was *not* to be learned as what *was* to be learned.

The systems approach was related to engineering psychology or human factors psychology, which conceived of psychologists and engineers as working on two parts of the same human–machine system.[23] Defined by Noble as "the study of human behavior with the objective of improving human interaction with systems,"[24] humans and machines were thought of as part of a single, irreducible system, and training consisted as much of adapting people to machines as the reverse. Engineering psychology became a major branch of military research and a lucrative one.[25]

At this time, the expression *educational technology* took on an expanded meaning, referring not only to instructional machinery, but to the whole idea of systematizing instruction. Audiovisual education specialist James D. Finn described in 1964 how "technology is not just hardware—or even hardware and materials. Technology is a way of organizing, a way of thinking, involving at the center, to be

[22]Noble, 1991, p. 86
[23]Smith and Smith, 1966, ch. 7
[24]Noble, 1991, p. 38
[25]See Noble, 1991, chapter 2, for a discussion of engineering psychology

sure, man–machine systems, but including systems of organization, patterns of use, tests of economic feasibility."[26] A prominent advocate of this view of educational technology, Robert Gagné, observed that "there is a growing tendency to relate educational technology in meaning to the *process of planning* by means of which an instructional system is developed, implemented, controlled, and evaluated."[27] According to this view, *educational technology* was the entire process of developing an instructional system, usually involving such things as identifying desired outcomes and describing them in detailed behavioral terms, performing task analysis to identify the steps to mastery of the desired behavior, and determining the optimal sequencing of task components.

The systems approach was a clear fit with military training, focusing on defining objectives narrowly, fitting the trainee to the assigned task to be learned, and accomplishing training quickly and cost-effectively. Although some people questioned the appropriateness of these priorities for public education, the methods of military training were carried into the realm of public education to a fairly great extent in the postwar years, particularly with respect to the promotion of educational technology.

APPLICATION OF AUTOMATED INSTRUCTION TO PUBLIC EDUCATION

As the principles of automated instruction found their way into issues of public education, they were generally promoted in the spirit of one or both of the two major issues dominating educational policy in the 1950s and 1960s—no doubt, in part, because large sums of federal funds were made available for research and development of educational technologies toward these two ends, while defense spending was being cut and defense contractors were turning their attention to public education. First, as described to some extent in chapter 4, cold war anxiety fueled a huge push for school reform, and these new techniques and technologies were promoted heavily in that spirit. Second, frustration over the general ineffectiveness of the *Brown vs. The Board of Education of Topeka* Supreme Court decision to inte-

[26]Murphy and Gross, 1966, p. 36

[27]Finn, 1972, pp. 135–136

grate schools, and growing tension over racial injustice more generally, led to intensified scrutiny of public schools and their role in per-
petuating inequality in American society. Automated systems of individualized instruction were often promoted for their potential to
equalize educational opportunity. These two strands of educational
reform are not entirely separable from one another, nor can the
applications of technology to them be clearly divided into two distinct
categories. Still, it is helpful to take each movement separately to
show how technology was promoted in the spirit of each argument
about what was wrong with American public education.

Cold War Impact on Automated Instruction

As discussed in chapter 4 and as summarized well by education historian Joel Spring, "most of the important discussions about education in the 1950s were against the background of an almost para-
noiac fear that if the United States lost the manpower race with the
Soviet Union, it would mean the end of all democratic institutions."[28]
Schools were under attack for allegedly neglecting core academic subjects, particularly math, science, and foreign languages, and reformers called for university scholars to involve themselves more deeply
in K–12 education as a way to improve instruction in those key academic areas.[29] In *Education and Freedom*, Vice Admiral H. G.
Rickover (1959) shared the belief that universities should set standards for public education, and added his concern that the United
States was particularly neglecting academically gifted youth by failing to separate them out from students of average ability. Although
schools were called on to improve the education of all students, they
were particularly expected to locate talented students and give them
special attention, channeling them into academic areas related to
national security.

The fear that substandard schools were threatening national
security prompted an unprecedented degree of federal involvement in
education. David Tyack described how, prior to the 1950s, schools
had involved themselves in war efforts and in the general goals of
patriotism building, "but not until the cold war did the needs of a

---

[28]Spring, 1989, p. 49

[29]Bestor, 1985 (originally published 1953); and Lynd, 1950

military-industrial complex assume lasting and great prominence in educational policy."[30] In 1950, Congress approved the establishment of the National Science Foundation, whose purpose, according to Joel Spring, was to be "a focal point for planning and supporting a scientific work force"[31] by improving science education in public schools. Vannevar Bush, the individual most responsible for the establishment of NSF, was director of the Office of Scientific Research and Development during World War II.[32]

Funding provided by the NSF prompted a flurry of curriculum development activity—first in physics, then in other sciences and mathematics (producing what came to be known as the *new math*). The emphasis on these new curricula, created primarily by university scholars and researchers, was on student inquiry and discovery, deemphasizing the acquisition of disciplinary content in favor of learning to think like a scientist or mathematician. The resulting curriculum materials were widely disseminated in public schools largely because the federal government provided funds to schools that wished to purchase them.[33]

Teaching machines and programmed instruction were promoted in the context of this curriculum reform movement, in part, in the spirit of bringing subject area experts to K–12 schools through their involvement in curriculum development. Given the concerns over the quality of teacher education, the goal of many reformers was to teacher proof the curriculum, and instructional technology offered one means to that end. It was adaptable to the key areas of math, science, and foreign languages, and it offered a variety of ways to systematize instruction and deliver course content regardless of whether or not the classroom teacher was strong in the content areas in question.

Shortly after the launch of Sputnik came passage of the National Defense Education Act of 1958, another major move into education by the federal government. The NDEA authorized the expenditure of approximately $90 million, which, combined with state matching funds, resulted in the allocation of over $1 billion on educational initiatives intended to address the perceived crisis.[34] It

---

[30]Tyack, 1974, p. 276

[31]Spring, 1986, p. 4

[32]Spring, 1989, p. 49

[33]Spring, 1989, p. 63

[34]Finn, 1972, p. 76

included funding to improve instruction in mathematics, science, and foreign languages, in part, through the development and implementation of technology-based curricular materials.

In short, then, the NSF and NDEA represented an unprecedented degree of federal effort to improve education. Joel Spring describes how

> The combination of the National Science Foundation and the NDEA was, therefore, to stem the tide of anti-intellectualism and U.S. losses in the race with the Soviet Union by the development of new curriculums, teacher training, student channeling through improved guidance, loans and fellowships, and the availability of money to purchase new scientific and mathematics equipment and materials for the schools.[35]

Among the provisions of these initiatives were those providing for the development of educational technology to support the educational reform goals given high priority by the federal government.

Related to the intensified focus on foreign policy and the associated purposes of schooling was the crisis of school overcrowding, discussed in chapter 4. The call to ensure that all Americans receive a quality education came at an inopportune time, given bulging enrollments and teacher shortages. As a result, efficiency of material and human resources was a prime consideration in school reform, and much of the promotion of automated methods of instruction carried the flavor of the efficiency experts of the early 20th century. For example, Edward Fry argued of programmed instruction that, "by limiting the program as strictly as possible, time-consuming learning that is not essential may be eliminated."[36] The only learning that should be going on, according to this view, was the learning that would prepare a particular individual for his or her place in the social order; the rest was wasteful.

Not all of the critics of public education advocated a narrow, specialized education based on vocational intentions. For example, Arthur Bestor (1953) argued in *Educational Wastelands* that all students should receive a liberal arts education, and he was highly critical of vocational tracks. Admiral Rickover (1959), in contrast, advocated tracking and ability grouping in *Education and Freedom*.

---

[35]Spring, 1989, p. 76

[36]Fry, 1963, p. 39

However, whether they advocated the same education for all or a tracked system, education reformers of the time agreed that national security demanded that all students receive a rigorous education. In that spirit, *instructional technology*—broadly defined as both technologies and systems-oriented techniques of instruction—offered the promise of increased achievement for all students. Its emphasis on operationalized, behavioral objectives and careful, efficient sequencing of instruction seemed to help guarantee that students would learn more effectively and economically. Moreover, evaluation and accountability procedures could be more systematic and objective because many systems of automated instruction—particularly CAI—included the recording of student responses and the tracking of student achievement through the program.

The transfer of military training practices to public education involved not only the promotion of programmed instruction and teaching machines, but the techniques of systems analysis as well, which offered the view that educational problems could be solved by making education more systematic, organized, rational, and efficient. This view was particularly apparent in the idea of mastery learning, popularized by Benjamin Bloom. Mastery learning emerged with the publication of Bloom's *Taxonomy of Educational Objectives* in 1956, and it received a fair amount of attention into the 1970s. It called for the precise statement of instructional goals and the breaking down of instructional sequences into small, graded steps. The assumption of mastery learning advocates was that all, or nearly all, students could achieve mastery of a given skill or topic if they were allowed to progress at their own paces, if mastery was clearly defined, and if the path to it was systematically laid out. It sought to replace the goal of equality of opportunity to equality of achievement in education.

In the spirit of ensuring a quality education for everyone came an interest in individualizing instruction, instead of giving all students a *one size fits all* style of mass instruction that seemed to prevent students from maximizing their learning potential. Individualization of instruction became the goal to strive for in the name of improving the education of all students, and programmed instruction and CAI were designed specifically for that purpose. Their origins in military training stemmed, in part, from the desire to reduce the costs of that training by designing systems that trained the trainee, thus eliminating the cost of instructors, so it was not a huge leap to imagine putting them to work in schools to that same end.

Although the strict training focus of military applications of instructional technology was not entirely appropriate to public education, the prospect of applying military methods of individualizing instruction was appealing to K–12 school reformers. Individualized systems of instruction were promoted for K–12 education in the spirit of allowing each student to work at his or her own pace, move through course material in a sequence most appropriate to the student (in the case of branching programs), and feel a sense of motivation and accomplishment by the instructional systems' tendencies to minimize student error. Robert T. Filep, a designer of CAI programs, praised the individualizing capabilities of the computer in 1967:

> Simultaneously, the computer can analyze and adapt teaching sequences to the learning abilities of each person, thus insuring true compatibility of individual and education. . . . Computer-aided instruction may also enable a student, while dealing with complex cognitive tasks, to gain satisfaction from responding and to develop a greater commitment to learning since contingencies for learning are so arranged that feelings of failure while at the terminal are minimized.[37]

Developers of military training methods had also claimed that their creations for individualized instruction had great motivational power. For example, J.C.R. Licklider, a researcher at—and later president of—research firm Bolt, Beranek, and Newman, coined the term *stimulus trapping* for the way the computer could *trap* students, drawing them in and holding their attention long enough for them to learn what they needed to learn. He experimented with continuous process drill and practice programs that continued indefinitely, rather than stopping when a particular lesson was completed, in the hope of maximizing the computer's holding power over unmotivated learners.[38] Other researchers believed that the carefully graded instructional steps in automated instructional programs nearly guaranteed student success at each step, which then inspired learners to continue onto mastery.[39]

Some teachers liked the degree to which students were made responsible for their own learning with individualized methods of

---

[37]Filep, 1967, pp. 102, 106

[38]Noble, 1991, pp. 124–125

[39]Goodman, 1947, ch. 1

automated instruction, observing that when students used these systems, they were "more independent, take more responsibility, and exhibit increased interest in school."[40] Additionally, advocates of CAI claimed, that the increased complexity of the individualized classroom could be handled by the computer, enabling teachers to keep track of each student's progress; and that high-speed computer test scoring would help teachers identify students' problem areas.[41] Moreover, it was frequently argued that the computer (or other programmed materials) would free teachers from their routine tasks, enabling them to work more closely with individual students.

In summary, the national security crisis was felt intensely in educational policy, and systems of automated instruction were developed to address this educational crisis. The other powerful force exerting itself on schools at that time was pressure for equality of educational opportunity, and educational technology advocates also found ways to apply their work to that cause.

Automated Instruction and Equality of Educational Opportunity

Although school segregation had been declared unconstitutional in 1954, that declaration did not carry with it sufficient means to integrate schools, and they remained, for the most part, as they had been. As tensions escalated over the persistence of racial inequality in American society, the continued segregation of public schools was a glaring example of that inequality, and civil rights actions under President Johnson put new pressures on schools to integrate.

The Civil Rights Act of 1964 forbade discrimination in federally funded programs; Title VI included the language that, "No person . . . shall, on the ground of race, color, or national origin, be excluded from participation in, be denied the benefits of, or be subjected to discrimination under any program or activity receiving Federal financial assistance." At the time of passage of the act, this threat was an empty one with respect to school segregation because there was no general federal aid to education. However, that was to change with the passage of the Elementary and Secondary Education

[40]Sponberg, 1968, p. 9

[41]Mikaelian and Thompson, 1969

2

03

Act in 1965, Title I of which provided funds for compensatory education to improve the academic achievement of underprivileged children. Most districts received at least some Title I funds. Therefore, the threat of losing federal funding carried more weight. Title VI was strengthened in 1966, and schools were integrated to unprecedented degrees.

Compensatory education was promoted as part of President Johnson's *war on poverty*. The idea of poor children as culturally deprived had gained currency, along with the recognition that social inequities were being reinforced by public schools. This perception of the problem of discrimination led to the belief that the proper intervention, such as giving poor children a good start, would prevent them from being discriminated against by the educational system.[42]

Diane Ravitch describes compensatory education as taking one of three main forms. One model was based on the belief that culturally deprived children needed intensive academic preparation to bridge the gap between them and middle class children. Head Start, she argues, was based on this model. In contrast, some advocates of compensatory education believed that culturally deprived children fell behind in school because they felt alienated from the middle-class culture being imposed on them, and that the solution was to respect the culture and values of these children. A third view, which was compatible with the others, was that schools should be social service centers for their communities.

Automated instruction was heavily promoted in the spirit of compensatory education. ESEA funding had attracted the attention of research and development firms whose budgets had been pinched by cutbacks in defense spending. Consequently, they shifted their focus to compensatory education applications.[43] In the early years of the ESEA, an estimated 90% of Title I funds were spent on audiovisual equipment, such as language labs. Title II provided for the purchase of such materials as textbooks, library resources, and programmed materials; Title III also provided funds for audiovisual aids.

As described earlier, a central feature of automated instruction was its potential to individualize instruction. Much as individualization had been (and was still) promoted in the spirit of national defense, it was also promoted in the 1960s as a way to equalize the

---

[42]Perkinson, 1968, p. 9

[43]Noble, 1991, pp. 124–125

educational experience. One of the most commonly cited advantages of automated instruction was that it would individualize instruction by freeing classroom teachers to spent more one-on-one time with students. Advocates also argued that automated, individualized instructional systems would help bring culturally deprived children up to speed with their more affluent counterparts in a nonjudgmental way without the risk of ridicule from their peers or teachers. Recent publications, including Jonathan Kozol's *Death at an Early Age* and Rosenthal and Jacobson's *Pygmalion in the Classroom,* were painting a picture of classroom teachers as cruel or at least indifferent racists whose low expectations of poor, minority students created self-fulfilling prophecies of failure in those students. In that climate, automated instructional programs were promoted for their neutrality. The argument went that children who might be discriminated against by their teachers, and therefore victimized by the self-fulfilling prophecy of low teacher expectations, would have a greater chance of academic success if they used programmed materials. Students would not fall victim to their teachers' subjective methods of evaluation because more objective measures were generally built into programmed instruction.

Automated instruction was promoted for its potential through nondiscriminatory instruction to develop students' self-esteem. Students who had rarely experienced academic success would do so with the carefully sequenced steps of programmed instruction designed to minimize failure. This success, in turn, would inspire them on to further academic success. The individualized pacing of instruction was offered as a way to remove the stigma of being behind grade level because children could progress at their own pace without having their deficiencies displayed before teachers and peers. Despite concerns at the time that automated instruction might be dehumanizing, advocates offered the argument that it was actually *more* humane than conventional instruction. The expression *child-centered* was often applied to automated instruction in that spirit.

Automated instruction was also promoted in the spirit of bringing the best instruction to all children regardless of where they lived or what the deficiencies of their local environment might be because that instruction would be contained in programmed materials designed by subject area specialists. One CAI advocate argued that CAI could offer "children across the country a highly specialized advanced curriculum equal to the best to be found in urban and suburban centers anywhere,"[44] regardless of the quality or the training of the classroom teachers in those schools.

Automated instruction was also appealing at the time because of an increased focus on accountability for learning outcomes. The ESEA included the requirement that all schools receiving funds provide regular, detailed evaluations of funded programs. The systems-oriented approach to automated instruction, involving precise statements of learning goals and procedures for reaching those goals, combined with the record-keeping functions of automated instructional systems, were well suited to an era focusing on accountability, cost-benefit, and quality assurance in compensatory education and in education more generally.[45]

In short, then, automated instruction was presented to schools to support two major reform efforts of the time: improving the quality of education for the sake of national security, and leveling inequalities of educational opportunity. A product of psychological research, it was closely tied to current theories about learning as well.

Automated Instruction Projects in Public Schools

Programmed instruction was developed and popularized somewhat before CAI, with the decline of programmed instruction roughly coinciding with the rise of CAI in the late 1960s. Despite some intense early enthusiasm for programmed instruction, including the involvement of many major electronics and publishing companies, communications theorist and educational technology scholar Wilbur Schramm reported in 1964 that it "has not exactly swept like a prairie fire through the schools. Rather, educators have experimented gingerly with it, and been slow to adopt it."[46] Still it is worthwhile to look at some schools that used programmed instruction as a way to get a sense of what was useful and problematic about it.

The Manhasset, New York, and Denver, Colorado, schools provide good case studies for attempts to use programmed instruction. Both began to use it in 1960—Manhasset using commercially

---

[44]Sponberg, 1967, p. 125

[45]Borich and Jemelka, 1981, p. 167

[46]Schramm, 1964a, p. 9

made programs, and Denver focusing on programs made by teachers. Although the Manhasset teachers had some reason to believe student achievement was improved by the use of programmed instruction, and they were professionally challenged to reconsider their assumptions about teaching, they only had one program in one grade in use after several years of work.[47]

The Denver schools were among the first large city school systems to use programmed instruction. They began in 1960, using both teacher-produced programmed materials and a commercial program in English. One teacher was released from his teaching duties to write programs because most commercially produced programs were a poor fit with the curriculum. That summer, an additional six teachers were freed from other duties and assigned to work with him to prepare programs in English. Over the course of the summer of 1960, they produced 2,800 frames covering 16 grammar units. These programs, after some initial experiments, were not much used; there was no systematic evidence of their effectiveness, they became outdated quickly, and they were not revised.[48]

Denver also experimented with foreign language programs in collaboration with Stanford University and UCLA's Center for Programmed Instruction. Although they experienced somewhat greater success with these programs, and some additional teachers took an interest in writing programs, programmed instruction was not catching on in any widespread fashion in the Denver schools.

The Brigham Young University Laboratory School, a private K–12 school in Provo, Utah, attempted to incorporate programmed instruction as part of a larger experiment. Having developed a curriculum designed specifically to permit students to progress at their own rates, they added programmed instruction in 1961 to 1962, the second year of the curriculum revision. Although the faculty seemed to support programmed instruction in principle, they found it hard to use effectively, discovering that students were getting bored and what they were learning with programmed materials was not transferring effectively to other tasks. Moreover, keeping track of each student's progress was complicated, requiring an array of forms, record books, and wall charts. The faculty and administration of this school also came to realize how thoroughly the organization of a school had

---

[47]Herbert & Foshay, 1964
[48]Schramm, 1964b

to change in order to accomplish the kind of individualized experience they had hoped to achieve with programmed instruction.[49]

Interest in programmed instruction seems to have peaked
around 1962, at which time 104 companies were involved in planning
or producing programmed materials. A report to the U.S. Office of
Education for 1961-1962 indicated that 233 localities in 42 states
were using programmed materials.[50] In other words, although use of
programmed instruction was widely dispersed at its height, it was
actually used by a small percentage of the nation's school districts.

CAI, particularly in its early days, was so prohibitively expensive that it was used primarily for research. However, some of that
research involved experimentation in public schools, even if it was not
thought reasonable to implement CAI in school systems to any great
extent. Three major CAI initiatives—the PLATO project, TICCIT,
and the work at Stanford University—provide a good overview of the
types of CAI that were developed and tested in public schools.

PLATO (Programmed Logic for Automatic Teaching
Operation) and TICCIT (time-shared, interactive, computer-controlled
information television) were "designed to study the cost and effectiveness of computer-based instruction (CBI) for teaching large numbers
of geographically dispersed students."[51] The first generation of
PLATO was developed in the Computer-Based Education Research
Laboratory (CERL) at the University of Illinois in 1959, its funding
being, according to Douglas Noble, "decidedly military."[52] The goals of
the PLATO experiment were to determine CAI's educational potential
and see if an educationally and economically viable CAI system could
be developed. PLATO I, completed in 1960, consisted of drill-and-prac-
tice programs based on the branching features of Crowder's programmed textbooks, in subjects like elementary math and vocabulary.
PLATO II and III, presented in 1964, offered more elaborate tutorial
and instructional capacities, such as simulations and games, and permitted more than one terminal to be in use at a time. PLATO IV,
which had NSF funding, was produced by CERL and Control Data
Corporation in 1972 and was in use in 70 locations by 1974 (although
those locations were generally industrial, military, or collegiate).

---

[49]Edling, 1964

[50]Smith and Smith, 1966, p. 275

[51]Borich and Jemelka, 1981, p. 164

[52]Noble, 1991, p. 101

TICCIT, another NSF-funded project, was developed at Brigham Young University in 1969 and focused on concept and rule learning. TICCIT programs had specific objectives, which showed students what they were to learn. Mini-lessons gave an overview of each unit and lesson, and each lesson had a test to go with it. TICCIT differed from PLATO in the degree of control it gave to the learner. In his chapter in O'Neil's (1981) *Computer-Based Instruction: A State-of-the-Art Assessment*, C. V. Bunderson contrasts TICCIT and PLATO as follows:

> TICCIT posited a mainline instructional approach in which a total student-centered culture was introduced. This was an individualized system where the machine, the books, and even the teachers serve in a resource role to the students. In a teacher-centered culture, the teacher retains the control of the schedule, the grading, and the pacing. PLATO maintained a teacher-centered culture, but TICCIT tried to introduce the student-centered culture into two community colleges.[53]

The Educational Testing Service (ETS) conducted evaluations of both PLATO and TICCIT, finding that teachers and students had generally positive attitudes toward PLATO and that PLATO classes had high completion rates (the study was conducted at the community college level). However, student performance in the PLATO classes was not any better than student performance in conventional classes. By contrast, TICCIT students showed significantly higher achievement than students in conventional classes, but had lower completion rates and expressed negative attitudes toward TICCIT.[54] In any case, both projects failed in their primary goal of developing a cost-effective CAI system, and neither saw much use in public schools.[55]

Another major CAI experiment—this one with direct application to K–12 education—began in 1963 by Richard C. Atkinson and Patrick Suppes at Stanford University, with funding from the Carnegie Corporation, the NSF, and the ESEA, and extensive collaboration with IBM. The goal of this project was to study CAI over an extended period of time in a CAI laboratory in a public elementary school. Suppes and Atkinson developed a number of different drill-

---

[53]Bunderson, 1981, p. 113

[54]Bunderson, 1981, p. 115

[55]Saettler, 1990, p. 310

and-practice and tutorial programs in subjects like elementary math, reading, spelling, logic, and elementary Russian; some of their programs were in use by approximately 3,000 students in California, Mississippi, and Kentucky by 1968.[56] The projects were focused on remedial education for culturally disadvantaged students, in the spirit of compensatory education funded by the ESEA.

Much of the school-based work with automated instruction, particularly CAI, was primarily in the name of research. That is, learning theories and machines developed in research laboratories had to be tested on schoolchildren, and it was often through participation in these tests that schools came into contact with automated instruction. However, it never spread extensively beyond those school sites. As was the case with film, radio, and television, a number of factors made it difficult to implement automated instruction in schools. Some of them echoed earlier problems with those earlier media—if not in the particular details, then in the general character of the problem.

FACTORS PREVENTING THE USE OF AUTOMATED INSTRUCTION

Programmed instruction was declining in popularity by the late 1960s. CAI was on the rise at that point, but was never implemented in schools on any widespread basis. Apart from the obvious problem of the prohibitive cost of CAI, there were several major factors contributing to the decline of these automated instructional systems, which can roughly be categorized as conflicts with teacher interests and concerns, the changing tone of educational policy (in part in response to technological change), and changes in the focus of educational psychology.

Conflicts with Teachers

As with any educational innovation, teachers had a great deal of control over the extent to which programmed materials were used in their classes. It is not hard to imagine that some teachers resented

---

[56]Saettler, 1990, p. 308

anything that claimed to *teacher proof* their classes. Although some advocates had argued that automated instruction would professionalize teaching,[57] these instructional systems represented to many teachers a kind of deskilling of their profession. It implied that not only did they have no place in curriculum development (which was part of the message of instructional film, radio, and TV), but that they could not even be trusted to teach a curriculum designed by qualified experts, and that student learning in no significant way depended on the relationship between teachers and students.

Many teachers were dissatisfied with commercially produced programmed materials, which were often incompatible with the curriculum for which the teachers were responsible. A book by the Fund for the Advancement of Education reported on a 1961 to 1962 survey, which indicated that approximately four times as many programmed instruction materials in use in schools came from commercial sources as from local construction.[58] It was possible for teachers to produce programmed materials themselves, but it was hugely time-consuming, and difficult, to do. One estimate of the ratio of programming time to amount of instruction created was 80:1.[59] The process of programming involved working out goals and objectives, writing what amounts to a textbook, and then breaking the material down into frames. Once the program was completed, it still had to be subjected to "pedagogical debugging,"[60] repeated revision and retesting, because it had to stand on its own, being perfectly self-explanatory in the absence of a teacher. One programmer likened the author to a theatrical producer, "presiding over an especially unruly cast of characters, none of whom has a copy of the script. He must coax them along in spite of their aberrations, trying not to lose any of his players before the end of the last act."[61] The task of creating programmed materials was well beyond the expertise of most teachers, who were rarely given training in the use of programmed materials, let alone the creation of them.

Some teachers feared they would be replaced by automated instruction much as their predecessors had feared replacement by

---

[57]Finn, 1972

[58]Schramm, 1964a, p. 10

[59]Meredith, 1971, p. 10

[60]Meredith, 1971, p. 119

[61]Meredith, 1971, p. 70

film, radio, or television. More common, however, was that teachers objected to their loss of professional control to technicians. For example, some teachers were concerned that CAI was shifting control away from teachers onto the programmers producing CAI courseware, who typically did not have much educational background. In a 1968 issue of *Educational Leadership*, John M. Flynn, although optimistic about the computer, pointed out that those who were well versed in the technology were often not educators. He went on to write:

> Hence, educational decision makers are not only on the verge of losing control of the technological advents in their profession, but are in danger of losing much of this control to personnel with non-educational backgrounds. Further, many of the data processing experts who have been trained in education are academicians who are not involved with the daily problems of schools and school districts.[62]

Reformers who were not educators themselves tended to blame teacher apathy or hostility for the slowness of change in schools, rather than acknowledge that teachers' reactions might "merely reflect a healthy resistance to tools that either do not work or are more time-consuming than they are useful."[63]

In *The Teacher and the Machine*, P.W. Jackson (1968) described the incompatible ideologies of teachers and technicians, arguing that, "In a very fundamental sense the world view of many teachers . . . is incompatible with the view of those who serve as the spokesmen of educational technology."[64] He argued that technicians were bogged down in the particulars of learning, where teachers had a more holistic approach (e.g., where technicians would focus on how a reader discriminated between "saw" and "was," the teacher would want to know if the child was learning to read). Where technicians wanted to streamline and standardize instruction, Jackson argued that teachers enjoyed the unpredictability of their interactions with students. Moreover, teachers saw value in a degree of flexibility and reflection that educational technology did not permit, due to its predetermined paths and its insistence that the student keep moving through the designated material.

---

[62]Flynn, 1968, p. 24

[63]Silberman, 1967, p. 639

[64]Jackson, 1968, p. 14

Jackson pointed out that even when teachers and technicians agreed on a general goal, they did not think about it in compatible ways. For example, both expressed approval of the idea of individualization, but what each liked about it was different from the other. Technicians seemed to see it as a means of efficiency and economy through the use of machines, where teachers liked the way that working individually with students could make children feel important and create an emotional connection between teachers and students—the things that machines could not do.

In *Adoption of Educational Innovations*, R. O. Carlson (1965) pointed out that many teachers tended to feel that if they were not performing, they were not doing their jobs (or, at least, that they were not doing their jobs well). Teachers would not be comfortable with CAI, he argued, unless they were able to adopt a different teaching model than the one to which they were accustomed. Otherwise they would feel undermined by CAI. Carlson described how some teachers using programmed instruction pulled back from its individualizing capacity by introducing "their own innovations which enabled them to recapture some of the role of 'director of learning' which was lost to the program."[65] CAI advocates were promoting the idea of the teacher as manager of a learning environment, as director of learning, not as transmitter of information, and that required teachers to rethink their roles and find a place for themselves, if possible, in this conception of schooling. Additionally, the kind of manager automated instruction required teachers to be was different from the conception of *teacher-as-manager* or *teacher-as-facilitator*, originating in child-centered pedagogy, that was often appealing to teachers. In *Using the Computer in Education: A Briefing for School Decision Makers*, P. G. Watson (1972) argued that "the key to the solution of the teacher acceptance obstacle is the definition of a meaningful role for the teacher to play."[66] *Teacher-as-lab-assistant* was not meaningful enough for most teachers to embrace automated instruction.

True integration of individualized automated instruction would not only require a different conception of teaching, but would also require a thorough reorganization of schools (a change advocated by promoters of automated instruction). If students progressed at

---

[65]Carlson, 1965, p. 84
[66]Watson, 1972, p. 109

their own paces, eliminating the need or relevance of same-age grouping, how would schools be organized? If all students would ultimately succeed, albeit some faster than others, what purpose would grades serve? Advocates of individualized instruction were often in favor of nongraded schools, which, regardless of their potential advantages, were difficult to establish after more than a century of organizing students in grades. Additionally, although automating instruction was often described as a time- and labor-saving benefit to teachers, their work was actually made more complicated because they had to keep extensive records of all the individualized work being done by students.[67] Rather than freeing teachers to focus on the more professionally challenging aspects of their work, automated instruction simply increased the workload by adding seemingly endless quantities of paperwork.

On top of intensified workload and loss of control over curriculum and instruction, automated instruction carried with it an unprecedented degree of surveillance of teachers and students and new forms of accountability made possible by that surveillance. P.G. Watson pointed out in 1972 that, "with the computer monitoring both the teacher's prescription and the student's achievements, the success and failure of the teaching process will become more public and subject to review by supervisors."[68] This was a time when people were increasingly concerned about technology's threats to privacy through things like polygraph tests and phone tapping, and certain aspects of automated instruction seemed to be yet another invasion of privacy.

Instructional technology had become more than just a new medium or method; it had acquired a broader definition that implied a whole mind set—an orientation toward schooling that ran contrary to the way many teachers viewed their profession and their students. They questioned the value of such precisely defined and predetermined goals, of behaviorist models of teaching and learning, and of individualization as practiced through these methods. They were increasingly concerned with issues of equity and community, and with resisting what they perceived to be dehumanizing practices. In that spirit, a new orientation in curriculum theory emerged, providing a critique of the orientation of automated instruction and systems

---

[67]Van Allen, 1968, 1968

[68]Watson, 1972, p. 110

approaches to educational issues. The reconceptualists, although
varying widely in their individual concerns and orientations, shared
an interest in raising awareness of the political implications of the
curriculum. The work of Michael Apple, Elliot Eisner, Maxine
Greene, and others focused new attention on the ideological biases of
the curriculum, the dangers of mechanistic thinking and methods,
and the conflicts surrounding the nature of teachers' work. This work
provided a counterargument to the orientation that had fueled the
development of automated instruction.[69] For example, Robert Gagné,
a prominent advocate of the systems approach, arued that one of its
virtues was that it made no judgments about educational goals; it
could be used equally well by anyone regardless of the person's objectives.[70] However, scholars in curriculum theory feared the amorality
of such an orientation, arguing instead that the form and content of
education cannot—and should not—avoid moral questions, particularly if an important purpose of public education is to support and
cultivate democratic citizenship.

Another concern that some critics voiced about automated
instruction was the commercial aspect of it, and how commercial
interests were both pushing automated instruction too aggressively
into schools, compromising the quality of programmed materials, and
ignoring the needs of teachers. In a 1967 article in *Phi Delta Kappan*,
Fred M. Heddinger described how industry leapt at what it saw to be
a potentially lucrative market:

> Under the Great Society, industry suddenly sensed new profit
> opportunities. . . . Industrial attention was particularly directed
> to the Office of Education because it was apparent that large-
> scale funds would become available which would have good likeli-
> hood for continuity.[71]

What ensued were "near frenetic efforts of business and industry to
relate to educational enterprises."[72] Many major publishing and electronics companies paired up to produce programmed materials; for
example, Sylvania Electrical Products merged with *Reader's Digest*,
RCA acquired Random House, Xerox purchased American Education

---

[69]Flinders and Thornton, 1997, p. Part III

[70]Gagné and Briggs, 1974, p. 227

[71]Heddinger, 1967, p. 216

[72]Bern, 1967 p. 231

Publications, Inc., and General Electric joined with Time, Inc. to form the General Learning Corporation.[73] In the same 1967 issue of *Phi Delta Kappan* as the Heddinger article quoted earlier, John R. Stark observed that,

> Educational technology has become an important source of investment for many U.S. corporations, and it is estimated that expenditures on educational "hardware" now exceed $1 billion a year. A brief review of the companies now involved in its manufacture looks like a Who's Who of the corporate world.[74]

Some observers believed that these industries would merely aid in the dissemination of new instructional materials, rather than assert themselves inappropriately in curricular matters.[75] However, others were much more concerned that these companies were motivated entirely by profit, not by an interest in improving education, and that their interest in finding the widest possible audience for their products meant they were afraid to experiment with any kinds of programmed materials that deviated from standard, only marginally useful, formulas. In 1964, Wilbur Schramm expressed his concern as follows:

> Regretfully, in a private enterprise country, one must admit that commercial activity in this field, so far, has been largely counterproductive to better programs and more imaginative uses. . . . Faced with the need to risk large financial stakes in an unfamiliar situation, they made little attempt to find new kinds of programs or new uses of programs—rather they sought the more conservative types of programs and the more familiar uses. Faced with field reports on their programs, they tried to avoid expensive revisions. The incarnation of programs in programed books tended to harden the form at the moment when it should have been most flexible and most responsive to test findings and new technical developments.[76]

This was neither the first nor the last period in which the motives of commercial organizations for involving themselves in education

---

[73]Murphy and Gross, 1966, pp. 80–81

[74]Stark, 1967, p. 196

[75]See, for example, Keppel, 1967

[76]Schramm, 1964c, p. 102

would be questioned by educators. These concerns echoed criticisms of industrial film makers and commercial radio broadcasters and foreshadowed later criticisms of software companies and other telecommunications industries.

Industry's apparent indifference to educators' criticisms and concerns was evident not only in their products, but in the practices that produced them. For example, in 1966, the Department of Defense, the Office of Education, and the National Security Industrial Association co-sponsored a "Conference on Engineering Systems for Education and Training," where 700 people from military agencies and industrial organizations gathered to discuss educational technology. F. M. Heddinger reported in 1967 that one of the planners of the conference, when asked why no educators had been invited, answered that, "education is now too important to be entrusted to the educators."[77] It was apparent to many educators that industry had little interest in meeting their needs, and that the involvement of these major industries in education threatened to further remove teachers from decisions about curriculum.

The Changing Tone of Educational Policy

One of the primary concerns about automated instruction was that it would harm children by dehumanizing education. These concerns about dehumanization had much to do with larger trends in education at the time, when major shifts were taking place in what schools were called on to do and how they were to do it. A renewed interest in the orientations of child-centered progressivism and social reconstructionism emerged in the 1960s in the form of open schools, free schools, alternative schools, and the call to *deschool,* altogether.[78]

Although each of these movements was different, taken together they reflected an interest at the time in trying new (or old, but rarely practiced) forms of school organization and methods of instruction, and in connecting schools to larger efforts at social reform.

In public schools of the 1960s, there was a reemerging emphasis on community, on more informal instructional styles, and process

---

[77]Heddinger, 1967, p. 218

[78]See, for example, Illich, 1970; Neill, 1960; Postman and Weingartner, 1969; Silberman, 1970

over product. For example, Herbert Kohl's (1969) *The Open Classroom* rejected traditional, authoritarian models of education, favoring loose classroom organization, flexible use of time and materials, emphasis on interaction and discovery, not planning too specifically, taking cues from students, and rejecting all things standardized or objective. The character of concerns about equity shifted as well. As it became apparent to many Americans that attempts to equalize educational opportunity were not producing a just society, educational policy focused more intensely on school reforms that would further the cause of social reform. Automated instruction had been advocated in the spirit of compensatory education as equalization of opportunity, but now schools were shifting to a focus on relationships between teachers and students, and between students and their peers. A new emphasis was placed on fostering a sense of community and connection among people of different backgrounds. Automated instruction, designed specifically to individualize instruction, had little to offer when the social context of learning was reemphasized.

Criticisms of the goal of using individualizing instruction to level opportunity through compensatory education were part of larger criticisms of individualized instruction. Many teachers questioned not so much the idea of individualization, but the means through which it was accomplished. Automated instruction individualized the pace of instruction and, sometimes, the path through the curriculum. However, many teachers believed that true individualization meant that the curriculum would originate from, or at least be shaped by, students' questions and concerns. For example, Charles E. Silberman (1970), author of *Crisis in the Classroom*, argued that individualized instructed forced students

> into a passive, almost docile role. . . . [The student] cannot "internalize" or apply what he has learned, for he cannot reconstruct the material in his own way—he cannot express a concept in his own words or actions or construct his own applications and examples.[79]

Moreover, teachers often believed they could individualize instruction far more significantly than any program or machine could because they could respond to students' personal needs and idiosyncracies in ways that automated instruction could not even begin to

---

[79]Silberman, 1970, p. 210

do. They argued that automated systems could not tell, as they could, when a student would benefit from a correction and when he or she would be demoralized by it. P. W. Jackson pointed out that teachers did not necessarily believe it was a good idea to correct all student errors, sometimes opting to let one mistake go by to keep a student focused on a different mistake or so as not to demoralize or humiliate the student. Advocates had promised that individualization was the best way to teach students, but Jackson felt that "whether they would learn more and what they would learn more of is by no means clear."[80]

Changes in the Focus of Educational Psychology

Researchers in educational psychology were beginning to question whether automated instructional systems were really modeled after the way people learn. First of all, many programmed materials followed a set, linear format, whereas cognitive psychologists were suggesting that learning actually takes place by a more circuitous route. Second, although branching materials permitted multiple pathways, psychologists were questioning the larger assumption that learning can be effective when it takes place in such decontextualized activities. They were revisiting the question of transfer of learning, and arguing that learning had to be situated and had to take place in the context in which it would be used. Along with the idea that learning had to be situated materially was the belief that it had to be situated socially, and that there were important social components to learning.

Behaviorism was giving way to theories of cognition that focused more on thinking strategies and processes. In their contribution to O'Neil's (1981) *Computer-Based Instruction: A State of the Art Assesement,* J. W. Rigney and A. Munro describe this shift as follows:

> The past 10 years has seen a remarkable shift of the center of interest in psychology from input-output to what goes on in between. In rapid succession, psychologists discovered mental imagery, mnemonics, and long-term memory. It became fashionable to think about thinking. Increasing numbers of psychologists fled the austere bastions of behaviorism, abandoning its fetish of

---

[80]Oettinger, 1969, p. 117

the empty organism for an organism with its head full of busy demons.[81]

Although work in automated instruction had moved away from behaviorism—for example, in Gagné's and Bloom's development of hierarchies of learning that included thinking skills at the top—it did not go so far as to conceive of those skills as part of the process of all learning as cognitive scientists later did.[82] Moreover, its focus on behaviorally stated objectives and precisely organized instructional material kept it more in the spirit of behaviorism than not.

Cognitive psychologists' new view of the mind as an information processor generated new interests in educational technology. They were particularly interested in using computers as simulators of human thought and, in turn, as cognitive tools for shaping thought. As the computer came to serve as psychologists' dominant metaphor for the human mind, its applications to education shifted as well.

CONCLUSION

In *Using the Computer in Education* P.G. Watson (1972) wrote that, "it is fairly evident that the question of whether the computer should be used in education and/or instruction is no longer relevant."[83] He was not exactly wrong. Computers remain, without doubt, a heavily promoted educational technology 30 years after Watson's observation. He was referring specifically to CAI, which is still produced for and used in schools. It is glitzier than its parents thanks to the development of computer graphics and multimedia capabilities, but the behaviorist underpinnings remain essentially the same. However, to say that CAI is still around is not to say that it has had any dramatic impact on what goes on in schools. All in all, CAI and automated instructional systems in general never quite lived up to its promoters' hopes that it could be used to support fundamental changes in the character of American public education.

---

[81]Rigney and Munro, 1981, p. 132

[82]Resnick and Klopfer, 1989, p. 2

[83]Watson, 1972, p. 3

6

NEW MEDIA

We are at the onset of a major revolution in education, a revolution unparalleled since the invention of the printing press. The computer will be the instrument of this revolution. . . . By the year 2000 the major way of learning at all levels, and in almost all subject areas will be through the interactive use of computer.

—Alfred Bork, in *The Computer in the School: Tutor, Tool, Tutee* (Ed. R. Taylor, 1980)

To say that the focus shifted away from automated instruction—computer based or otherwise—is not to say that interest in using computers for instruction disappeared. As educational psychologists increasingly questioned the behaviorist orientation of such forms of instruction, they shifted the nature of their interest in computers accordingly. Changes in educational policy also had their impact on educational technology as public education once again came under attack by those who felt schools were not adequately preparing young Americans for a technologically and economically competitive world. Meanwhile the computer was changing in such a way as to move it more prominently into the lives of many Americans, fueling an interest in acquainting children with computers through contact with them in school. All of these issues have contributed to the present thrust to use new technology in schools for a wide variety of purposes.

CHANGES IN EDUCATIONAL PSYCHOLOGY AND EDUCATIONAL TECHNOLOGY

Cognitive researchers had been moving away from strict behaviorism for some time. For example, as mentioned in chapter 5, the systems approach began to challenge behaviorism in the 1960s. Gradually, cognitive science shifted the focus more dramatically from input–output and directly observable behaviors to internal thinking processes and strategies, and new ideas about learning led to new ideas about how technology might be used to support learning.

Mainstream educational practice had been based on behaviorist principles and the idea that learning involved the gradual accumulation of little bits of knowledge. Gagné and Bloom refined this orientation by acknowledging thinking skills, such as problem-solving abilities, and placing them at the top of their hierarchies of learning.[1] However, as the 1980s progressed, learning research was suggesting that thinking skills were not a higher order level of development, but were part of all successful learning. For example, Lauren Resnick promoted her Thinking Curriculum in 1989, where thinking skills were infused in the educational program from kindergarten through graduation as opposed to being treated as end goals for those advanced students who manage to reach the top of the learning ladder.[2]

One fairly early challenger to behaviorism was the developmental approach offered by Piaget. Piaget is probably best known for his theory that cognitive development takes place in a series of stages, characterized by different ways of understanding and interacting with one's environment. He believed that development takes place through a fairly fixed and predictable series of shifts, occurring at fairly predictable ages. One key characteristic of these shifts was a change from focusing on concrete thinking, based largely on sensorimotor experience, to more abstract, logical thought. This develop-

---

[1]Gagné and Briggs, 1974; Bloom, 1956

[2]Resnick and Klopfer, 1989

mental process, according to Piaget, cannot be accelerated through any particular training or instructional approach. Of greatest importance, then, is that a child be provided with developmentally appropriate experiences, and that material be presented in a way that a child in a particular stage of development can understand it.

Piaget's theories were applied to educational technology most directly and influentially by Seymour Papert, whose computer program, *Logo,* was designed in part to embody Piaget's theories and connect them to classroom instruction. *Logo* was also one of the most influential factors in the widespread introduction of computers to schools. *Logo*'s origins trace back to work begun in 1964 at the research and development firm of Bolt, Beranek, and Newman, where attempts to develop a programming language for children were first sponsored by the Office of Naval Research and later by the National Science Foundation and the Air Force Office of Scientific Research. Seymour Papert was first brought into the project as a consultant and, together with a number of collaborators, developed *Logo*, a program based on LISP, a programming language for artificial intelligence. *Logo* was first used to teach elementary mathematics at an elementary school on an Air Force base.[3]

Although teaching general thinking skills and problem solving were not initially goals for *Logo*, a shift took place in the late 1960s when Papert began to promote the idea of *Logo* as a tool for cognitive simulation. That is, he felt that the process of programming a procedure led students to a deeper understanding of the thought processes involved in that procedure. He believed that children would become epistemologists of sorts with *Logo* because they would recognize that *Logo* required a particular thinking style of them, and would then become more thoughtful about the variety of possible thinking styles and the reasons for choosing one over another. He also believed that children would be able to transfer the learning style they learned in *Logo* to other contexts where it might prove useful.

Having studied with Piaget, Papert shared Piaget's belief that a child's cognitive growth would come through active participation with a learning environment, and that one should start from the knowledge or experience with which the child is familiar. Papert believed that *Logo* provides a sensorimotor point of entry into a variety of abstract concepts. It drew on children's knowledge of their bod-

---

[3]See Noble, 1991, for the story of the military origins of *Logo*.

ies to the extent that the goal in *Logo* was to make a turtle move, the turtle being either a graphical image on the computer screen or a robot that moved around on the floor. Either way, Papert's idea was that children could construct patterns with *Logo* that would tap into their innate understanding of their own body movements, making abstract concepts more concrete. He argued that, "children can *identify* with the Turtle and are thus able to bring their knowledge about their bodies and how they move into the work of learning formal geometry."[4] Papert conceived of children as builders in need of building materials, and he believed that *Logo* provided them with an object to think with. He criticized traditional education for being too abstract, which he believed made many concepts unnecessarily inaccessible to young children.

Papert particularly emphasized the process of *debugging* in *Logo,* which was based on the Piagetian idea that loss of equilibrium requires accommodation. The turtle would not always behave as predicted, requiring the child to figure out why not (and resolve her disequilibrium). Papert hoped that children would then apply this process to learning experiences apart from *Logo*—that debugging a computer program would become a model for solving problems in other aspects of life. He also hoped that children would come to value mistakes as a good way to learn, rather than fearing them or fearing that they would be punished for making mistakes.

Logo was appealing to many educators, and it was adopted on a fairly widespread basis by American public schools. However, despite its quick, dramatic acceptance into schools and a general agreement among critics that Papert's intentions were good ("One wants so badly to *like* what Seymour Papert has done"[5]), educators ultimately became disenchanted with it, particularly as more and more research findings suggested that *Logo* did not do all it purported to do. Criticisms of *Logo* generally fell into one of three categories: that it was not as concrete as it was argued to be, that it privileged and reified one form of reasoning over all others, and that what was learned with *Logo* did not transfer effectively to other contexts.

One common criticism of *Logo* was that it was too abstract especially for young children. Although one of Papert's primary claims about *Logo* was that it made abstract concepts more concrete

---

[4]Papert, 1980, p. 56

[5]Talbott, 1995, p. 151

for young learners, critics pointed out that the computer is an inherently abstract symbolic form. For example, Steven Talbott pointed out in *The Future Does Not Compute: Transcending the Machines in Our Midst* that, "it is a strange definition of 'concrete' that places all its stress upon the student's active involvement, and none at all upon whatever it is he is involved with. The only fully concrete thing a computer offers the student is its own, perhaps enchanting presence. Beyond that, it hosts a mediate and abstract world."[6] Although *Logo* might have effectively made highly abstract knowledge more concrete for children, it was fairly easy to point out that many of its applications made activities more abstract than was useful or necessary for children (e.g., drawing a picture with *Logo* required an ability to abstract the drawing process to a far greater degree than drawing the same picture with paper and crayons). Although Papert claimed to be doing a service to children by concretizing powerful ideas earlier than Piaget would have believed them to be developmentally capable of handling such ideas, some critics believed that it was more in the interests of children to provide them with rich sensory experiences, especially at early developmental stages.[7]

Another criticism of *Logo* was that it presented one particular form of thinking over others without providing children with any mechanism for encountering or cultivating a variety of thinking styles. Papert claimed that children would, through *Logo*, develop awareness of other thinking styles, but some critics argued that "the entire temper of his work is in the spirit of instrumental reason,"[8] and that *Logo* implicitly taught children that this mechanical, amoral way of thinking was superior to others. Papert was fully aware that *Logo* cultivated a mechanical way of thinking, but he believed that children would learn that this was but one of many cognitive styles from which to choose. However, critics questioned the extent to which children would be aware that *Logo* shaped their thinking in a particular way, and that there were other ways to approach a problem.

Logo's emphasis on instrumental reason seemed particularly dangerous to these critics because they believed it reinforced a contemporary cultural predisposition, even obsession, toward such

---

[6]Talbott, 1995, p. 152

[7]See Sloan, 1984, for a number of critiques

[8]Davy, 1984, p. 17

thinking. Developmental psychologist John Broughton expressed his concern that *Logo* presented instrumental reason as just another way to think when it really is much more than that. He believed that instrumental reason "presents itself as the definitive *rationality*, the exclusive and exhaustive principle of intelligent and objective understanding or action. It is an ideological world view embedded in a mystifying technology."[9] The danger of this form of thinking, he argued, is that it "communicates to children a way of actively pursuing cognitive control while actively fleeing examination of their lives."[10] This concern echoed that of Joseph Weizenbaum, perhaps the best-known critic of instrumental reason, who argued in *Computer Power and Human Reason* that instrumental reason

> actively hides, buries, the existence of real conflicts . . . instrumental reason converts each dilemma, however genuine, into a mere paradox that can then be unraveled by the application of logic, by calculation. All conflicting interests are replaced by the interests of technique alone.[11]

Weizenbaum believed that, "when instrumental reason is the sole guide to action, the acts it justifies are robbed of their inherent meanings and thus exist in an ethical vacuum,"[12] and that "the attribution of certainty to scientific knowledge by the common wisdom . . . has virtually delegitimatized all other ways of understanding."[13]

Besides criticisms of *Logo*'s lack of ethical context were accusations that *Logo* decontextualized knowledge, and out of these accusations came a different way of thinking about educational technology. Papert argued that what children learned while using *Logo* would transfer to other task environments, but a variety of research studies suggested otherwise. Meanwhile many cognitive scientists were focusing on the question of transfer, placing new emphasis on the importance of situating learning in appropriate social and material contexts, and they were critical of the way in which learning with *Logo* was decontextualized.

---

[9]Broughton, 1984, p. 107

[10]Broughton, 1984, p. 111

[11]Weizenbaum, 1976, p. 251

[12]Weizenbaum, 1976, p. 276

[13]Weizenbaum, 1976, p. 16

Advocates of *situated learning* challenged prevailing ideas about transfer of learning, which derived from Thorndike's common elements theory. Early in the 20th century, he argued that transfer of learning would occur between tasks that shared common or identical elements. Situated learning theorists offered the idea that transfer is affected by situation reading—that a learner's perception of a situation affects what he or she thinks should be transferred to it.[14] Such a theory emphasized not only the importance of resemblance between the learning and transfer contexts, but the values of the learner that inform what is perceived appropriate for transfer—and therefore the sociocultural contexts in which the learner is immersed.

Those who advocated situated learning generally argued that school instruction tends to artificially separate what is learned from how it is used, whereas most learning outside of school—both by expert practitioners and "just plain folks"—is deeply rooted in sociophysical contexts. They emphasized the need to learn and adopt the culture of practitioners in a discipline, regarding education as a kind of *cognitive apprenticeship*. John Seely Brown, Allan Collins, and Paul Duguid describe cognitive apprenticeship as follows:

> Unfortunately, students are too often asked to use the tools of a discipline without being able to adopt its culture. To learn to use tools as practitioners use them, a student, like an apprentice, must enter that community and its culture. Thus, in a significant way, learning is, we believe, a process of enculturation.[15]

A crucial component of this enculturation process was participation in authentic activities in a particular domain—activities that require the learner to think and work like a mathematician, historian, scientist, and so forth, and to use the tools and strategies that are commonly employed by practitioners in the domain in question. A serious shortcoming of school-based learning, these researchers argued, was that the classroom context tended to be "wholly absent from and alien to authentic activity."[16] Meanwhile people outside of school tended to solve problems "within the framework of the context that produced them,"[17] drawing on the environment and community.

---

[14]Pea, 1988

[15]Brown, Collins, and Duguid, 1989, p. 33

[16]Brown, Collins, and Duguid, 1989, p. 34

[17]Brown, Collins, and Duguid, 1989, p. 36

Some of the prominent advocates and researchers of situated learning and cognitive apprenticeship were particularly interested in the potential of computer technology to support such learning. One of their interests stemmed from the notion that humans' memory capacities are limited, and that there is value in *off-loading* parts of cognitive tasks onto cognitive tools such as computers.[18] This use of technology was particularly advocated for novice learners, who have yet to make any aspects of a task habitual or automated, and therefore have to use a good deal more mental capacity and energy than an expert on the same task. For these learners, computer-based cognitive tools could perform parts of the task while novices get up to speed, and a number of software programs were designed to support this process.[19]

Related to the idea of off-loading is the process of *scaffolding*, which "refers to a process of initially limiting a novice's access to all the features of the context and then removing those constraints as soon as possible."[20] The learner is given the opportunity for practice in context, where supports are gradually removed as the learner is able to take on more of the task. Researchers developed computer-based tools to support the scaffolding process—for example, by performing parts of tasks or prompting the learner to the extent he or she requires at a particular stage of mastery.

Another goal toward which situated learning theorists designed computer applications was *anchored instruction*. The term was coined by the Cognition and Technology Group at Vanderbilt University, referring to a learning environment that is "sufficiently rich and complex to be meaningfully viewed from several perspectives"[21] (such as using one film or book as the central element of a whole course). "This is the evidence of a successful situated learning event—it serves as an anchor for multiple perspectives, all equally valid and fully justifiable within the context of the situation."[22]

These researchers also designed computer applications with the goal of transfer in mind. Roy Pea described these applications as follows:

---

[18]Brown, Collins, and Duguid, 1989

[19]Resnick and Johnson, 1988

[20]Young, 1993, p. 47

[21]Young, 1993, p. 49

[22]Young, 1993, p. 50

> The general aim is to create tools that enhance the chances that
> students adopt a self-aware transfer state of mind, and that they
> be provided with the transfer-relevant access skills and heuristic
> strategies, and a sufficiently rich taxonomy of problem types for
> each domain of study to make the application of such search
> heuristics worthwhile. [23]

A primary goal in such tools was to help students cultivate
their metacognitive capacities—that is, their ability to reflect on their
own thought processes. Also referred to as *self-regulation*, *metacognition* can be defined as "knowledge about one's own thinking, as well
as the ongoing planning, monitoring, and evaluation of one's performance on a task."[24] Metacognitive activity is central to transfer in
that it helps learners form generalizations that enable them to recognize situations where knowledge or skills might be applicable.

Some software programs have been developed specifically to
support the development of certain kinds of metacognitive activity.
The goal of these programs is to make the transfer processes more
visible, and to make them available for replay, analysis and reflection. Such a program can "act as a mirror of the learner's thought
processes by providing an external representation of internal cognitive processes."[25]

The idea of metacognition raises another important way in
which technology and cognitive science converged. As Gavriel
Salomon describes, psychology scholars tend to base their theories on
the dominant technology of the time. In the computer age, the idea of
the mind as a computer, an information processor, gained currency to
the point that it has come to dominate the field of psychology. For
example, metacognition describes the executive functions or routines
of the mind, much as one can describe the workings of a computer. As
Robert B. Kozma describes,

> The computer is an important resource for designers not only
> because of its unique control capabilities, but because these
> attributes are so isomorphic with the representations and
> processes involved in human learning . . . [the computer] can
> model, activate, or amplify cognitive strategies. It is this last possibility that may hold the most promise, for learners may inter-

---

[23]Pea, 1988, p. 195

[24]Thornburg and Pea, 1991, p. 122

[25]Kozma, 1987, p. 24

nalize the very processes in which the computer excels and thus become better learners.[26]

Researchers in the field of artificial intelligence (AI) took a particular interest in using computers to simulate human thought and decision making, the idea being that if one can simulate the thought process, one can understand that process. Out of this interest came AI, or simulations of human thought, as well as intelligent CAI (ICAI) and intelligent tutoring systems (ITS). These systems go beyond ordinary CAI in that they can monitor student performance and prescribe courses of study to a more sophisticated degree than can CAI. What they also do is provide the learner with a simulated "expert" after whom the learner can model his or her own thinking. Wallace Feurzig describes such a program as:

> . . . capable of performing the same kinds of tasks that it trains and explaining its actions as it performs them. The object is to provide students with concrete models that prepare them for their own attempt to solve similar problems in the reasoned and articulate way exemplified by the expert.[27]

In other words, these programs use AI—a simulation of human thought—to actually *shape* human thought.

Douglas Noble refers to this process as *cognitive engineering* or "the redesign of the human mind, according to specifications of advanced technologies."[28] Gavriel Solomon calls it "AI in reverse":

> what I have in mind is the use of the system's intelligence not just to simulate human cognition but rather *to have human cognition come to simulate the system's unique intelligence.* By so doing, one would hope to equip learners with "cognitive tools" that simulate or reflect the essence of computerized tools that capitalize on their own artificial "intelligence." This, then, would constitute AI in reverse: using artificial "intelligence" to allow learners to emulate it and come to use it as part of their cognitive apparatus.[29]

---

[26]Kozma, 1987, p. 21
[27]Feurzig, 1988, p. 109
[28]Noble, 1991, p. 182
[29]Salomon, 1988, p. 124

In summary, cognitive scientists were actively involved in research agendas in which technology played a central role—partly out of an interest in bringing these cognitive tools into schools and largely for the purposes of conducting learning research. Clearly their work was based on different theories than earlier technologies for automated instruction, and the computer applications that were promoted for school use were different as well. These applications were also different, in part, because of changes in the tone and focus of educational policy at the time.

CHANGES IN EDUCATIONAL POLICY AND EDUCATIONAL TECHNOLOGY

In the late 1970s and early 1980s, American public education was criticized for having once again gone soft, allegedly neglecting academic skills in the focus on civil rights, equality of opportunity, and neoprogressive pedagogy. Evidence was mounting that compensatory education was not working, and critics were claiming that the focus on equity had resulted in the lowering of educational standards. The back to basics movement was in full swing, combined with a renewed emphasis on holding schools accountable for student achievement.

Logo and other microworld technologies had attracted some attention by educators, but were out of keeping with the focus on basic literacy and numeracy skills. In the meantime, the invention and popularization of the personal computer cast a different tone on calls to use computers in schools. *Computer literacy* became a buzz phrase in the early 1980s and was even promoted as a new basic in important educational policy documents. Generally referring to programming skills or proficiency with software programs like word processors, the push for computer literacy was generally premised on the notion that computer skills were fast becoming fundamental— basic skills in an increasingly computer-based technological world, particularly in the world of work. Its advocates came from a variety of places outside of public education, as described by H. Besser (1993) in *Computers in Education: Social, Political and Historical Perspectives*:

> Major advocates of computer literacy included corporations, higher education leaders, the military, the federal government and

the scientific community. The corporate world saw mandatory computer literacy as a way of creating a more trained work force through direct computing skills . . . as well as general skills and habits.[30]

This priority was not necessarily that of teachers, but became a high priority of educational reform in this era, which was characterized by educational agendas pressed by economic and business leaders.

The 1980s came a number of scathing reports about how public schools were failing, generally linking the inadequacies of schools to problems in the national economy. The publication of *A Nation at Risk: The Imperative for Educational Reform* marked a radical— some like to call it *seismic*—shift in perceptions of public education and beliefs about the primary purpose of schooling. This report, published in 1983, represented the work of the National Commission on Excellence in Education, created in 1981 by Secretary of Education T. H. Bell. The report warned:

> Our nation is at risk. Our once unchallenged preeminence in commerce, industry, science, and technological innovation is being overtaken by competitors throughout the world. . . . the educational foundations of our society are presently being eroded by a rising tide of mediocrity that threatens our very future as a Nation and a people. . . . We have, in effect, been committing an act of unthinking, unilateral educational disarmament.[31]

A Nation at Risk emphasized the increasing need for skilled workers, that need being fueled by technological change and global economic competition. The report stressed that the United States had to become a Learning Society, a society of lifelong learners with high learning standards and discipline. No longer could people count on a high school diploma leading to one job that would provide a living wage and sustain them throughout their working years. Now success in the world of work would demand much more.

In the late 1980s, a number of initiatives were announced that were intended to address the concerns voiced in *A Nation at Risk*. In 1989, national political leaders and governors met at what came to be known as the Charlottesville Summit to discuss biparti-

---

[30]Salomon, 1988, p. 124

[31]National Commission on Excellence in Education, 1983, p. 5

san plans for school reform. One of the key ideas that emerged was that of developing national goals for education. Congress and state governors ultimately developed eight national education goals[32] (which first were six) intended to "help provide a national framework for education reform and promote systemic changes needed to ensure equitable educational opportunities and high levels of educational achievement for all students."[33] Following the summit also came the development of a number of institutions and organizations charged with developing, implementing, and evaluating those goals. For example, the National Education Goals Panel was established in 1990 to measure the nation's progress in meeting the national education goals.

Another federal component to this era of reform was the challenge President Bush issued to Americans to create innovative, break-the-mold schools. To that end, members of the corporate world

---

[32]The goals are as follows:

1. By the year 2000, all the children will start school ready to learn.
2. By the year 2000, the high school graduation rate will increase to at least 90%.
3. By the year 2000, all students will leave grades 4, 8, and 12 having demonstrated competency over challengeing subject matter including English, mathematics, science, foreign languages, civics and government, economics, arts, history, and geography, and every school in America will ensure that all students learn to use their minds well, so they may be prepared for responsible citizenship, further learning, and productive employment in our Nation's modern economy.
4. By the year 2000, the Nation's teaching force will have access to programs for the continued improvement of their profesional skills and the opportunity to acquire the knowledge and skills needed to instruct and prepare all American students for the next century.
5. By the year 2000, United States students will be the first in the world in mathematics and science achievement.
6. By the year 2000, every adult American will be literate and will possess the knowledge and skills necessary to compete in a global economy and exercise the rights and responsibilities of citizenship.
7. By the year 2000, every school in the United States will be free of drugs, violence and the unauthorized presence of firearms and alcohol and will offer a disciplined environment conducive to learning.
8. By the year 2000, every school will promote partnerships that will increase parental involvement and participation in promoting the social, emotional, and academic growth of children.

[33]NEGP web site: http://www.negp.gov/webpg50.html

formed the New American Schools Development Corporation
(NASDC), a private foundation created in 1991 with substantial
financial support from such sources as the Annenberg Foundation
(with Walter Annenberg serving as NASDC's founding director),
AT&T, Exxon, IBM, and the U.S. Department of Education. NASDC
awarded contracts to 11 design teams in 1992 to promote comprehensive, whole-school reform. The NASDC was replaced in 1998 by a
successor organization, the New American Schools, which has continued the work of NASDC.

　　Along with calls for new school visions came "America 2000,"
plans put forth in April 1991 by President Bush and Secretary of
Education Lamar Alexander to attain the national education goals.
President Bush delivered to Congress the "AMERICA 2000
Excellence in Education Act" in May 1991, which was signed into law
as the "Goals 2000: Educate America Act" under President Clinton on
March 31, 1994 (later amended on April 26, 1996). This act supported
the development of state-level content and performance standards,
along with new state assessments aligned with those standards (to
be in use by 2001) and systems for holding districts and schools
accountable for state standards. Goals 2000 has allocated billions of
dollars for states to develop learning standards and assessments
aligned to those standards.

　　At approximately the same time as the proposed America
2000 legislation came the formation of the Secretary's Commission on
Achieving Necessary Skills (SCANS), formed by the Secretary of
Labor to "examine the demands of the workplace and whether our
young people are capable of meeting those demands."[34] The
Commission was asked to do four things: "define the skills needed for
employment; propose acceptable levels of proficiency; suggest effective ways to assess proficiency; and develop a dissemination strategy
for the nation's schools, businesses, and homes."[35] SCANS delivered
its initial report in June 1991, arguing that:

> The message to us was universal: good jobs will increasingly
> depend on people who can put knowledge to work. What we found
> was disturbing: more than half our young people leave school with-
> out the knowledge or foundation to find and hold a good job. . . .
> Two conditions that arose in the last quarter of the 20th Century

---

[34]SCANS web site: http://www.ttrc.doleta.gov/SCANS/work.html
[35]SCANS web site: http://www.ttrc.doleta.gov/SCANS/work.html

have changed the terms of our young people's entry into the world of work: the globalization of commerce and the explosive growth of technology on the job. These developments have barely been reflected in how we prepare young people for work or in how many of our workplaces are organized.[36]

The Commission called for World Class Standards for educational performance, as well as the transformation of all American businesses and schools into high-performance organizations. Their report identified five competencies and three skills or personal qualities they believed were essential to job performance: (a) ability to use resources; (b) interpersonal skills; (c) ability to acquire, evaluate, organize, and interpret information; (d) understanding systems; and (e) using technology. Additional skills or qualities of effective workers identified in the report were strong basic skills, thinking skills, and a sense of personal integrity and responsibility. It urged American businesses to make clearer to schools what they feel students need to know and be able to do.

Related to these SCANS competencies came a push toward school-to-work reforms, including the 1994 School-to-Work Opportunities Act. School-to-work advocates argue that schools and businesses have not typically communicated adequately with one another, leading to a mismatch between what schools teach and what graduates need to know when they enter the workforce. By contextualizing academics in such on-the-job experiences as apprenticeships and internships, the argument goes, students see the reason for studying academic subjects and are more motivated to do well academically. School-to-work, advocates emphasize, is for all students, providing an authentic context for, and a sense of purpose behind, academic work. At the same time, critics maintain that school-to-work initiatives tend to focus too heavily on the *work* part, thus taking on a vocational feel.

Out of all of these concerns about American high school graduates lacking the necessary skills for work, then, came a new era of education reform promoting national economic prosperity in a global, technological age as the primary goal of schooling. Along with the national education goals expressing this focus came state-level learning standards, as well as standards documents emanating from a host of discipline-specific professional organizations and a variety of

[36]SCANS web site: http://www.ttrc.doleta.gov/SCANS/work.html

organizations devoted to developing, promoting, and/or measuring learning standards. Tied to these standards-based reforms came calls for the development of new forms of assessment that would capture and measure the extent to which the standards were being met *and* that could be used toward the high-stakes end of holding schools accountable by comparing their performance to other schools across the nation.

Although high-stakes, standards-based reform has been a dominant aspect of recent efforts at school reform, it would be inaccurate to say that it has had universal appeal or support. Certainly it has prominent and diverse critics. At one end of the spectrum are those who believe that public education cannot be fixed, and that the only solution is to open public education to market competition. Among these critics are people like Myron Lieberman (*Public Education: An Autopsy*) and Lewis Perelman (*School's Out*), who see popular choice initiatives (such as charter schools and school vouchers) as inconsequential tinkering around the edges. Instead they believe that the only way for a school to effectively promote learning is if it is fully part of a market system, operating for profit and in competition with other providers of its services.

Then there are people like Theodore Sizer, founder of the Coalition of Essential Schools, whose criticisms focus (among other things) on the process through which schools are held accountable. Sizer supports the idea of schools having high standards and being held accountable for them, but he opposes the way in which accountability is most often imagined and practiced. He argues that not enough attention is given to important questions about *what* schools are being held accountable for and *to whom* they are accountable. He advocates a type of schooling where schools must be responsive to their local communities, who get to see the progress students are making through public demonstrations of mastery of learning objectives. Otherwise, Sizer argues, the authority of those communities is seriously undermined, and their educational needs are not met.

Sizer is also critical of the mismatch between new standards and old assessment strategies, which do not adequately measure achievement of many new standards, but *do* provide score data in a form that can be easily compared for high-stakes purposes. He is concerned that "some people want to reduce evidence of world-class standards to immediate scores on expensive tests—and habits are extremely difficult to score. Paradoxically, then, we accept low-quality criteria to define high-quality work."[37] He also objects to the punishing quality of the current high-stakes climate:

> At my sourest I compare this with Vietnam War bombing strategies, measured with body counts. When bombing does not appear to win the war, just bomb more. When the test scores do not go up, just give "tougher" tests.[38]

Sizer envisions a kind of standards and accountability that provide dignity rather than punishment, where students feel that by being held to high standards, they are being taken seriously.

Then there are those who focus particularly on this issue of human dignity, arguing that simply raising the bar and expecting that all children will thus be inspired to learn is a grossly insensitive (and ineffective) way to help those children who are most in need. For instance, Jonathan Kozol (*Savage Inequalities*) documents the huge inequities in American public education and the implicit message that those inequities send to poor children about their worth. From this point of view, it is grossly unrealistic to believe that these children, who have spent years in schools where the most basic conditions of comfort and safety, to say nothing of instruction, are not met will somehow be inspired to learn because of tougher standards and penalties. Standards then start to look like a huge distraction from the deeper question of why a prosperous nation permits so many children to be so mistreated—particularly in public schools, which could be the one part of their lives that provides hope and genuine opportunity.

In other words, there are many different ideas in circulation at the present time about what schools are for, whose purposes they should serve, and how those purposes should be served. Politicians and policymakers are heavily promoting standards and high-stakes accountability and focusing on the preparation of competitive workers in a global information economy. However, as always, there are other views providing counterarguments to the dominant tone of school reform.

---

[37]Sizer, 1996, p. 45
[38]Sizer, 1996, p. 133

TURN OF THE CENTURY TECHNOLOGICAL CHANGE AND AMERICAN PUBLIC EDUCATION

Recently, new technology has been promoted as being compatible with just about everything being advocated in the way of school reform. Frequently, it is named as the reason for such reform. Even though various school reform movements have points of disagreement and often arise as reactions against one another, what nearly everyone seems to share is the belief that new technology is an important mechanism for accomplishing school reform. As in the past, an underlying faith in the synergy between educational and technological progress fuels many an American educationist today. Some of the educational reform purposes to which new technology is being put are described next.

Information Literacy

For starters, technological change today is, once again, cited as the reason that schools should change. Calls for one or another kind of computer-related literacy (e.g., *computer literacy, technological literacy, information literacy*) have been multiplying and intensifying. Each of these terms refers to something different, and none of them has a single, clear definition of its own.[39] However, the argument generally goes something like this: Technology is changing the world, and schools are not preparing students to use technology professionally or personally after graduation; nor are they "harnessing these powerful tools" to enhance student achievement. President Clinton wrote an "Open Letter to Parents" on October 11, 1995, which reads:

> In order for us to ensure that all our children have their shot at the American dream, we need to empower them with the technological literacy they'll need to succeed in a new and ever-changing information economy. By 2000, 60% of the new jobs in America will require advanced technological skills. Unfortunately, only 20% of our workforce possesses these skills today.
>
> We have a long way to go, but there is no better place to start than in our schools. While our workplaces are moving swiftly into the information age, our classrooms are not keeping pace. Today,

---

[39]See Tyner, 1998, for changing definitions of literacy

millions of children have more contact with technology in an afternoon at the video arcade than they do all year in school. We need to change that. We need companies to develop software that is as exciting to learn from as video games like Mortal Kombat are to play. We need schools equipped with the right technology.

If we fail to ensure that all our children are technologically literate, our nation will be poorer economically and spiritually. We will allow our nation to face a new divide—the divide between those children who have access to technology and those who never have.[40]

In this spirit, the classroom use of computers is promoted as a way of making sure that all children know how to operate computers and use them to locate information.

Equity

Another school reform issue in which technology is central is that of equality of educational opportunity. Contemporary discussions of equity often focus on the *digital divide*—the disparities in access to technology that exist among different socioeconomic and ethnic groups—and look to technology as the great equalizer in education. Rural children, poor children, and children with unqualified teachers are all promised an adequate education through technology.

In this spirit, President Clinton's technology literacy agenda included federal iniatives for schools in underserved communities. For example, the Technology Literacy Challenge Fund and the Technology Innovation Challenge Fund have provided millions of dollars in federal funds to technology projects serving schools with high proportions of poor and/or minority children. The Telecommunications Act of 1996 included a provision for the establishment of "e-Rate" funds, or funds collected from telecommunications companies and awarded to schools and libraries in the form of discounts on telecommunications services. e-Rate funds were first made available to schools in 1998 and have provided millions of dollars to schools and libraries for telecommunications services.

Another equity issue that relates to the use of technology is that of motivation. In much the same way that educational technolo-

---

[40]http://www.whitehouse.gov/WH/EOP/OP/edtech/letter.html

gists in the Johnson era argued that culturally deprived students would show higher achievement if taught by nonjudgmental, nondiscriminatory machines, some educators of at-risk students seem to find that their students' achievement improves markedly when students learn through direct contact with computers. Some argue that these students tend to feel that their teachers dislike them, and treat them unfairly, so they prefer the impartiality of a computer-teacher. Other students are reportedly less afraid to make mistakes with a computer than they are in front of their peers. Still others appear to gain a sense of mastery as they learn to operate the computer, and as they learn from computer-based experiences, and some take greater pride in the more professional-looking work they can produce with a computer.

Constructivism

A great deal of contemporary reform talk is in the constructivist spirit. *Constructivism* is a tricky term because it seems to be becoming a term broadly used to refer to many different things, much as *progressive* has been. Overall, the constructivist view "holds that teachers should be facilitators who help students construct their own understandings and capabilities in carrying out challenging tasks."[41] Deriving most directly from the cognitive apprenticeship theorists, constructivism considers the whole to be greater than the sum of its parts; that is, learning is treated as a social process, and knowledge is distributed among members of a group, the group's knowledge being greater than that of any individual.

Many of the ideas about using technology to support constructivist ends were expressed more than a decade ago by people like John Seely Brown, Allan Collins, Paul Duguid, and Roy Pea. However, much of what they imagined with regard to the use of technology was not feasible before the widespread availability of relatively inexpensive computing power sufficient to support such features as graphical user interfaces and hypermedia. In many ways, then, the same ideas that they put into circulation in the 1980s are now being presented as ends for which new media are useful means.

First of all, central to constructivism is a model of teaching that deemphasizes traditional notions of teachers as experts who dis-

---

[41]Collins, 1991, p. 29

pense information to students. In the constructivist spirit, new media are advocated for the ways in which they might transform the classroom into a more project-oriented, collaborative environment where teachers orchestrate learning experiences and coach students through those learning experiences. The argument, in brief, is that digital information resources are so vast and accessible that no one can be an expert anymore, and that we should shift our focus to using, evaluating, and understanding information. In this spirit, teachers become learners along with their students.

Another important aspect of constructivism is the idea of providing students with authentic learning experiences, where students acquire knowledge in the context of its use. New media can be helpful in this regard; for example, many students participate in programs where they, along with children all over the country, collect scientific data and report it to a central group of adult researchers, who use those data in legitimate scientific research. Web sites and CD-ROMs give students access to the same data that adult researchers use in a variety of disciplines, and primary source documents are more readily available online than they ever were through older media. Simulations attempt to provide computer-based environments where students can work and learn in ways that resemble the real-life counterparts of those environments. Some schools have students publish newsletters or research reports online or use desktop publishing software to produce student publications for community distribution, which gives students a sense of their work having significance to a substantial readership beyond their teacher.

Learning in authentic contexts often requires scaffolding, particularly for novice learners. As described earlier, computers can help by permitting the learner to offload certain parts of cognitive tasks until they are able to perform them without help. Computer-based learning can also incorporate scaffolding and the means for gradually withdrawing it in a variety of ways. For example, hypermedia texts are constructed in layers, where advanced information or activities can be embedded in such a way that novices do not have to encounter it and be confused or distracted by it. Some computer software can offer different features at different skill levels, where advanced users have access to features not made available to beginners. Software programs can vary the degree to which they prompt users—for example, by reading a word aloud upon request or waiting a longer or shorter time before offering a suggestion or solution to a student.

New media can help with the anchoring process by linking information to some designated focal point. Again the layering feature of hypermedia permits many strands to be linked off a central point and to be linked to one another in a variety of ways. The advantage over other media is that anything—text, diagram, moving or still image, sound—can be digitized and incorporated into the knowledge web, providing a nonlinear, but not necessarily haphazard, way of organizing resources. Well-designed hypermedia learning environments always lead the learner back to the central point when they need to reorient themselves.

Constructivism also emphasizes interdisciplinary studies. Rather than containing learning into rigidly separated subjects, constructivist reformers would prefer to see learning take place more as it does outside school, which usually involves some overlap of disciplines. New media are promoted for interdisciplinary studies for their tendency to blur the distinctions among disciplines. Interactive multimedia provide links and webs that connect information in new combinations, permitting the user to explore a subject from a variety of angles, rather than the one that an isolated textbook allows. New media can also fit with a renewed interest in the project method, which tends to be inherently interdisciplinary. Students develop skills and knowledge in a variety of areas in the context of working on a project (such as designing a building or planning a political campaign). In the process of working on these projects, students might consult digital resources, manipulate data with computers, or create computer-supported presentations or demonstrations.

Constructivism promotes higher order thinking skills, such as inquiry, critical thinking, and problem solving. The argument generally asserts that schools have tended to feed students predetermined questions and the proper answers to those questions. This approach seems to go against children's natural inquisitiveness, and their capacity to ask questions, explore their environment, and relate what they learn to what they already know. The push is to make children more active learners by encouraging discovery over delivery of knowledge.

Technology can be used to support these learning processes by making more information readily available to consult and use in the classroom or by giving students a simulated experience to think about. For example, Internet resources provide children with access to information sources and resources previously unavailable to them.

Digitized resources, particularly primary source documents, permit students to compare different accounts of events. They can use online resources during class discussions and debates to verify their assertions, thus developing the ability to form reasoned opinions and keep discussions well grounded in accurate information. Simulations allow students to see the probable outcomes of certain choices or actions. In some cases, simulations shift the focus from the mechanics of conducting an experiment to the interpretation of the findings. In other cases, simulations allow students to conduct experiments that would otherwise be impossible because they are too difficult, dangerous, time-consuming, or expensive. Databases and spreadsheets permit users to manipulate data in a variety of ways, which might allow them to revise a hypothesis or challenge an assumption that they are making. Students can work with a variety of representations of information to see how many different ways the same facts can be interpreted, thus providing a point of entry into thinking about how to evaluate arguments and the evidence used to support them.

Constructivist approaches take a particular interest in tools software programs—that is, software where users provide the content, rather than the software leading the user through its premade content. Examples of such software would be programs for creating multimedia creations, Web pages, text documents, databases, spreadsheets, music compositions, or digital images. In *Education and Technology: Reflections on Computing in Classrooms*, Charles Fisher (1996) writes of "the power of composition environments,"[42] arguing that "where students and teachers are composing, cognitive engagement is focused and intense."[43] Composing requires students to collect information, then reflect on it, and organize it into some form that makes sense to others, which many argue is much more meaningful work than memorizing prepackaged content or working with drill material. It also means a lot to some students to have physical products to show for what they have learned.

Constructivism also acknowledges the variety of ways in which children learn and advocates the mobilization of many different types of intelligence. Howard Gardner is well known for his idea

---

[42]Fisher, 1996, p. 122
[43]Fisher, 1996, p. 122

of multiple intelligences, identifying some seven intelligences,[44] only two of which—logical and linguistic—are really emphasized in school. Children lose out, Gardner argues, because some are strong in one type of learning (e.g., kinesthetic, musical, or interpersonal), but do not have the opportunity to use those strengths as points of entry into the kinds of learning most often required by schools. Additionally, he adds, a well-rounded individual should try to cultivate all seven intelligences, and school fails to do so. New media can be used to address different ways of learning by providing a variety of modalities through which children can approach a topic. Interactive multimedia can engage a student through music, recorded speech, video, animation, graphics, and text—alone or in one or more combinations. Multimedia can "present different characterizations of the same situation or process simultaneously,"[45] not to mention provide immediate feedback to learners.

In addition to acknowledging multiple intelligences, some educators also acknowledge multiple literacies. The idea behind critical literacy is that it conceives of literacy as proficiency in understanding a variety of discourses or communication styles, recognizing which ones are privileged in society, and understanding how those privileged discourses are tied to particular arrangements of power. In other words, literacy is not merely the ability to read and write in a particular language, but the ability to employ a variety of discourses and understand the relationship between discourse and the existing social order.

Paulo Freire and Donald Macedo promoted critical literacy, describing it as "reading the world" and "writing the world." That is, in the same way that traditional literacy is considered to be the abilities of reading and writing, literacy today must encompass not only the ability to read a variety of media texts, but to write or create them as well. Engaging students in the production of texts in a variety of media both helps reveal the biases of those media to them and enables students to express ideas that might run counter to those advanced by mainstream media. It gives them access to a wider variety of discourses, particularly in media often monopolized by large commercial interests.

---

[44]Those intelligences are musical, spatial, bodily kinesthetic, interpersonal, intrapersonal, logical-mathematical, and linguistic. See Gardner, 1993, for a discussion of multiple intelligences.

[45]Collins, 1996, p. 58

In other words, critical literacy expands the concept of literacy to include both a variety of media beyond traditional texts and the
cultivation of personal power. In *Literacy in a Digital World,*
Kathleen Tyner (1999) argues that this vision of literacy could
"enable each person to at least join the debate by skillfully negotiat-
ing within the existing power structure, as well as outside it. And
this is why it is urgent that everyone has access to literacy in its
most powerful forms."[46]

Another central idea to constructivist learning is collaboration and community. Many people question the potential of new technology to support collaborative projects, but there are some education
reformers, such as Tom Snyder, who see this as a particularly strong
point of technology. The idea is generally to have groups of students
working together to solve a problem and for them to use new technology as one means through which they work on that problem. For
example, a group of children might be discussing the implications of
the choices that political leaders make and then use a simulation to
see what happens when attention is given or denied to health care,
the elderly, schools, or infrastructure. Students preparing a debate on
freedom of speech might consult Internet resources, such as the Web
site for the American Civil Liberties Union, as they refine their arguments. In these ways, children are not isolated at machines so much
as they are using them to gather or reflect on relevant information.

The focus on community building is not just on students; new
media are promoted for their potential to support teachers' professional development by connecting them with one another. Teachers
have traditionally led relatively isolated lives, coming into contact
with their colleagues only if they have the time and inclination to
visit the faculty lounge during lunchtime. Computer-mediated communication enables teachers to share ideas with one another;
through e-mail, teachers can send questions or comments to others
when their schedules allow. E-mail lists, bulletin boards, Web sites,
and chat rooms devoted to teacher concerns have proliferated, providing teachers with such things as lesson plans, ideas for projects, tips
on classroom management, guides to using technology in their teaching, and information on where to obtain classroom materials.

The interest in collaboration for students is not restricted to
classmates; technology is sometimes promoted in the context of con-

---

[46]Tyner, 1999, p. 4

necting children to their communities. For example, some schools conduct authentic research on some issue of community interest, such as an environmental problem or unusual matter of local history, using technology to conduct and/or disseminate their work. The interest in community building often extends beyond the immediate geographical region as well; computer-mediated communication, such as e-mail and chat rooms, can be used to establish links between students in different areas so they can learn about one another and work on projects together.

The spirit of collaboration has also taken on a global sensibility of late, and computer-mediated communication seems to be the technology of choice to this end. For example, children use e-mail to establish pen pals (*e-pals* or *keypals*) with children in other countries, or they engage in some kind of collaborative research or writing project where they share their work and ideas with children in other locations. Some such projects, like the Global SchoolNet Foundation, a nonprofit consortium providing free technology services to schools, has as one of its goals "fostering development of global, cultural, geographical, environmental, and socio-political understanding (*and ultimately world peace!*)"[47] (emphasis original). A lofty goal, perhaps, but a much-named one among technology advocates.

Assessment is another area in which constructivist reformers see uses for new technology. For example, some teachers have students compile portfolios of their work, which contain selections of a student's work over time. Students are also encouraged to reflect on that work as they select new additions to their portfolio, revisiting learning goals and taking stock of the progress they have made and wish to make. Interactive multimedia are potentially useful in portfolio assessment because they permit the collection of a wide variety of student work in one convenient, digital form. A multimedia portfolio can contain student writing, artwork, audio, and/or video, and all of those works can be linked to one another. Students might include written commentaries about their work, with links in the text to those specific works that illustrate their observations about their work. They might also use the nonlinear format of multimedia in their self-analysis, by taking advantage of its potential to suggest connections among different components.

---

[47]http://www.gsn.org/who/gsn.visions.html

Another recently promoted type of assessment is the public demonstration of mastery, such as that promoted by Theodore Sizer and the Coalition of Essential Schools. Rather than taking a test to show mastery of a learning goal, students give a demonstration to a group of people that might include teachers, peers, experts, parents, and other community members. The idea here, according to Sizer, is that "teachers and students have to work out how a topic can be deployed intellectually to go beyond the immediate facts covered in class and be displayed in some form for interested observers."[48] New media are useful to the extent that they might be used to organize information for presentation to an audience. For example, a student might use a slideshow presentation program to organize what he knows and explain and present it to others.

Basic Skills

It is also important to point out that there is still a great deal of concern over the teaching of basic skills to students, although there are many different ideas about how and in what context those skills should be taught. Much reform talk focuses on the higher order skills that will supposedly be increasingly necessary to live a reasonable life, but many parents, employers, and college professors are more concerned that young people are coming out of high school lacking the basic skills they need as they enter adult life.[49]

Technology can be used to support education in basic skills, particularly through what are most often called *integrated learning systems* (ILS). An ILS covers basic skills in a systematic way all the while monitoring each student's progress:

> Integrated Learning Systems (ILS) are touted by enthusiastic supporters as the complete solution to teaching basic language and mathematics skills to students. Essentially, an ILS is a comprehensive, computer-based K-8 basic skills curriculum, accompanied by a management system that can link learning objectives with particular lessons, as well as track students' progress throughout the system.[50]

---

[48]Sizer, 1996, p. 85

[49]www.publicagenda.org

[50]Knapp and Glenn, 1996, p. 159

At the same time, integrated learning systems have been criticized for isolating basic skills in such a way that children are "less skilled at applying them successfully in the context of real work."[51] Research exploring the impact of ILS on student achievement has produced contradictory results. In particular, "it seems that the vendors report high gains in test scores, while independent sources show modest or negligible gains."[52] Still it is important to recognize that many teachers and administrators believe that integrated learning systems are a valuable way to support instruction in basic skills.

Many of the methods of cultivating basic skills, particularly those involving technology, are reminiscent of the 1960s systems approaches to instruction. They seek to standardize instruction, reducing ambiguity and making learning as efficient as possible. In many ways, although contemporary standards documents make many references to constructivist pedagogy, they also provide a detailed, fixed structure of learning expectations and behaviorally stated performance objectives. In that sense, they reflect a somewhat mechanized view of education, where all desired learning can be specified in behavioral terms that detail the outcomes of instruction that would serve as indicators of that learning.

Although a great deal of reform talk promotes the idea of teacher as facilitator, not everyone is interested in removing teachers from their didactic role. Specific to educational technology, distance learning tends to hold to the view of teachers as content providers more than it promotes other models of teaching. Distance education advocates often argue that distance learning will bring the best teachers to all students, both by providing students with lessons from master teachers and exposing classroom teachers to more models of good teaching. Distance learning technology can also enable schools to offer subjects that their own teachers are not qualified to teach or the school lacks the resources to offer. Additionally, with distance learning a district can hire only one person in a specialized area because that one person can be spread out over the entire district. G. R. Jones, founder of a variety of distance learning projects, points out:

---

[51]Knapp and Glenn, 1996, p. 159

[52]Knapp and Glenn, 1996, p. 149

The problem is shared by both rural and urban schools. Often schools cannot afford the luxury of hiring teachers for courses such as trigonometry or Latin if only a few students will enroll. And some schools cannot convince subject-qualified teachers to relocate to their geographic area.[53]

This advantage might look more and more appealing in light of predictions that school enrollments will increase by some 3 million by the year 2006, while some 2.2 million teachers are expected to retire.

Some advocates argue that new technology can teach better than human teachers or that certain aspects of teaching should be handed over to computers so that teachers can focus on other aspects where being human is essential. For example, Frederick Bennett's book, *Computers as Tutors*, describes a vision where all delivery of content takes place directly from computers, and teachers focus on individual conferences and small seminars. He believes that students will learn more through computers because their program will be individualized, they will not be humiliated by making mistakes in front of teachers or peers, and the instructional software can be kept up to date with the current state of knowledge in a particular field.

In summary, there are many different ideas about teaching, learning, and school reform for which new technologies are promoted, and there is a wide variety of technology-based projects and experiments underway in schools across the nation. Although it is far too soon to judge the success or effectiveness of these projects, it is worthwhile to look at some of the problems that are emerging, particularly in terms of the degree to which they do or do not resemble problems encountered in technology reforms in the past.

FACTORS PREVENTING THE USE OF NEW TECHNOLOGY IN SCHOOLS

Generally when educational technologists are asked to name the obstacles preventing the use of new technology in schools, they name the obvious culprits: inadequate funds, technical problems, and teacher training. Certainly these are obstacles; the money factor alone is enough to kill aspirations to incorporate technology into the

---

[53]Jones, 1996, p. 26

classroom experience. In *High Tech Heretic: Why Computers Don't Belong in the Classroom and Other Reflections by a Computer Contrarian*, Clifford Stoll (1999) asks, "What's the cost of computers in the classroom? Around the country, communities float thirty-year bond issues to buy computers which will be obsolete within five years."[54] However, these are obstacles with fairly straightforward solutions, and no shortage of publications and professional organizations devoted to them. Meanwhile, there are other issues that need to be examined that are rarely given attention because so much of the focus is at the level of implementation, of execution. It is also important to consider issues like the way technology changes teachers' work, impact of intense corporate involvement in public education, inequities in access to technology, concerns about the effects new media might have on children, and ideas about what constitutes knowledge and how knowledge is cultivated. All of these issues have a great deal to do, as they always have had in the past, with the extent to which new technology is integrated into classroom practice.

Issues Related to Teachers' Work

As in the past, the introduction of new technology into the classroom does not simply give teachers a valuable new resource with which to transform the teaching and learning experience. It changes the nature of their work and the character of their relationships with students, often in ways that are not perceived desirable or valuable by teachers.

Not surprisingly, advocates are once again offering the argument that new technology will professionalize teaching—for example, by bringing to the teaching profession the kind of productivity that has purportedly come to professionals in other fields through their use of technology. However, many teachers are experiencing something different when they start to use new technology. The amount of time required to produce appropriate and valuable curricular materials is staggering. On top of that is the time involved in locating useful Web sites and software programs, evaluating possible software purchases, and keeping up to date with new hardware and software offerings, not to mention figuring out how to coordinate computer use in classrooms that typically have only a few computers for a tradi-

---

[54]Stoll, 1999, p. 23

tional size class. It is also a huge misconception that technology training need only happen to get teachers "up and running"; in fact, the more they use technology, the more training they need. Meanwhile teachers are already facing overwhelming expectations that they prepare all their students to meet local, state, national, and international learning standards and to pass new tests aligned to those standards.

Rather than professionalizing teaching, this speedup stands to deskill the teaching profession. Teachers are increasingly forced to look for ways to streamline their work or cut corners, often becoming more dependent on experts to provide them with materials they used to produce for themselves. With so much of their time taken up by the detailed record-keeping required in their increasingly professionalized role, teachers have no time to keep up in their fields or engage in meaningful collaborations with one another, and they lose many of the skills they once possessed because they have few opportunities to use them.[55]

Many teachers resist using technology, not because they find it inappropriate or uninspiring, but because they perceive as yet another task added to an already overwhelming burden. If software is not specifically designed to meet a goal to which they are being held accountable and ready to use with their students, they are likely to avoid using it. Deskilling of teaching happens when teachers, in an effort to make their workload reasonable and manageable, accept forms of technology that involve the use of commercially or otherwise premade content. That is, using tools applications requires more of the teacher, who must design the associated activities. Without the time, resources, or opportunity for collaboration with colleagues needed to produce curricular materials, teachers have little choice but to turn to content made by someone else who is thinking in terms of making a product for national distribution, which cannot be too closely tailored to any particular school or community.

Teachers lose even more autonomy as new technology increasingly chips away at their privacy. In this age of accountability, integrated learning systems record all student activity on those systems. Although the overt purpose is to monitor students' progress and individualize instruction, the potential exists for that information to be accessed and used in less appropriate manners. More troubling are

---

[55]Apple, 1988; Apple and Jungck, 1998

the ways in which students' and teachers' Internet and e-mail activity can be monitored and punished. Again the stated purpose is to ensure proper use of the system and to protect children from inappropriate online experiences. However, at the same time as the Internet is hailed as an inherently decentralizing, democratizing medium, it is also being used to more carefully monitor the actions of students and teachers and, in some cases, to diminish teacher autonomy.

The threat to autonomy is perhaps clearest in the use of Internet-filtering devices on school computers. There are several different types of filters, each working in a somewhat different way, but the overall purpose of them is to prevent users from accessing certain Web sites (usually those with pornographic or otherwise adult material). The problem is that in many cases teachers have little or no ability to override the filter even if they know that a site they wish to use, or to have their students use, is appropriate for those students. For example, the filtering criteria of an Internet filter installed in the New York City public schools blocked sites that many teachers had found to be valuable, and many teachers were unable to override the block. In this particular case, the filtering criteria reflected a conservative ideology to which teachers objected—for example, by permitting access to prolife Web sites, but blocking sites expressing prochoice positions.

Educational technologists do not typically talk about *teacher proofing* anymore, but it is understandable that teachers sometimes feel that it is still the goal. Regardless of whether critics' characterizations are accurate, teachers do not generally appreciate being accused of poor judgment, incompetence, discriminating against students, losing patience, or not knowing their fields. What might be genuinely useful in those reformers' plans is often lost in their failure to engage teachers or involve them in those plans. Too often teachers are described as impediments and technology as the way to get past them. For example, in *Computers as Tutors: Solving the Crisis in Education*, Frederick Bennett (1999) emphasizes that he does not mean to criticize teachers, but cites their diversity of styles (by virtue of being human) as the *problem* that computer teaching would *solve,* if only we gave teaching over to computers:

> In recent years, software producers have been trying to overcome the financial handicap of this diverse market by directing their sales pitches to school boards and superintendents. These authorities can choose programs for the entire system and can buy

many copies and impose them on groups of teachers. Software companies avidly embrace this plan of marketing because it allows them to sell larger quantities of the same program. Teachers, however, don't like it.[56]

Lewis Perelman was more blunt, arguing that "perhaps the most pernicious myth thwarting progress in education today is the shibboleth that 'Technology will never replace the classroom teacher.' The truth: It already has. . . . Classrooms and teachers are far too costly and slow to meet the Information Age's exploding demand for learning."[57] He went on to advocate the "wholesale replacement of lecturers and classrooms with silicon chips and glass threads."[58]

Teacher concerns about being replaced by technology are exacerbated by a dominant rationale behind distance education, which, according to L. R. Knapp and A. D. Glenn (1996) in *Restructuring Schools with Technology*, "has become popular in recent years with the emerging financial difficulties experienced by many school districts and the development of new technologies that enable districts to employ one teacher to instruct students in multiple schools."[59] If the predictions of teacher shortages in the near future come true, it is likely that distance learning will be heavily promoted to fill the gap and to stand in for classroom teachers. Whether distance learning will ever actually be used to that end, particularly in K–12 education, is an entirely different question, but the possibility is enough to worry teachers and raise their suspicion.

In other words, it is possible that if educational technology is not being used as much as advocates would like, it may be due, in part, to resistance on the part of teachers to something that has been forced on them—generally without their real participation or consent—and that does not always serve their professional interests very well.

Commercialism and Corporate Involvement in Schools

In response to charges that teachers are not up to par have come others—particularly from the corporate sector—stepping up to provide

[56]Bennett, 1999, pp. 64–65

[57]Perelman, 1993, p. 5

[58]Perelman, 1993, p. 7

whatever schools are lacking. As mentioned earlier, although *A Nation At Risk* never explicitly called on corporate interests to involve themselves in schools, the years since the publication of that report have been characterized by a variety of styles of corporate involvement in public education.

Some of the ways in which new technology has been promoted for school use raise questions about whose interests are really being served. For example, hardware and software manufacturers have an interest in schools, at least in part, because schools are a potentially enormous market for them. Not only can they sell their products to schools, but they can hope that their presence in schools will lead students and parents to choose those brands when they make home computing purchases. Industries and interest groups have a new way to promote their point of view through Web sites with educational components or teacher resources sections. In much the same way that teachers used to write away for free teaching materials, they can now access those materials online. Companies providing Internet service to schools see the potential for online advertising revenue from companies marketing products to children and teenagers.

The topic of new media, commercialism, and public education is a book all its own. For the moment, the point is simply that in an age where partnerships between schools and business are heavily promoted, it is important to think carefully about who really benefits from those partnerships and how to ensure that students are not made a captive audience to corporate promotions.

The Digital Divide

Despite ever-dropping costs, computers are expensive relative to many other instructional materials. As a result, like many other resources, computers are more prevalent in relatively affluent school districts than in poor districts. The expression *digital divide* generally refers to a variety of ways in which access to new technology is unequal,[60] and it certainly can be applied to imbalances in access to technology across school districts.

Access to new technology in schools is unequal in a variety of ways. Schools vary not only in the number of computers they have,

---

[60]National Telecommunications and Information Administration, 1998

but in the age, capability, and state of disrepair of those machines. Having Internet access in a school might mean having one computer wired or having several wired computers in every classroom and in one or more computer labs. Although the divide has been closing, it is still unacceptably large (by virtue of the fact that it exists at all), and its closure depends on programs and funds that are constantly in jeopardy. As of 1998, 89% of public schools had Internet access. As high as this number might look, it is disturbing that Internet access in schools with 50% or more minority students was 82%; in schools where 71% or more of students were eligible for free or reduced-price lunch, the percentage dropped to 80%. This pattern also held for percentages of instructional rooms with Internet access, which was 51% overall, 37% in schools with 50% or more minority students, and 39% in schools where 71% or more of students were eligible for free or reduced-price lunch. It was also evident in disparities in ratios of students to computers, which was generally in the 9:12 range (of students per computer) overall, but jumped to 17 for schools with large numbers of non-white and/or poor children.[61]

   Programs like the e-Rate, which provides discounts on telecommunications services to schools and libraries, are not popular with political conservatives and are forever in danger of being cut. As a result, even if the access gaps narrow or close, those gaps are far from being welded shut. Additionally, the differences in student-to-computer ratios and Internet access suggest that if poor and/or minority children are using technology, they are using it differently from the ways in which other children are using it, to the extent that different ratios imply different technology configurations in schools. This is significant if different kinds of technology use cultivate different kinds of thinking skills; we stand to create different classes of thinkers as a result. As it is, there is a persistent tendency for more affluent schools to make more use of technology applications that support higher order cognitive development, where schools in poor districts are more likely to have the kinds of hardware and software that provide practice in basic skills.

---

[61]National Center for Education Statistics, 1999

Concerns About New Media's
Effects on Children

Many teachers, and adults in general, have huge reservations about new media and their potentially negative effects on children. Adults worry that children will encounter pedophiles or other kinds of predators online or they will gain access to pornography or other sexually explicit material. They are concerned about the proliferation of hate speech and the celebration of violence on the Internet and in video games. (Consider the shooting at Columbine High School in the spring of 1999. Some aspects of the shootings that received a great deal of attention were the gunmen's use of e-mail, their affection for a violent video game, and the existence of a Web site for the "Trenchcoat Mafia" to which they allegedly belonged. The day after the shooting, a Gallup poll showed that 82% of 659 adult respondents believed the Internet was at least partly to blame.[62])

Just as in the early days of public education, many American parents want schools not only to foster academic achievement, but to provide some kind of moral education or guidance as well. This is a time (perhaps not so different from other times in this regard) when adults fear that society is in peril because children are not learning or adopting the kinds of values that adults believe will lead to a stable, safe, good society. When adults try to attribute a cause to the change, the new technology of the day fits the bill—and even if it cannot be proved to be a whole or partial cause of the problem, somehow it feels like the problem to many people. As a result, enthusiasm about using new technology in schools is always accompanied by some degree of ambivalence.

Other difficulties in using new media in schools have to do with new patterns of access that students have to each other and the outside world, and to the access that the outside world has to students. New media have raised a number of free speech and privacy questions as they relate to students. For example, a number of lawsuits have been making their way through the courts involving students who criticized or threatened their teachers or principals on personal Web pages. Other suits concern questions of whether student access to certain kinds of Web sites—such as those on reproductive health or religion—should be restricted in school. Then there are concerns about putting student work or photos of students on school Web pages. In particular, many parents and educators are fearful that including students' names on those pages might endanger the student if the page is accessible to anyone with a Web browser.

The World Wide Web (WWW) has raised large questions about what is appropriate information to bring into schools, and whether and how to restrict what comes into schools through that medium. It is fairly customary now for schools to use filtering software, which in one way or another (depending on the filtering program) blocks students' (and sometimes teachers') access to sites deemed unacceptable. Schools are also developing *acceptable use policies* that they require students and parents to sign, which essentially outline a student's obligations with respect to technology use, and throw in a disclaimer that no matter how hard the school might try, students might still manage to find their way to information that parents find objectionable.

In other words, new media challenge old monopolies on information. For good or ill, they make it easier for students to express their views large audiences, be brought to the attention of large (unknown) audiences, and to locate information considered appropriate only for adults. All of these aspects of new media make them hard to bring into existing school structures and practices because of the challenges they present to them.

Information Overload

There is also the possibility, familiar to many teachers, that more information is not high on the list of what students need the most despite that many promotions of educational technology stress this aspect heavily. New media, above all else, have vastly increased the volume of data available to people. Teachers then have to apply themselves all the more to helping students maintain a sense of coherence in an environment characterized by its huge volume of tiny fragments of unrelated information. Even when students only had an encyclopedia and the school library's supply of books for their research, they had trouble locating and using relevant information. Even then, developing an idea was a challenge. Now the media environment works against both of those aims, and teachers have to either redouble their efforts at cultivating those skills in students, or to reconsider their goals.

Related to the issue of information overload is something of a misconception that knowledge is changing so fast that the only way to keep up with it in schools is to use new technology. In keeping with the notion that the world is changing at breakneck speed is the belief that the state of our knowledge about the world is not keeping up with the pace of change. The solution? Whatever medium is new at the time, and that offers a quicker or otherwise superior means of keeping people up to date.

It is popular to claim today that books are obsolete—that teachers should work from online resources because knowledge is changing too fast for more traditional media to keep up. Certainly this is sometimes the case in highly specialized aspects of disciplines and at advanced levels of study, where digital journals and other publications help keep research moving at a fast clip. However, it takes a long time for those changes to make their mark on lower levels of instruction in those disciplines—not because of the media used to convey the information, but because there is little need to make those changes rapidly. For example, new music, literature, and visual arts are created every day, but how much and how fast do the texts used in teaching the fundamentals of music, literary, or art theory have to incorporate those changes lest the integrity of those courses be compromised? The same can be asked about mathematics, chemistry, world history, French, or nearly any academic discipline. Is it really accurate to say that teachers are unable to keep those courses up to date because print media change too slowly?

Part of the problem here is the confusion of information or data with understanding, knowledge, or wisdom. Data change at a dizzying pace; wisdom is a little more durable. If teachers are in the business of delivering the most up-to-date data to students, then digital media probably are essential. If wisdom is the goal or even just a little understanding or insight, then technology may or may not be useful, and it certainly will not do the trick on its own.

Many teachers are keenly aware these days of the challenges that new media pose in terms of flooding the classroom with huge volumes of information, much of it extraneous to students' needs or purposes at the moment it pours in. Novice researchers are generating bibliographies with thousands of citations or downloading hundreds of pages of text, from which they are supposed to choose that which is relevant to their research question. This task was hard enough when the student worked from an encyclopedia and the school library's holdings. What now?

There is also the danger that the celebration of sheer volume of information creates the illusion that information collection is the answer to any problem that society faces. Meanwhile the real challenge is to take what we already know—which, in many cases, is quite a bit—and put it to use once we have determined which information is relevant. Seemingly intractable problems like hunger, poverty, and racism do not continue to plague us because we are waiting for the new information that will enable us to solve them; we need to start using the knowledge we already possess and stop using lack of information as an excuse that perpetuates misery and injustice.[63] The state of our information is changing rapidly, the state of our knowledge somewhat less so. It is not a matter of mere semantics to choose one term over the other.

CONCLUSION

At the present time, it is no great challenge to find people describing computers and related technologies as accessories to, catalysts of, or rationales for school reform. At a time when every imaginable educational change seems to be promoted—from emphasizing solid basic skills to focusing on higher order skills, improving student performance on traditional standardized test to replacing those tests with new forms of assessment, increasing the subject-matter content of the curriculum to focusing on deep knowledge in just a few key areas, promoting individual achievement to encouraging collaboration—one or another kind of new technology is promoted as a key component in educational change.

The machines have changed, but the idea of using them to solve almost anything that is wrong with public education has not. For that matter, ideas about what is wrong with schools have not changed that much, either. For example, we are still trying to decide whether schools should help children adapt to a changing world by fitting them to it or by making them critics of it. We are still debating whether a democratic education is one that provides all students

---

[63]Postman, 1999, chapter 5

with the same experiences or one that offers different programs tailored to different kinds of students. The verdict is still out on whether schools should focus primarily on the transmission of academic content or on the cultivation of social skills. Although there are many ways in which we are different from those who have thought about education and technology in the past, there is also much that we share with them. It is important and valuable to be aware of those points of common ground, and to use them to inform our understanding of the present situation.

7

COMMON THEMES

. . . there is something disturbingly familiar about the current vision of on-line resources. It has some of the quality of the early arguments for technology revolutionizing education: if we just get the materials right, then substantial changes will naturally follow.

—Jan Hawkins, in *Education and Technology:*
Reflections on Computing in Classrooms (1996)

Having now arrived at the present, it might be worth taking a long glance back over the stories of each of the media discussed in earlier chapters. It should be apparent by now that certain common themes and assumptions emerge out of the stories of all the major educational media of the 20th century. The details change, but many of the hopes, plans, fears, problems, and oversights follow common themes that weave their way through each story and are still with us today.

The point here is not so much to warn that history is bound to repeat itself or that trends in education follow a simple pendulum cycle, swinging between high hopes and disillusionment. It probably *is* fair to say that attitudes toward technology appear to follow a sort of pendulum swing, with a new technology providing each new push after the old one comes back with disappointing outcomes. However, that pendulum does not swing in perfect time with other ones or with changes in education that move according to other kinds of patterns. For example, Tyack and Cuban point out the problems that arise when reform talk is out of sync with reform action. Generally, the rhetoric of policymakers swings away from a reform long before any substantive efforts at implementing that reform have been made, leaving the reform out of joint with the issues at the forefront of policy talk.[1] This is certainly the case with respect to technology, in the sense that educational technology is generally promoted in the context of some particular school reform. When that reform falls out of favor, so does that particular technology application, and typically educators have not had nearly enough time with the technology to complete the process of assimilating it into the classroom environment.

Even if ideas about educational media tend to follow something of a pendulum swing, other changes are meanwhile taking place in school practices, politics, and philosophies. As a result, when the pendulum swings back, it never returns to exactly the same conditions from which it departed. So it is not always possible simply to apply what has been learned about earlier educational media experiments to new ones, because some of the conditions leading to past successes and problems will have changed. In other words, this is a complicated business—too complicated to warrant a simple warning that history repeats itself unless we heed its lessons.

Still historical context has much to offer in efforts to understand the present and to live and act successfully in it. Contemporary educational technology talk tends to be glaringly ahistorical. When it does acknowledge the past, that past rarely extends back very far. Consider, for example, this excerpt from an editorial in *eSchool News*, entitled "Memory Lane" and focusing on the controversies over internet filtering in schools:

> In simpler days—before answering machines, voice mail, and Caller ID—the barely stifled giggle on the other end of the line was the tip off: You'd just picked up a prank phone call.
> One might be angry or amused, but hardly anybody thought to slap a ban on telephones or limit their use by school-age children.

---

[1] Tyack and Cuban, 1995

> The telephone was seen as a neutral medium. You could use the
> phone to call your dear old mother or to make a bomb threat.[2]

Although this reference to the telephone is meant simply as an entertaining introduction to the piece, and perhaps should not be too closely scrutinized, it deserves attention because it embodies precisely what is wrong with much ed-tech talk. It places *the past* too recently, thus missing all of the controversy that raged in the truly early days of the telephone over its disruption of family stability and social interaction.[3] Moreover, it paints an idealized picture of the past as a simple time with simple problems, as opposed to today, where advanced technological development presents us with supposedly unprecedented challenges. It is as if we are all alone, embarking on a venture never before attempted or imagined, and the past has nothing to offer in the way of guidance or context.

Rarely in the history of educational technology has there been any concerted effort to understand what went wrong. Instead a new technology is embraced as the old one is discarded; some feature of the newcomer is named as the shortcoming of whatever came before and as the reason for the ascent of the new technology and the decline of the old. However, simply being different is not enough for the story to turn out differently. It is popular to argue today that computers play a different role than earlier media in our lives or that their educational applications are grounded in more solid psychological research than earlier media were, and that these differences mean that computers will be more extensively used in schools than those earlier media. Those claims about what is new about computers might be true, but that basic argument—that difference will make the difference—was used in American education to promote every new educational medium over the past century and a half. Clearly, difference alone does not lead to widespread implementation of a new medium in schools.

A long-range historical view helps reveal some of the assumptions that have been, and continue to be, deeply embedded in efforts to use new media in schools. Such assumptions are hardest to see when looking only at the present; they are more readily apparent in contexts that are farther removed in time and emotional investment.

---

[2]Downey, 1998, p. 6

[3]Marvin, 1988, chapter 2

For example, it is probably easier to find and rationally evaluate the 1920s assumption that film would make children violent than it is to do so with respect to the Internet today. We also have the benefit of hindsight to see how it all turned out. That does not mean that we can assume that things will happen again in roughly the same way, but it does remind us that predictions made in the heat of change are frequently flawed and should be regarded as hypotheses not prophecies.

Identifying and criticizing assumptions is not the same thing as rejecting them. It is important to know what assumptions are being made and what their potential flaws, weaknesses, or limitations might be because, as Terry Astuto et al. (1994) argue in *Roots of Reform: Challenging the Assumptions that Control Education Reform*, each assumption about school reform "constrains the proposition, let alone the implementation, of changes"[4] that take place while they are dominant. Unless we can play devil's advocate with our own assumptions, we risk being their captors, our thoughts contained within their framework. For that matter, some ideas that are now taken for granted and have been naturalized to the point of invisibility were not always that way. For example, much of what is today referred to as the *hidden curriculum* of schools was not hidden at all by the administrative progressives and scientific curriculum makers who promoted those functions of schooling in the early 20th century. However, all that has made it to the present, for most people, are the practices those reformers popularized, which, according to Michael Apple, "have become so commonplace that in a few more years we may have lost from our collective memory the very possibility of difference."[5]

It is important to understand this process by which the explicit becomes implicit, particularly in the story of educational technology. Although each individual story—that is, the story of educational film, or radio, or television—can be described as a story of ultimate failure to reform education, the larger story of all these media, taken as a whole, is one of success in building into American thought the acceptance of the assumption that new technology belongs in schools. New technology and American public education have always been linked by reformers as our primary means of progress, but more so today than ever before. Consider the variety of

[4]Astuto et al., 1994, p. 3

[5]Apple, 1998, p. 133

conflicting educational goals for which technology is advocated today. Whatever one seeks to change about schools, it is barely permissible to question the value of new technology as a means to the desired end. As Douglas Noble argues:

> The impact of computer-based education . . . is not to be found in an examination of the current, rather pedestrian, uses of computers in classrooms . . . the impact is to be found in fundamental reconceptualizations of human intelligence, thinking and learning . . . which have entered the schools alongside this technology, and which frame, as well, the latest directions in educational research.[6]

Unless education reformers question technology more carefully, they will be missing key issues that help explain why efforts to use it in schools turn out the way they do.

There are many common themes to be drawn out of the stories of the educational media discussed in this book. A look through contemporary educational technology journals, Web sites, and conference schedules suggest that what I call issues of implementation and execution—money, system configurations, teacher training—are the most important. Certainly they are important; no attempt to integrate new media into classroom practice can succeed without them. However, the near exclusive focus on them is misplaced because, until a number of other issues are identified and considered, these issues are more or less beside the point.

There is no shortage of publications or conversations about implementation or execution questions. In fact, they are far too numerous and multiplying too fast for any individual to keep up with them. For that reason, I have chosen to exclude them from this chapter and to focus instead on some of what I think is being overlooked. Following are several themes that recur in chapters 2 to 6, organized into four general categories, although these categories do overlap, and some ideas could as well be placed in one as in another. Surely readers will see other themes that are not included here. My purpose is primarily to open up the possibility of thinking differently about the relationship between new media and education, not to exhaust the topic in a single volume.

---

[6]Noble, 1991, pp. 6–7

IDEAS AND ASSUMPTIONS ABOUT TEACHERS
AND TEACHING

The stories of educational film through educational computing are full of ideas about how these media would change the nature of teachers' work by making them better at what they do or altering their relationships with students, administrators, parents, and each other. What is harder to locate, because it was rarely stated explicitly, is what teachers thought about those claims and how they chose to respond to them. What I would like to suggest is that teachers might have felt (and might feel today) a kind of ambivalence that is more complex than standard portrayals of teachers as Luddites permit.

First it is necessary to identify some of the common elements in these stories. A standard claim was that each new medium would make teachers better by providing them with interesting new ways to enhance their teaching. Film, radio, television, automated instruction, and contemporary digital media were all promoted for making lessons more exciting through some feature of the medium that made instruction snazzier than the teacher alone. Another popular claim for each medium was that it would help teachers by serving as a supplement in their weak areas because the film, radio, television, or distance learning teacher would be a master in those areas, or because the computer programmer would build into programs the content and/or the instructional methods the teacher did not know.

A hope expressed for each of these media is that its introduction into schools would professionalize teaching by enhancing the profession through state-of-the-art innovations and techniques. With film and radio, the media represented an effort on the part of educators to use the newest resources to enhance the latest developments in pedagogy and learning theory. Television and automated instruction were supposed to professionalize teaching by transferring the routine, mundane aspects of the job from teachers to machines, freeing teachers to focus on the more important and challenging aspects of their work. Automated instruction and digital media, to the extent that they embody theories of learning, have sometimes been said to require that teachers know more about educational psychology than they have typically known in the past. The expectation that teachers become highly technologically literate is also offered as a kind of professionalization of teaching.

However, an equally common theme throughout each of these stories is the belief that the new medium could be used to teacher proof the classroom. Film and broadcast media were frequently promoted as a way to spread out master teachers to larger student audiences and to replace classroom teachers in the process (although it was rarely described as replacement so much as enhancement). Television and automated instruction were developed in the heyday of curriculum revision focused on teacher proofing. Military research in televised and automated instruction literally and overtly sought to deskill teachers, standardize instruction, and reduce the time it took to train both students and instructors. Many contemporary software packages and integrated learning systems do their best to minimize the chance that a teacher will get in the way of student achievement.

It is difficult to know what teachers, on a whole, felt about these various claims about what new media could do for them. In each case, there are frequent promises that no one means to replace teachers, and yet in each case there are also expressions of fear on the part of teachers that they will be replaced by new media. Even if teacher replacement was never a dominant motive on the part of school reformers who promoted new media, it seems to have been on the minds of teachers—either as literal fear of job loss or as concern that the new medium would change the nature of their work in ways that would be dissatisfying to them and detrimental to their students and their relationship with them.

Although advocates of new educational technologies have always tended to stress that the teacher still has an important role to play, the effect of these technologies has often been to remove teachers from the instructional process or assign them a role that both devalues them and prevents students from learning effectively with new technologies. Technologists and teachers sometimes use the same language when they talk about the ways they would like to change education. However, what they mean can be quite different. For example, both tend to support the idea of the teacher as a coach or guide, but the kind of coach envisioned by technologists is too often a technician that simply helps students use the technology, not a person who selects technology (or some other resource) as a way to help students learn. In recent years, learning theorists have reemphasized the centrality of the teacher in student learning and in effective transfer of learning to new settings. Educational technologies have to be designed in such a way as to give teachers a meaningful role to play or students are not likely to learn much with those technologies that they will be able to bring with them to other situations.

Certainly there were many teachers who were excited about experimenting with a new resource as there are many enthusiastic teachers using new media today. However, the types of obstacles they tended to encounter suggest that new media might deskill teaching and take away teacher autonomy and professionalism at least as much as they offer teachers exciting new opportunities to enhance their work. For example, the scheduling problems associated with broadcast media (airing at the wrong time of day or year to be useful), film (where rentals could not always be obtained when needed, and films could not be shown in the classroom), and computers (where using labs or cycling an entire class around three or four classroom computers is a problem) all require that teachers adapt their practices to the restrictions of the technology, rather than providing them with a resource responsive to their needs. All of these media, when used to transmit content rather than to produce projects, deskill teachers by removing them from the production of curricular materials, which are instead delivered wholesale through the radio or TV broadcast, film, or software package. Rarely have teachers been brought into the production process in any substantive way.

This "separation of conception from execution," as Michael Apple calls it, is a problem in contemporary education generally and certainly with respect to educational technology. Technology has often been used to systematize instruction and break it down into its smallest components, making teachers merely the executors of a small part of a larger process without a clear sense of what it is or how they might have been brought in on conceptualizing it.[7] Although using technology might appear, even to teachers, to professionalize their work, it may merely add additional tasks onto an already difficult workload, thus creating a work speed-up that leaves teachers looking for shortcuts and ready-made solutions to their problems. In the process, they become more dependent on experts and prepackaged materials, rather than becoming more autonomous as skilled professionals. The degree to which this tendency is exacerbated by the standards movement makes the situation even more problematic. In *Education / Technology / Power: Educational Computing as a Social Practice*, Michael Apple and Susan Jungck (1998) describe the problem as follows:

---

[7]Skornia, 1955, p. 85

> The tendency for the curriculum increasingly to become planned, systematized, and standardized at a central level, totally focused on competencies measured by standardized tests, and largely dependent on predesigned commercial materials and texts written specifically for those states that have the tightest centralized control and, thus, the largest guaranteed markets, may have consequences exactly the opposite of what many authorities intend. Instead of professional teachers who care greatly about what they do and why they do it, we may have alienated executors of someone else's plans.[8]

As well intentioned as many promoters of standards may be, it is possible for their efforts to have the unintentional effect of further devaluing the teaching profession.

Although new educational media are often celebrated as tools for decentralization, a persistent problem with them is the tendency for them to be used to further centralize the curriculum, which poses a substantial threat to teachers' autonomy. First of all, if media content is to be commercially viable to those producing it, it must appeal to a large audience. It is nearly impossible for producers to adapt their products to the specific desires or requirements of a particular school or community. This problem emerged over and over again throughout the century, whether it was films that were too general to be useful or that came to town months before or after that unit had been taught; radio broadcasts on the right topic, but aired at the wrong time of year; or computer software that does not quite match the goals of a local curriculum. This push for national schools of the air, national distribution of films, nationally adopted programmed materials, and nationally marketed computer software all reflect a huge debate that has gone on in educational policy for generations—a debate over centralization versus local autonomy. The push for centralization has shown itself in the consolidation of school districts at the opening of the 20th century and the later development of comprehensive high schools, the creation of national and state learning standards and standardized tests, and a variety of other moves that assume that bigger is better. Technology has often been offered as the ideal facilitator of centralization particularly in terms of its potential use to manage complex bureaucracies.

---

[8]Apple and Jungck, 1998, p. 137

Another danger of the tendency to use technology for centralization is the invasion of privacy that comes with it, particularly where the computer is concerned. The record-keeping functions of automated instructional systems provided new ways to watch teachers and students and closely scrutinize classroom activities. Today the Internet activities of both teachers and students are often monitored to ensure that children are using the Internet safely and that teachers are not wasting taxpayers' money by goofing off at work. Internet browsers, depending on how they are configured, routinely store information about recently visited sites, and e-mail is not nearly as private as many people wish to believe. A number of recent court cases have had to do with school administrators or school boards possessing information about teachers' or students' online activities and taking disciplinary action based on that information.

Certainly there are computer-based activities that are inappropriate for teachers and/or students to engage in during school hours. However, the line between appropriate and inappropriate is not always clear, and teacher autonomy is jeopardized when they are not given adequate opportunity to make the choices they feel are appropriate for their students. Monitoring is particularly problematic when it becomes the norm, when teachers and students come to assume that they are always being watched. Howard Rheingold discusses the dangers of this "panoptic" climate, where, as in Jeremy Bentham's 1791 vision of the ultimate prison (the Panopticon), people are controlled by establishing in them the constant sense they are under surveillance even when they are not.[9] The work of Foucault, too, describes *panopticisim* and the ways in which the Panopticon "assures the automatic functioning of power."[10] The implication for teachers is that the more they feel they might be monitored by (often invisible) technology, the more they will lose any sense of autonomy they may have had, and the more hostile they are likely to be toward the introduction of new technology into schools.

In short, it seems likely that part of the reason that new media have not had the dramatic educational successes hoped for by their advocates relates to the fact that using them is a much more complex process for teachers than many of those advocates realize. For many teachers, the aggressive promotion of new technology may

---

[9]Rheingold, 1993
[10]Foucault, 1977, p. 201

represent a lack of understanding of, and respect for, their interests and concerns. Furthermore, the quality of educational media is often compromised by the relative absence of teachers in the planning, production, and insructional process. It seems almost too obvious to say that anything that is promoted as a *teacher proofer* is bound to be offensive to teachers. In *Teachers and Machines: The Classroom Use of Technology Since 1920*, Larry Cuban (1986) argued forcefully that teachers' use of technology cannot be understood without really thinking carefully about the nature of teachers' work, the reasons that teachers make the choices that they do, and the questions that teachers most often ask about technology. As obvious as it might seem that this kind of understanding is crucial, it is still lacking among many top–down education reformers.

School administrators across the nation scratch their heads, wondering why so many teachers make such little use of the computers at their disposal (or that appear to be at their disposal, but whose use is limited by a variety of obstacles). Rarely do those teachers overtly oppose the use of technology or speak openly against it. However, it is important to keep in mind that resistance can take many forms, one of which is inaction. As Michael Apple points out, "We need to remember that doing nothing is a form of action itself. Though it is not always the result of a set of conscious decisions, it can have serious consequences."[11] It may often be the case that teachers simply go on with their business without doing much with new technology because, consciously or otherwise, they recognize that it is not always in their best interests and it requires a huge investment of time and effort with unclear professional gains. Much of the nonuse of technology has likely been, and continues to be, a form of teacher resistance against centralization, control, and surveillance expressed in resistance to those machines that seem so often to embody such goals.

It should not be news that teachers want to be treated as professionals and that their commitment to any school reform is central to the success of that reform. John Dewey wrote nearly 100 years ago about the importance of giving teachers a central role in shaping reform efforts, lest they "remain an external thing to be externally applied to the child."[12] Yet the prevalence over the decades of top–down reform efforts and movements that originate (and substan-

---

[11]Apple, 1998, p. 154

[12]Dewey, 1969, pp. 30–31 (originally published 1904)

tially remain) apart from teachers suggests that this aspect of school reform is still inadequately acknowledged. Furthermore, acquiring the equipment and giving teachers basic training should be just the beginning, but is frequently the end of the support teachers receive. Researchers in the Apple Classrooms of Tomorrow project, one of the most comprehensive attempts to transform schools with technology, have discovered that massive infusion of technology into schools can help catalyze interesting changes, but that teachers need more support, not less, the farther they go with those changes.[13] The more teachers do with new technology, the more the entire character of the classroom experience changes—often for the better, but not without causing them a lot of anxiety about their changing role, and they need to be supported in a variety of ways as they make the transition.

IDEAS AND ASSUMPTIONS ABOUT STUDENTS AND LEARNING

Given that many of the claims about new media were about how they would change teaching and the relationship between teachers and students, it naturally follows that there were many popular arguments about how new media would change students and learning. First of all, advocates of each of the media discussed in chapters 2 to 6 believed that new media would democratize education by offering all students, regardless of their background or location, the best possible education. By placing instruction in a form that could be mass produced and widely disseminated, the hope was (and continues to be) that local inadequacies can be corrected and all children would have a chance at learning in ways previously available to only a privileged few.

Whether providing something a local teacher could not, or being used by a highly qualified teacher, each new medium was promoted for increasing student engagement. Each medium, in its entertainment form, was known to be loved by children, and some advocates hoped that children's enthusiasm for the medium would translate into enthusiasm for learning with it. Film, radio, and television were all promoted, in part, as ways of appealing to expanding school populations and ever-increasing numbers of noncollege-bound

[13]Fisher, Dwyer, and Yocam, 1996

high school students. Computer applications have frequently been promoted as ways of making learning more appealing to unmotivated students.

Advocates of educational technologies have often argued that learning is more effective when multiple senses, modalities, or learning styles are employed, and that the technology they are promoting can be used to that end. Radio and television provided a sense of immediacy. Film and television added images to words. Automated instruction and digital media allowed students to take their own individualized paths to learning. Computer simulations and interactive multimedia are said to have sensorimotor appeal and immerse learners in rich, inspiring microworlds.

In general, the belief throughout the century has been that new media are good motivators, that children find them appealing, and that children will therefore want to learn with them in school. They will come to school more faithfully and promptly, and they will learn more, better, and faster. Children will be more connected to the world outside the classroom because outside events will be brought in via new media. Automated systems will *trap* the unmotivated, tricking them into learning. New media will animate (literally or figuratively) the learning process, making the invisible visible, the unimaginable imaginable.

New media have been linked to learning theories of their day to the point that a substantial shift has taken place from using the medium to *support* a learning theory to believing that the medium *is* the learning theory. That is, media of the first half of the 20th century were sort of applied to learning theories after the fact, where media from the 1950s on were designed in the context of learning research and were used as models and metaphors for the learning process. Film and radio were often used to support child-centered progressive pedagogy in a variety of ways, discussed in chapters 2 and 3. Television was promoted apart from any particular learning theory of the time, its appeal being mainly to deliver instruction to as many students as possible in overcrowded schools. (Then again to the extent that the focus was on delivering ever-increasing quantities of information to students, the transmission of a TV signal *was* resonant with the idea of instruction as transmission—which, although not a learning theory per se, contains assumptions about how learning takes place.) In roughly the same era, automated instruction represented a major shift in the connection between learning theory and educational technology. Teaching machines had their origins in learning theories, in psychological research. The link between technology and learning theory was further strengthened during the development of cognitive science and was fully fused in the concept of "AI in reverse," or the use of computer simulations of human thought processes to be turned around and used to shape those process.

In *The Cult of Information*, Theodore Roszak (1994) argues that "no other teaching tool has ever brought intellectual luggage of so consequential a kind with it. A conception of mind—even if it is no better than a caricature—easily carries over into a prescription for character and value."[14] Although the firm link between learning theory and technology might result in the creation of cognitive tools that are more compatible for school use than earlier technologies, we must also avoid reifying those tools to the point that they inappropriately constrain the way we think about learning and learners. Again it is more important to provide an instructional setting where students learn with and from talented teachers than it is to design the ultimate cognitive tool, which however powerful it might be, cannot compensate for the absence of a good teacher. As Steven Talbott insists:

> The information that the child can receive from a Knowledge Machine—or any other source, including the encyclopedia—is hardly what matters. What counts is *from whom she receives it.* . . . Her need is not to gather facts, but to connect imaginatively with the world of the adult—and to find that her own lofty fantasy (which makes an animate toy of every stick or scrap of cloth) can progressively be instructed and elevated so as to harmonize with the adult's wisdom even while remaining true to itself.[15]

Learning researchers are currently placing a great deal of emphasis on the relationship between teachers and students, and on the role that relationship plays in learning. Designers of educational technology would do well to stay informed about this research and to incorporate its findings into their projects.

Another common theme running through the history of educational media is that they have been promoted for students of every imaginable ability level, learning style, or socioeconomic background. The actual results of the countless effectiveness studies that have

---

[14]Roszak, 1994, p. 241
[15]Talbott, 1995, p. 171

been performed over the decades are less important than the fact that new media have typically been tested on whatever student groups were in the limelight of educational policy when a particular medium was being tested. For that reason, it is impossible to tell a consistent story about who seems to be most benefited by educational media because children were sorted into different experimental categories in different eras. For example, the 1950s were years when there was a heightened interest in knowing if new media helped gifted students. Shortly thereafter, the attention shifted to the culturally deprived child. The larger point here is that whatever students are capturing the attention of education reformers will be the focus of effectiveness studies of new educational media.

While these media have been promoted for their educational benefits, there have been underlying fears that they have negative effects on children, that they foster behaviors or habits of mind that are antithetical to what is expected of them in school. These concerns address the issue not only of the relationship between teachers and students, but more generally between adults and children. Each of these media frightened adults, who believed that the new medium of their age had some kind of damaging effect on children. Film corrupted children's morals and damaged their health; radio gave them bad taste in music and overstimulated them through action-packed serials; television lured them away from books and brought sex and violence right into their living rooms; and computers made them antisocial. Today the Internet is seen as a land where predators lurk waiting for the opportunity to victimize children. It puts adult secrets in full view of children. It serves as a mouthpiece for anyone who wishes to be heard, including those who promote hatred and violence.

These fears about media, and the belief that schools have an obligation to protect children by somehow immunizing them against the dangerous influences of media, have deep roots. The 19th century superintendents who sought to purge their schools' libraries of pernicious novels were acting on essentially the same fear as those administrators today who put filtering software on all school computers. As long as Americans have thought of children as different from adults, and therefore as deserving of special protection from the evils and perils of adult life, they have wanted schools to participate in the sheltering of children from information deemed inappropriate for the young. Ambivalence on the part of adults about the effects of media on children has always influenced the way those media are used in schools.

Teachers and students, teaching and learning cannot be discussed in a vacuum. What they do is greatly affected by the prevailing ideas about what public education is for and about whose interests are to be served by schools. For that reason, it is also important to look at the ways in which a variety of external interests have influenced the path that the story of educational technology has taken.

IDEAS AND ASSUMPTIONS ABOUT THE PURPOSES OF SCHOOLING, AND WHO DECIDES WHAT THOSE PURPOSES WILL BE

It should be a given that it is impossible to know how new media fit into schools without first deciding what public education is for. The question "What are schools for?" is a deceptively complex one, and one that, when explored in any depth, reveals a variety of possible answers. As a result, those with an interest in having their purposes served by public education have always vied with one another for control over school practices. George Counts expressed it well enough in 1934 for his words to remain relevant today:

> . . . the school has become a major social institution and one of society's most powerful agencies of propaganda. That rival groups should strive to possess it is entirely to be expected. The curriculum at any moment is to some extent a resultant of the play of these battling forces upon the school—professional educators within and conflicting interests without.[16]

In particular, the promotion of educational media has often had something to do with military, government, and/or corporate interests as much as—or more than—it has had to do with the enhancement of the classroom experiences of teachers or students.

It is sometimes difficult to identify the underlying motives for introducing new media into schools in part because new media are often presented as their own rationale for school reform. That is, technological change is frequently named as the reason that new technologies belong in schools. It is presented as good, basic common sense to technologize the classroom. However, a deeper examination of the origins of those technologies, and the purposes they might be

---

[16]Counts, 1934, p. 272

used to advance, reveals questionable motives for their implementation in schools.

First, it should be clear by now that the U.S. military has been deeply involved in American educational technology for a long time, with their active involvement beginning with the use of training films (and, to a lesser extent, radio) during World War II and subsequent research on film and television as training media. As documented in some detail in chapters 5 and 6, the military was pivotal in the postwar psychological research that produced automated instruction and later forms of computer-based education. Douglas Noble sums it up well:

> . . . military research in "human engineering" has been the prime incubator, catalyst, and sponsor of educational technology throughout this century—from the classification and selection tests of World War I, to the programmed instruction and teaching machines of the 1960s, to the most sophisticated, computer-based "intelligent" tutoring systems of today.[17]

Although these media applications vary widely, they can all be seen as carrying some aspect of the military ethos into education. In one way or another, their military influence or origins are evident in the many uses of these media that focus on efficiency and economy, the conception of teaching as training, and enabling the student (the trainee) to self-instruct as a means of streamlining the functioning of the larger system.

The military influence on public education is intertwined with government influence, particularly in terms of foreign policy issues. Federal involvement in education, particularly during the cold war, was directly related to national security concerns. The educational technologies emerging from military laboratories, or from projects conducted under military contract, were often applied to school contexts with those questions of national security in mind.

Government and military interest are both related to economic interests in schools, particularly in an age where technology is central to the nation's economy. Douglas Noble describes how

> Education is increasingly being viewed in terms of its contribution to the viability of the American economy, and particularly to the efficient and productive utilization of the technological apparatus that is the centerpiece of that economy; thus, the military

---

[17]Noble, 1991, p. 2

prerogatives shaping economic and technology policy are indirectly shaping educational policy as well.[18]

From the publication of *A Nation at Risk*, with what Michael Katz refers to as its "slightly more than thirty pages of military metaphors,"[19] to the present day, national security is seen as being threatened by the demands of a global information economy, and American schools are frequently accused of failing to prepare their graduates to compete in that economy. However narrowly that report might have presented the purpose of public education (as James Carey argues, "We are told rather often these days that our nation is at risk, but the only risks that interest anyone are economic and military ones"[20]), its tendency toward hyperbole was frightening enough to many Americans as to trigger greatly intensified attacks on schools. This anxiety created an opportunity for corporate interests to move into schools to an unprecedented degree.

Conflicts over commercializing the classroom can be traced much farther back than *A Nation at Risk*. As described in chapters 2 and 3, conflicts over the appropriateness of involving commercial film makers and radio broadcasters in educational ventures created intensely bad feelings among those interested in using film and radio in schools and often divided them into separate (and competing) factions. Commercially produced programmed instruction materials were frequently criticized for sacrificing quality of content for profitability. "Free and inexpensive materials" have been made available to schools for decades, providing product samples, coupons, and pro-industry brochures and instructional aids.

Contemporary corporate influence in schools takes a variety of forms. One involves the training of the workforce and the desire on the part of employers that schools provide that training. Generally, the argument goes that jobs of the future will require a high level of technological skills, and that it is the responsibility of schools to provide students with those skills. The cost benefit to employers of this conception of schooling is clear, but the rationale is questionable. For all the talk that future jobs will require complex skills, there is also evidence that most jobs will be relatively low skill or that do not require any preparation or education in advance of being hired.

[18]Noble, 1991, p. 2
[19]Katz, 1987, p. 130
[20]Carey, 1997, p. 293

According to the Bureau of Labor Statistics, although computer engineer is currently considered the fastest growing occupation (with 299,000 jobs in 1998 and a projected 622,000 by 2008), among the 10 occupations with the largest projected job growth are retail salespeople, cashiers, truck drivers, and personal care and home health aides, with 2008 projections of 4,620,000, 3,354,000, 3,463,000, and 1,179,000, respectively.[21] More jobs of 2008 are predicted to require "short-term, on-the-job training" than any other kind of preparation, with "moderate-term, on-the-job training" coming in second.[22]

What then is the point of organizing education around high-tech skills? James Carey argues:

> There is, in short, hardly anything revolutionary in the effect of computerization upon employment except to make the conditions of work generally less satisfactory, and computer education hardly presents a challenge to education except in preparation of relatively small numbers of mind workers in computer science. This hardly provides a warrant for reshaping education in the image of computer literacy.[23]

Although the information industries might not have as many high-skill jobs in the future as we would be led to believe, they have a clear interest in having a presence in schools. For these industries, American public schools are a huge market for their products and services, as well as a means to build credibility and brand loyalty. Besides their interest in selling computers, telecommunications services, and software to schools, these industries hope that the presence of their products in schools will lead to purchases for home use as well. Perhaps the push to increase students' technological skills is less about preparing them for jobs and more about inspiring schools to purchase new technology—which, in turn, intimidates parents into making purchases of their own, lest their children's scholastic achievement fall behind that of their computer-owning classmates. In much the same way that some educational radio programs were advertisements, of sorts, designed to increase home sales of radio sets, the use of a particular brand of computer or software program is desirable to the industries producing them because that use might

---

[21]http://stats.bls.gov/news.release/ecopro.t07.htm

[22]http://stats.bls.gov/news.release/ecopro.t04.htm

[23]Carey, 1997, p. 298

translate into further profit. *Why* children use technology in schools is less important, from this perspective, than *that* they use it.

Commercial interest in educational technology is not confined to those industries with products to sell in or through schools. New media are also a popular way for all kinds of industries and interest groups to bring their messages into schools. For example, free or inexpensive Internet access is sometimes provided to schools through services that place advertising on the Web sites students will use, often further requiring that schools guarantee a certain number of hours of student exposure to those ads and/or a minimum number of students exposed. Classroom materials that have been produced for decades by companies marketing products to children are now distributed via Web sites. For example, the Web site for M&M's candy provides pie charts showing the proportions of each M&M's color in a typical package and lessons on how to teach probability through student use of M&M's packages.

A more elaborate chocolate undertaking comes from Hershey Foods, the teacher section of whose Web site offers an entire interdisciplinary, middle-school curriculum centering around Hershey chocolate. Among the goals of one unit in the Hershey program are for students to "describe chocolate's place in a well-balanced diet" and "make a favorite chocolate snack or dessert"; teachers are reminded that "Flavored milk, such as chocolate, is well liked by children and helps to increase milk and nutrient intake."[24] In 1934, Arthur E. Morgan, chair of the Tennessee Valley Authority, expressed his concern about the dangers of commercial involvement schools—dangers that, at that point, he felt had been averted:

> Suppose our public schools had been established on a purely commercial basis. . . . There might be no charge to the public for our public schools; the teaching staff might be supplied by the toothpaste manufacturers or patent medicine manufacturers . . . and they would have textbooks describing the values of toothpaste or patent medicine.[25]

Although his scenario was meant to be regarded as ludicrous, it is not far from many contemporary commercial schemes to tap into a lucrative market and a captive audience of schoolchildren.

---

[24]www.herseys.com/consumer/teacher/dream_machine/index.html
[25]Morgan, 1934, p. 81

These criticisms are not meant to imply that new media have no place in schools or that those who are helping to get new media into schools have no benevolent motives. Rather, they are meant as a reminder that, despite the apparent neutrality of much policy talk advocating the increased use of educational technology, there are often powerful agendas behind it—agendas that promote particular conceptions of public education that have important implications for American society.

IDEAS AND ASSUMPTIONS ABOUT TECHNOLOGY AND TECHNOLOGICAL PROGRESS

One of the standard arguments in favor of bringing new media into schools is that technological change demands it. Technology is transforming how we live, work, play, interact, worship, and so forth, and so schools must undergo the technological transformation as well. Every medium discussed in this book was promoted for school use, in part, because reformers believed that technological change required school reform. Either the new technology seemed to have something to offer teaching, learning, or administration or it needed to be brought into schools to tame its dangerous influences on children, or it was changing the world outside schools so much that schools had to respond or be rendered obsolete. Whatever the particular claim, the general idea has always been that technologies are powerful things, and their power will be felt in schools for good or ill.

It is ironic, then, that one of the most popular claims made by educational technology advocates is that new technology is just a tool. *It's just a tool* is generally used as a preemptive strike against a variety of anticipated accusations: teachers are sitting back while computers do their jobs for them, the school is becoming a dehumanizing place, that everything's been turned topsy-turvy by the introduction of new technology into the classroom. It is typically an expression used by teachers and principals to soothe the nerves of parents and skeptical colleagues and reassure them that everything is okay—that they are all still in the same business they have always been in only now they have something new and exciting at their disposal. Despite its apparently transformative powers in all other aspects of life, and the use of those transformations as rationales for bringing it into schools, in education new technology is presented as simply one more way to make education better in whatever way its users wish to mobilize it to that end.

When applied to education, new media are typically presented as neutral tools, with no biases or predispositions of their own or of their creators. However, the form of any medium structures in a particular way what is expressed through that medium, which affects the meanings we make when using that medium. (Anyone doubtful that the content of a message is affected by the medium used to convey it should imagine the difference among learning of the death of a loved one through, say, a face-to-face conversation, a message on an answering machine, and a TV broadcast. The content of the message—"Your loved one has died"—is more or less the same, but the way that message is understood, processed, and responded to is likely to be different in each case.)

Some scholars attribute the biases of media to the media themselves (i.e., the form of a medium is believed to alter information configurations, power structures, and, therefore, social institutions in ways that individuals in the media environment cannot entirely predict or control). Others think more in terms of the ways in which those in power are in a position to build their own purposes and biases into new media, whereas others remain unaware or incapable of changing the course of events. A combination of these two views is probably most appropriate, envisioning media as environments that act on their inhabitants and on which those inhabitants act—often in the hope of securing or maintaining power or otherwise realizing their goals. In any case, the key to avoiding falling into a cynical determinism—surrendering either to the power of technology those who control it—is a heightened awareness of the media environment and how individuals and groups participate in shaping it. As Hank Bromley writes, "the attributes built into the technology do not fully determine how it may be used and to whose benefit."[26] Still "the environment in which a technology is developed—especially the power relations prevailing there—does nonetheless instill in the technology traits that favor some uses (and beneficiaries) rather than others."[27] What is important, then, is to maintain or restore a sense of human agency in technological change.

---

[26]Bromley, 1998, p. 13

[27]Bromley, 1998, p.13

This sense that a particular course of technological development is *not* inevitable is fostered, in large part, by knowledge of historical context, which exposes the path a technology took on its way to becoming whatever appears today to be its logical or natural form. Douglas Noble makes a good case for being aware of historical context:

> The perspectives embodied in a technology reflect a history of decisions made throughout the development of the technology, decisions influenced, more often than not, by the particular goals of those parties or institutions with the resources and the power to determine the shape of the technology. . . . Thus, some technologies get developed while others do not, and those that do are shaped by particular interests and by the historical and political circumstances surrounding their development.[28]

Looking historically at the development of a technology helps reveal the debates that surrounded its development and the tone of the times in which it seemed to be a viable solution to a perceived problem. It sometimes shows how different groups responded in different ways depending on whose problem was being solved and what the consequences might be. When looking only at what a mature technology has become, it is difficult to know how it came to be what it is. Still the path it took helps to shape the uses to which it can now be put and the interests it can effectively serve. As John Broughton argues, "Material products of human labor contain the policies through which they were intentionally constituted, whether those subjective purposes ever reach consciousness or not."[29]

Specific to education, it is important to think not only about whose knowledge may be privileged by one or another educational medium's form or content, but what kinds of learning and what ways of knowing are favored. Discussions of the *hidden curriculum* allude to the biases of media, but do not always directly address them, generally focusing more on issues like the physical organization of schools and the implicit messages of the rules and procedures governing the school day. Broughton, however, describes how "instrumentation such as that provided by computer technology exemplifies a particular curricular and pedagogical orientation."[30] The classroom

[28]Noble, 1991, p. 4

[29]Broughton, 1984, p. 103

[30]Broughton, 1984, p. 103

media environment has particular epistemological biases, and changing that environment will change those biases as well. Whether and
how that environment should be changed is a complex question—
should the school's symbolic environment be brought more in line
with that of the world outside schools or should schools be thermostatic, providing the counterargument to the dominant culture?[31] The
answer to such a question can only be derived from a kind of discussion of education and technology that has yet to adequately take
place.

Marshall McLuhan was aware of the short sightedness of
most talk about education and technology:

> Had any of our current testers of media and various educational
> aids been available to the harassed sixteenth century administra-
> tor they would have been asked to find out whether the new
> teaching machine, the printed book, could do the full educational
> job. . . . Using the methods the testers now use for radio, film, and
> TV, our testers would have reported in due course: "Yes, strange
> and repugnant as it may sound to you, the new teaching
> machines enable students to learn as much as before. Moreover,
> they seem to have more confidence in the new method as giving
> them the means of acquiring many new kinds of knowledge."

The testers, that is to say, would have entirely missed the character
of the new machine.[32]

Once again discussions of new educational media tend to
revolve around questions of effectiveness, impact on test scores, and
curriculum delivery. That is to say, people having these discussions
today have, like their predecessors, entirely missed the character of
the new machine. Rather than trying to determine what the medium
offers in the way of enhancing learning differently than what is possible with other symbolic forms, they focus on the relative effectiveness of moving information via one medium as opposed to another.

As on many matters, John Dewey seemed to recognize
decades earlier what McLuhan expressed in the prior quote. Dewey
seemed to clearly understand the difference between the overt message that comes from the content of communication and the implicit
message that comes from the means through which the content is
conveyed. Early in the 20th century, Dewey foreshadowed McLuhan

[31]Postman, 1979

[32]McLuhan, 1962b, p. 177

in his ability to distinguish between the form and content of the medium of school and his sensitivity to the invisible, but powerful, communicative or educative influence of one's surroundings:

> . . . in general it may be said that the things which we take for granted without inquiry or reflection are just the things which determine our conscious thinking and decide our conclusions. . . . We never educate directly, but indirectly by means of the environment.[33]

Dewey was aware of the ways in which the technological changes of his time were challenging the monopoly that print had held on education. His writings on education predate the massive growth of film, radio, television, and computers, but he was already noticing that electronic media were altering the information environment in ways that called into question the print bias of traditional schooling—a type of education whose means and ends rested in the book and in the cultivation of typographic habits of mind. In *The School and Society*, Dewey wrote that, "our school methods, and to a very considerable extent our curriculum, are inherited from a period when learning and command of certain symbols, affording as they did the only access to learning, were all-important."[34] He saw that access to knowledge was no longer confined to print media, and so he challenged the absolute authority of print in schools.

Part of Dewey's concern was that, over the centuries, the volume and complexity of what was to be learned had grown to the point that most of it was learned indirectly by means of symbol systems that, by definition, are removed from direct experience:

> Much of our experience is indirect; it is dependent upon signs which intervene between the things and ourselves, signs which stand for or represent the former. . . . All language, all symbols, are implements of an indirect experience; in technical language the experience which is procured by their means is "mediated." It stands in contrast with an immediate, direct experience, something in which we take part vitally and at first hand, instead of through the intervention of representative media.[35]

---

[33]Dewey, 1916, p. 22

[34]Dewey, 1976, p. 17 (originally published 1899)

[35]Dewey, 1916, pp. 271-272

Dewey recognized that these media had the capacity to "enlarge the range of purely immediate experience and give it deepened as well as wider meaning by connecting it with things which can only be signified or symbolized."[36] However, he also understood the tradeoff involved in mediated experience, particularly in terms of print's hold on education:

> . . . there is always a danger that symbols will not be truly representative; danger that instead of really calling up the absent and remote in a way to make it enter a present experience . . . media of representation will become an end in themselves. Formal education is peculiarly exposed to this danger, with the result that when literacy supervenes, mere bookishness, what is popularly termed the academic, too often comes with it.[37]

Fifty years later, McLuhan expressed a similar sentiment when he argued that, "it is a matter of the greatest urgency that our educational institutions realize that we now have civil war among these environments created by media other than the printed word."[38] He understood Dewey's attempts "to dislodge the school from the . . . idea of it as immediate adjunct to the press and as the supreme processor or hopper through which the young and all their experience must pass in order to be available for 'use.'"[39] McLuhan wrote of Dewey:

> In our time John Dewey worked to restore education to its primitive, pre-print phase. He wanted to get the student out of the passive role of consumer of uniformly packaged learning. In fact, Dewey in reacting against passive print culture was surf-boarding along on the new electronic wave. That wave has now rolled right over this age.[40]

Now nearly 40 years after McLuhan wrote of the electronic wave rolling over us and our schools, there is still little understanding as to precisely what that means for schools or what they might or should do differently as a result. For that matter, most people have

---

[36]Dewey, 1916, p. 272
[37]Dewey, 1916, p. 272
[38]McLuhan, 1967, p. 100
[39]McLuhan, 1962b, p. 176
[40]McLuhan, 1962b, p. 178

little sense of how schools are, in many ways, products of print media and typographic habits of mind. In *Ramus, Method, and the Decay of Dialogue: From the Art of Discourse to the Art of Reason*, Walter Ong (1958) describes how Peter Ramus, the 16th century French professor and textbook writer, found in the medium of print the opportunity to systematize knowledge in ways that are still the basis of textbook organization. Living, as he did, in an age that was making the transition from the manuscript to the printed book, he took advantage of print's potential to organize information spatially and uniformly from copy to copy, organizing subjects into hierarchies and methodically arranging them in books.[41] Robert Logan (1986) also acknowledges Ramus' contribution to contemporary conceptions of mass education in *The Alphabet Effect*, describing how books were different from manuscripts, in that books could serve as effective "teaching machines" upon which mass education could be based.[42] In *No Sense of Place: The Impact of Electronic Media on Social Behavior*, Joshua Meyrowitz (1985) describes further how public education derives much of its form from the dominant medium of the age in which it was conceived:

> The idea of stages and sequences of texts was an innovation that followed the spread of printing. Education in oral cultures involves relatively few "sequences" of courses and little separation of people into many different groups based on age and years of learning. School systems in literate societies, however, are usually designed to divide people into groups based on differences in reading ability.[43]

He goes on to describe how graded schools are "closely related to the informational characteristics of print. Print allows for information segregation and gradation."[44] Granted, print is not the only medium that permits or encourages this methodical, standardized, hierarchical organization of information; it was also a hallmark of automated instruction, whether in the form of books, teaching machines, or CAI programs. Still it is important to consider how a medium configures information in a particular way, and might influence the character of educational institutions and practices.

---

[41]Ong, 1958

[42]Logan, 1986, p. 216

[43]Meyrowitz, 1985, p. 78

[44]Meyrowitz, 1985, p. 254

McLuhan claimed that "Peter Ramus and John Dewey were
the two educational surfers or wave-riders of antithetic periods, the
Gutenberg and the Marconi or electronic."[45] He felt that, "just as
Dewey, in a very confused way, was trying to explain the meaning of
the electronic age to educators, Ramus had a new program for all phases of education in the sixteenth century."[46] However, where Ramus'
reforms took hold and are still deeply embedded in public education as
we know it today, Dewey's attempts to change schools to match the
changing media environment were markedly less successful.

Dewey's interest in adjusting education in light of media
change, and his insistence that schools be agents of social reform, are
a pair of ideas that work together powerfully. With them in mind, it
is possible to conceive of a different relationship between technology
and schools—namely, there should be a way for schools to acknowledge and understand technology in its larger social context and to
prepare students to live in a world characterized by significant technological change. In all of the hustle to prepare children for this
information age that appears to be on us, and in all the various ways
that such preparation is imagined, new media have been embraced
as an important part of the answer to an urgent problem. Meanwhile
only occasional lip service is paid to the larger question of who and
what we are becoming in the process of being made over by technological change. The typical responses of educational institutions to
technological change focus on accommodating students to a changing
world, either by teaching them computer skills or utilizing new technologies to increase the quantity or quality of their knowledge in
accordance with the apparent demands of the age. It is reasonable to
argue that schools have to be in keeping with their times, but there
should be a way to be so that does not resign itself to change without
offering criticism or resistance. Indeed no school is truly preparing its
students for the information age without providing them with the
means both to understand the character of such an age, and to
redress its deficiencies.

Discussions of educational media seem stuck at the level of
execution of how and where to set things up, who needs training, and
how to pay for it all. What is neglected is more broad thinking about
what the new medium is doing in schools in the first place, whose

[45]McLuhan, 1962b, p. 176

[46]McLuhan, 1962b, p. 178

interests are served by its implementation, and whether the whole thing is worthwhile in the context of a well-formed educational philosophy that conceives of schools as serving some important social purpose. Until it is clear what schools are for, it is impossible to know what role new media can play in the service of education. There is no question that matters of execution need huge amounts of time and attention; otherwise new media projects are doomed. However, those matters cannot be addressed in a reasonable way until it is clear *why* the projects are being undertaken in the first place, and that comes around to the fundamental question of what American public education is for. Michael Apple argues of technology and education that "it is more than a little important that we question whether the wagon we have been asked to ride on is going in the right direction. It's a long walk back."[47] To the extent that technological change cannot be undone, it is a one-way trip.

It is also important to understand that technology is not merely the means to an end in schools, although it is frequently argued to be just that. If schools are to be meaningfully connected to society, then educators need not only to have a clear sense of what they think the relationship between schools and society should be, but what technological change means for all of society's institutions. That can only be understood if technology is regarded not simply as the means to an end in schools or as one or more machines with which students must achieve proficiency, but as the subject of inquiry and criticism in its own right.

---

[47]Apple, 1988, p. 174

AFTERWORD

We need education for a real and thorough cultural literacy and a
real and thorough public purpose. Plans to save education via
technology reveal a deep and pervasive nostalgia for the future: a
desire to escape and outrun our problems by the simple turning
of the wheel of technological progress.

> —James Carey, "Salvation by Machines: Can
> Technology Save Education?" (1997)

The long-standing American belief in improvability does not seem to
be accompanied by a sense that we need to know where we have been
to forge a path ahead. Despite exhortations from a variety of scholars
in education, history, media studies, and cultural criticism, American
talk about the future continues to inadequately reference the past.
Apple Classrooms of Tomorrow researcher Decker F. Walker
describes how this attitude works against the goal of school reform:

> As a society, we squander the limited resources available for
> innovation in education by overinvesting in the search for the
> next revolution and underinvesting in efforts to learn from and
> build on the achievements of the last one. In this never-ending

ideological struggle no one has an incentive to look back, to study
their failures, to salvage what worked, to fix what didn't, and to
avoid making the same mistake next time.[1]

When it comes to thinking about education and, in particular,
about educational technology, it is crucial to have a sense of historical context. As described in chapter 7, much of what is today considered commonplace and natural in public education, constituting the
hidden curriculum, was not hidden at all when it was new. Ignorance
of those early days enables people today to believe that such changes
took place without struggle or resistance—that they were either
desirable to all or so powerful as to be inevitable regardless of their
desirability. Either way, such a view removes us as citizens from any
active role in determining what is to be, leaving it instead to the tide
of technology or the wishes of the powerful.

With respect to education, situating technology talk in the
context in which it took place reveals the ways in which ideas about
technology tend to be isomorphic with ideas about curriculum, pedagogy, and learning. Debates about new educational media are often
couched within debates about what should be taught and how it
should be taught, what schools are for and who should decide. Media
and education are also alike in that both are expected to be agents of
American progress—to "redeem modernity," to use Joli Jensen's
phrase. Jensen describes how ideas about modernity include hopes
that the age offers unprecedented promise for progress as well as
fears of unprecedented alienation and misery. Media and education
both are looked to as a means of realizing the promise of modernity;
when they fail, they are blamed for the shortcomings of modern life.
Jensen argues:

> "Education" has at least as complex and contradictory a location
> as "the mass media" in American social thought. Both institutions
> serve as touchstones for unresolved hopes and fears, and thus
> there are parallel charges, and tensions, in the criticism of both.[3]

A particularly interesting interaction between media theory
and education studies is related to James Carey's distinction between

---

[1]Walker, 1996, p. 97

[2]Jensen, 1990

[3]Jensen, 1990, pp. 154–155

the transmission and the ritual function of communication. Where the transmission function of communication focuses on moving messages accurately from sender to receiver, across space, the ritual function is concerned more with binding a culture together through time. Carey explains:

> A ritual view of communication is directed not toward the extension of messages in space but the maintenance of society in time (even if some find this maintenance characterized by domination and therefore illegitimate); not the act of imparting information or influence but the creation, representation, and celebration of shared even if illusory beliefs. If a transmission view of communication centers on the extension of messages across geography for purposes of control, a ritual view centers on the sacred ceremony that draws persons together in fellowship and commonality.[4]

Carey is concerned that American society, with its long-standing emphasis on the transmission function of communication, is in need of a revitalization of the ritual function. In particular, he sees ritual communication as crucial in the restoration of civic life and democratic participation.

The tension between the transmission and ritual purposes of communication is clearly evident in debates education in general and educational technology in particular. Debates about the purpose of public schooling often come around to the question of which is more important: the transmission of content or the establishment of a sense of community. Joli Jensen describes the distinction:

> . . . the contradiction between ritual and transmission views of communication appears also in education, supporting a tension between views of education as socialization (the creation and maintenance of group life) and knowledge acquisition (the absorption of a body of necessary information).[5]

A great deal of talk about educational technology throughout the 20th century has focused on its potential to deliver the content of the curriculum more effectively than more conventional methods of instruction. Advocates of educational technologies have generally had less to say about how those technologies can support community

---

[4]Carey, 1989, p. 43

[5]Jensen, 1990, p. 155

building and strengthen the relationships between a student and the other people involved in that student's learning experiences. Yet learning theorists are once again asserting the primacy of the social context of learning and the relationships between students and their teachers. No matter how effectively a technology can move content, it is not effectively learned by students outside the context of a social environment that has been well cared for by a skilled teacher. That is to say, the preoccupation with transmission at the expense of attention to the ritual function of communication and instruction pretty much guarantees that new technologies, despite their potential to support learning, are not likely to be used effectively to that end.

Calls for this kind of shift in focus are hardly new. A century ago, John Dewey stressed the need for education to focus more on its ritual function. Susan Barnes and Lance Strate describe how Dewey, through his emphasis on experience, discovery, and the connection of schools to communities, "sought to retrieve elements of oral culture's dispersal of the educational function throughout society, and of chirographic culture's reliance upon discourse and dialogue as opposed to texts."[6] Dewey's insistence that the school serve the purpose of social criticism and improvement was also consistent with his emphasis on the ritual function of communication. He was critical of pedagogues who regarded language as merely the means for transmitting information:

> At present we lose much of the value of literature and language studies because of our elimination of the social element. Language is almost always treated in the books of pedagogy simply as the expression of thought. . . . but it is fundamentally and primarily a social instrument. Language is the device for communication; it is the tool through which one individual comes to share the ideas and feelings of other. When treated simply as a way of getting individual information, or as a means of showing off what one has learned, it loses its social motive and end.[7]

His contemporary, George Counts, had similar views on the relatively impoverished quality of a transmission-focused conception of education:

> A fact never to be forgotten is that education, taken in its entirety, is by no means an exclusively intellectual matter. It is not

---

[6]Barnes and Strate, 1996, p. 188

[7]Dewey, 1997, p. 21 (originally published 1929)

merely, or perhaps even primarily, a process of acquiring facts and becoming familiar with ideas. The major object of education since the beginning of time has been the induction of the immature individual into the life of the group.[8]

A central purpose of American public education has always been the cultivation of citizens capable of making sound decisions in a democracy. What constitutes education in a democratic nation, however, has always been a subject of debate. For example: Is education more democratic if it provides the same experience for all students, or if it tailors experiences according to individual differences? Is education equal if all students have the same opportunities or only if all students reach the same level of achievement? Similarly, the transmission and ritual views of communication and education offer different conceptions of a democratic education. If one adheres to a transmission view, then the goal is to provide equal and ample access to information for all citizens. Education is amply democratized so long as everyone has access to the information they need. To a degree, enthusiasm over film, radio, and TV's potential to bring the best teachers to all students (and the reiteration of that hope today with respect to distance learning) reflect this view. So did the curriculum reform movement of the 1950s and 1960s and the teacher-proof automated systems that emerged from it. In general, reforms that regard teachers primarily as conduits of curricular content, and that seek to reduce noise in that conduit or improve the quality of message delivery, are in keeping with this view.

By contrast, a ritual view would focus on the role of shared experience in learning and on the role of teachers in supporting learning regardless of the materials or machinery employed. It would conceive of schools as preparatory institutions for later participation in democratic life—as places where people come together to learn how to ask (and answer) questions about their society, identify its key problems, and imagine and implement solutions.

It is conceivable that new technologies could be used toward these ends. However, it is more often the case that the assumptions implicit in educational technology talk are less about community building and democratic participation than they are about narrowly conceived technical solutions to equally narrowly conceived problems.

---

[8]Counts, 1934, p. 536

Such a focus provides a convenient distraction from the deeper (non-technological) problems of public education, and the complex (and probably nontechnological) solutions to them. For example, it is much easier for politicians and policymakers to talk about—and follow through on—wiring schools in poor neighborhoods to the Internet than to figure out ways to address the social inequality that produced those neighborhoods. James Carey argues that,

> The purpose of modern technology is not to reconstruct democracy. From the outset it is designed to exercise more effective control over the population. Therefore, it should not surprise us that the current movement to save education with a new generation of technology is also a sustained attack upon democracy and democratic institutions.[9]

Redirecting technology toward democratic ends, in schools and otherwise, would require that Americans rethink their relationship with their machines. Jensen describes how "technology embodies progress in American social thought, rather than being seen as a means to achieve desired political, economic, social, and cultural changes."[10] The satellite dish on top of the school, or the mere installation of a computer lab, has become a powerful symbol of educational excellence regardless of the purpose to which those technologies are put. Until we demythologize technology—until we make it problematic—it will continue to elicit this type of response, and its trajectory will remain out of our control.

George S. Counts emphasized that schools should never imply that the nation's work toward building a democracy is completed:

> If the school is to function at all in the betterment of the social order, it must expose pitilessly and clearly the shortcomings in contemporary society. It should never convey the impression that the democratic ideal has been fulfilled in the United States.[11]

Similarly, schools should expose—pitilessly and clearly—the shortcomings of technology. Neil Postman advocates a form of technology education not as it is typically conceived—that is, as training in the use of machines and in accommodating oneself to those machines—

[9]Carey, 1997, p. 301
[10]Jensen, 1990, p. 96
[11]Counts, 1934, p. 552

but as a branch of the humanities—an inquiry into the social, political, and moral implications of technological change.[12] In that sense,
technology education would serve what he earlier referred to as a
thermostatic function—it would provide a counterargument to the
technological dominance of American culture.[13] Naturally, as in all
cases when schools are called on to correct the deficiencies of a society, it is unrealistic to believe that a rigorous, thermostatic technology education, by itself, would dramatically change the direction or
character of technological change or its impact on American society.
However, Postman argues that, "it is well to remember that in
designing a thermostatic education, what one is trying to control is
not which set of biases will win the competition but what the score
will be. The narrower the margin, the better."[14]

  The classroom media environment is a complicated one where
technological change reveals itself to be a complex process. This environment is shaped by people in schools and by people with an interest in schools. It is also affected by schools' firm grounding in the
book, and in the epistemological biases of print media. Decisions
about how—and whether—to change the media environment of
schools need to take into account these types of issues, recognizing
the beliefs, assumptions, and aspirations that Americans have
embedded into their schools and their technologies for as long as they
have had both. At the least, placing the present situation in its historical context reminds us that we are not the first to struggle with
the question of how technology and schools fit together. It shows us
how we got to where we are. Finally, it helps us set a meaningful
agenda for the discussions that we are bound to have, and that we
will need to have, on this topic in the future.

---

[12]Postman, 1995

[13]Postman, 1979

[14]Postman, 1979

REFERENCES

Ackerman, J., & Lipsitz, L. (Eds.). (1977). *Instructional television: Status and directions*. Englewood Cliffs, NJ: Educational Technology Publications.

Adams, H. (1999). *The education of Henry Adams*. New York: Oxford University Press. (Original publication 1918)

Advisory Committee on Education By Radio. (1930). *Report of the Advisory Committee on Education By Radio*. Columbus, OH: F.J. Heer Printing Co.

The American School of the Air. (1930, March). *The Instructor, 39*(5), 6-7.

American School of the Air enlarges program. (1930, October). *The Instructor, 39*(10), 15-16.

Among the producers. (January, 1923). *Educational Screen*, 2, 41.

Anderson, C. (1948). Selection and projection of films. In D. L. Bock et al. (Eds.), *New tools for instruction* (pp. 11-14). New York: Hinds, Hayden & Eldredge, Inc.

Annual report of the superintendent of common schools of the State of New York. (1843).

Annual report of the superintendent of common schools of the State of New York. (1845). Albany: Carroll and Cook.

Annual report of the superintendent of public instruction of the State of New York. (1867). Albany: C. Van Benthuysen & Sons.

Apple, M. W. (1988). *Teachers and texts: A political economy of class and gender relations in education*. New York: Routledge.

Apple, M. W., & Bromley, H. (Eds.). (1998). *Education/technology/power: Educational computing as a social practice*. Albany: State University of New York Press.

Apple, M. W., & Jungck, S. (1998). You don't have to be a teacher to teach this unit. In M. W. Apple & H. Bromley (Eds.), *Education/technology/power: Educational computing as a social practice* (pp. 133-154). Albany: State University of New York Press.

Apter, M. J. (1968). *The new technology of education*. London: Macmillan.

Astuto, T. A., Clark, D. L., Read, A.-M., McGree, K., & deKoven Pelton Fernandez, L. (1994). *Roots of reform: Challenging the assumptions that control education reform*. Bloomington, IN: Phi Delta Kappa Educational Foundation.

Atkinson, C. (1942a). *Broadcasting to the classroom by universities and colleges*. Boston: Meador.

Atkinson, C. (1942b). *Public school broadcasting to the classroom*. Boston: Meador.

Atkinson, C. (1942c). *Radio network contributions to education*. Boston: Meador.

Baker, E. L., Herman, J. L., & Gearhart, M. (1996). Does technology work in schools? Why evaluation cannot tell the full story. In C. Fisher, D. C. Dwyer, & K. Yocam (Eds.), *Education and technology: Reflections on computing in classrooms* (pp. 185-202). San Francisco: Jossey-Bass.

Band instruction by radio. (1931, February). *The Instructor, 40*(4), 16.

Barnes, S., & Strate, L. (1996). The educational implications of the computer: A media ecology critique. *The New Jersey Journal of Communication, 4*(2), 180-208.

Bell, R., Cain, L. F., & Lamoreaux, L. A. (1941). *Motion pictures in a modern curriculum: A report on the use of films in the Santa Barbara schools*. Washington, DC: American Council on Education.

Bennett, F. (1999). *Computers as tutors: Solving the crisis in education*. Sarasota, FL: Faben.

Berkman, D. (1977). Instructional television: The medium whose future has passed. In J. Ackerman & L. Lipsitz (Eds.), *Instructional television: Status and directions* (pp. 95-108). Englewood Cliffs, NJ: Educational Technology Publications.

Bern, H. A. (1967, January). Wanted: Educational engineers. *Phi Delta Kappan, 48*(5), 230-236.

Berry, L. (1943). *Radio development in a small city school system.* Boston: Meador.

Besser, H. (1993). Education as marketplace. In R. Muffoletto & N. Nelson Knupfer (Eds.), *Computers in education: Social, political and historical perspectives* (pp. 37-69). Cresskill, NJ: Hampton.

Bestor, A. (1985). *Educational wastelands: The retreat from learning in our public schools* (2nd ed.). Urbana: University of Illinois Press. (Original publication 1953)

Bildersee, M. U. (1954, January). Radio: Common denominator of education. *The Instructor, 63*(5), 33-34.

Blake, F. (1927). Eastman movies in Newton. *Journal of Education, 105*(7), 177.

Blakely, R. J. (1979). *To serve the public interest: Educational broadcasting in the United States.* Syracuse, NY: Syracuse Univesity Press.

Bloom, B. S. (Ed.). (1956). *Taxonomy of educational objectives.* New York: Longman.

Bobbitt, F. (1997). Scientific method in curriculum-making. In D. J. Flinders & S. J. Thornton (Eds.), *The curriculum studies reader* (pp. 9-16). New York: Routledge. (Original publication 1918)

Bock, D. L., Cypher, I. F., Gardner, L. H., Siepmann, C. A., Anderson, C., & Hoban, Jr., C. F. (1948). *New tools for instruction.* New York: Hinds, Hayden & Eldredge, Inc.

Borich, G. D., & Jemelka, R. P. (1981). Evaluation. In H. F. O'Neil, Jr. (Ed.), *Computer-based instruction: A state-of-the-art assessment* (pp. 161-209). New York: Academic Press.

Briggs, L. (1960). Two self-instructional devices. In A. A. Lumsdaine & R. Glaser (Eds.), *Teaching machines and programmed learning: A source book* (pp. 299-304). Washington, DC: National Education Association.

Bromley, H. (1998). Data-driven democracy? Social assessment of educational computing. In M. W. Apple & H. Bromley (Eds.), *Education/technology/power: Educational computing as a social practice* (pp. 1-25). Albany: State University of New York Press.

Broughton, J. M. (1984). Computer literacy as political socialization of the child. In D. Sloan (Ed.), *The computer in education: A critical perspective* (pp. 102-122). New York: Teachers College Press.

Brown, H. E. (assisted by J. Bird). (1931). *Motion pictures and lantern slides for elementary visual education.* New York: Bureau of Publications of Teachers College, Columbia University.

Brown, J.S., Collins, A., & Duguid, P. (1989, January–February). Situated cognition and the culture of learning. *Educational Researcher, 18*, 32-42.

Buckley, H. M. (1934). Usefulness of school broadcasts. *Education on the Air, 5*, 80-86.

Bunderson, C. V. (1981). Courseware. In H. F. O'Neil, Jr. (Ed.), *Computer-based instruction: A state-of-the-art assessment* (pp. 91-125). New York: Academic Press.

Carey, J. W. (1989). *Communication as culture: Essays on media and society.* Boston: Unwin Hyman.

Carey, J. W., & Quirk, J. J. (1989a). The history of the future. In J. W. Carey (Ed.), *Communication as culture: Essays on media and society* (pp. 173-200). Boston: Unwin Hyman.

Carey, J. W., & Quirk, J. J. (1989b). The mythos of the electronic revolution. In J. W. Carey (Ed.), *Communication as culture: Essays on media and society* (pp. 113-141). Boston: Unwin Hyman.

Carey, J. W. (1997). Salvation by machines: Can technology save education? In E. S. Munson & C. A. Warren (Eds.), *James Carey: A critical reader* (pp. 292-307). Minneapolis: University of Minnesota Press.

Carlson, R. O. (1965). *Adoption of educational innovations.* Eugene, OR: University of Oregon Press.

Cassirer, H. R. (1960). *Television teaching today.* Paris: UNESCO.

Cawelti, J. G. (1965). *Apostles of the self-made man.* Chicago: University of Chicago Press.

Charters, W. W. (1933). *Motion pictures and youth: A summary.* New York: Macmillan.

Children and the films. (1933). *School and Society, 30,* 25-26.

Chisolm, M. (1967, December). Educational technology: How humane can it be? *Educational Leadership, 25*(3), 225-228.

Clarizio, H. F., Craig, R. C., & Mehrens, W. A. (1981). *Contemporary issues in educational psychology* (4th ed.). Boston: Allyn & Bacon.

Clausse, R. (1949). *Education by radio: School broadcasting.* Paris: UNESCO.

Collins, A. (1996). Whither technology and schools? Collected thoughts on the last and next quarter centuries. In C. Fisher, D. C. Dwyer, & K. Yocam (Eds.), *Education and technology: reflections on computing in classrooms* (pp. 51-65). San Francisco: Jossey-Bass.

Collins, A. (1991, September). The role of computer technology in restructuring schools. *Phi Delta Kappan, 73*(1), 28-36.

Confrey, J. (1996). The role of new technologies in designing mathematics education. In C. Fisher, D. C. Dwyer, & K. Yocam (Eds.), *Education and technology: Reflections on computing in classrooms* (pp. 129-149). San Francisco: Jossey-Bass.

Conrad, L. H. (1954, March). Schools can start using tv now. *Educational Leadership, 11*(6), 373-375.

Cook, G. S. (1931, March). How we are fed. *Educational Screen, 10,* 73-76.

Cooper, W. J. (1932, July 16). The future of radio in education. *School and Society, 36,* 65-68.

Counts, G. S. (1934). *The social foundations of education.* New York: Charles Scribner's Sons.

Cremin, L. A. (1980). *American education: The national experience 1783-1876.* New York: Harper Colophon.

Cremin, L. A. (1951). *The American common school: An historical conception.* New York: Bureau of Publications, Teachers College, Columbia University.

Cross, G., & Szostak, R. (1995). *Technology and American society: A history.* Englewood Cliffs, NJ: Prentice Hall.

Cuban, L. (1986). *Teachers and machines: The classroom use of technology since 1920.* New York: Teachers College Press.

Cubberley, E. P. (1909). *Changing conceptions of education.* Boston: Houghton Mifflin.

Czitrom, D. (1982). *Media and the American mind: From Morse to McLuhan.* Chapel Hill: University of North Carolina Press.

Dale, E., Dunn, F., Hoban, C., & Schneider, E. (1937). *Motion pictures in education: A summary of the literature.* New York: The H.W. Wilson Company.

Darrow, B. H. (1932). *Radio: The assistant teacher.* Columbus, OH: R. G. Adams & Company.

Davis, J. (1934). The radio, a commercial or an educational agency? In T. F. Tyler (Ed.), *Radio as a cultural agency: Proceedings of a National Conference on the use of radio as a cultural agency in a democracy* (pp. 3-10). Washington, DC: The National Committee on Education by Radio.

Davy, J. (1984). Mindstorms in the lamplight. In D. Sloan (Ed.), *The computer in education: A critical perspective* (pp. 11-20). New York: Teachers College Press.

Delon, F. G. (1970, November). A field test of computer-assisted instruction in first grade mathematics. *Educational Leadership, 28*(2), 170-179.

Desiderato, O.L., Kanner, J.H., & Runyon, R.P. (1956). Procedures for improving television instruction. *Audio-Visual Communication Review, 4*(1), 57-63

The demands of the age. (1854, November). *New York Teacher, 3*(2), 114-116.

Dennis, J. R. (1968, November). Geometry via PLATO. *The Instructor, 78*(3), 116.

Denno, B. H. (1941). Films and the world about. In R. Bell, L. F. Cain, & L. A. Lamoreaux, *Motion pictures in a modern curriculum: A report on the use of films in the Santa Barbara schools* (pp. 25-38). Washington, DC: American Council on Education.

Dewey, J. (1916). *Democracy and education: An introduction to the philosophy of education.* New York: Macmillan.

Dewey, J. (1938). *Experience and education.* New York: Collier.

Dewey, J. (1969). *The educational situation.* New York: Arno Press and the New York Times. (Original publication 1904)

Dewey, J. (1976). *The school and society.* Carbondale: Southern Illinois University Press. (Original publication 1899)

Dewey, J. (1997). My pedagogic creed. In D. J. Flinders & S. J. Thornton (Eds.), *The curriculum studies reader* (pp. 17-23). New York: Routledge. (Original publication 1929)

Dible, I. W. (1970, November). The teacher in a multi-mediated setting. *Educational Leadership, 28*(2), 123-128.

Dickinson, J. (1934). Radio and democracy. In T. F. Tyler (Ed.), *Radio as a cultural agency: Proceedings of a National Conference on the use of radio as a cultural agency in a democracy* (pp. 38-43). Washington, DC: The National Committee on Education by Radio.

Dorau, H. B. (1939). *An extemporaneous, exploratory, confidential statement for the use of Dean Madden.* New York University Archives.

Downey, G. (1998, August/September). Memory lane. *eSchool News,* p. 6

Dransfield, J. E. (1927). Is there a technique for the use of motion pictures in schools? *Educational Screen, 6,* 121-122.

Dr. Damrosch has audience of six millions. (1932, March). *The Instructor, 41*(5), 9.

Dwyer, D. C. (1996). The imperative to change our schools. In C. Fisher, D. C. Dwyer, & K. Yocam (Eds.), *Education and technology: Reflections on computing in classrooms* (pp. 15-33). San Francisco: Jossey-Bass.

Editorial. (1923, March). *Educational Screen, 2,* 101-102.

Edling, J. V. (1964). Programed instruction in a "continuous progress" school. In *The Fund for the Advancement of Education, Four case studies of programed instruction* (pp. 65-94). New York: The Fund for the Advancement of Education.

Fund for the Advancement of Education. (1964). *Four case studies of programed instruction.* New York: Fund for the Advancement of Education

Eisner, E. (1997). Educational objectives—help or hindrance? In D. J. Flinders & S. J. Thornton (Eds.), *The curriculum studies reader* (pp. 69-75). New York: Routledge.

Ekirch, A.A., Jr. (1969a). *The idea of progress in America, 1815-1860.* New York: AMS Press.

Ekirch, A. A., Jr. (1969b). *Ideologies and utopias: The impact of the New Deal on American thought.* Chicago: Quadrangle Books.

Eliot, C. W. (1903). *More money for the public schools.* New York: Doubleday, Page & Company.

Ellis, D. C. (January, 1923). What the association proposes to do. *Educational Screen, 2,* 36-37.

Ellis, D. C., & Thornborough, L. (1923). *Motion pictures in education: A practical handbook for users of visual aids.* New York: Thomas Y. Crowell Company.

Elwood, J. W. (1930). Radio and the three r's. *Education on the Air, 1,* 19-33.

Ensign, F. C. (1969). *Compulsory school atendance and child labor.* New York: Arno Press and the *New York Times.*

Eye and ear instruction. (1927, November). *Educational Screen, 6*(9), 435.

Fern, G.H., & Robbins, E. (1946). *Teaching with films.* Milwaukee: The Bruce Publishing Company.

Feurzig, W. (1988). Apprentice tools: Students as practitioners. In R. S. Nickerson & P. P. Zodhiates (Eds.), *Technology in education: Looking toward 2020* (pp. 97-120). Hillsdale, NJ: Erlbaum.

Filep, R. T. (1967, Spring). Individualized instruction and the computer: Potential for mass education. *Audio-Visual Communication Review, 15*(1), 102-112.

Film news. (1940, July). *Newsletter of the American Film Center.* New York University Archives.

Finn, J. D. (1972). *Extending education through technology: Selected writings by James D. Finn on instructional technology.* Washington, DC: Association for Educational Communications and Technology.

Fisher, C., Dwyer, D. C., & Yocam, K. (Eds.). (1996). *Education and technology: Reflections on computing in classrooms.* San Francisco: Jossey-Bass.

Fisher, C. (1996). Learning to compute and computing to learn. In C. Fisher, D. C. Dwyer, & K. Yocam (Eds.), *Education and technology: Reflections on computing in classrooms* (pp. 109-127). San Francisco: Jossey-Bass.

Flinders, D. J., & Thornton, S. J. (1997). *The curriculum studies reader.* New York: Routledge.

Flynn, J. M. (1968, October). "Computer appreciation" courses in education. *Educational Leadership, 26*(1), 24-27.

Forman, H. J. (1935). *Our movie made children.* New York: Macmillan.

Forsdale, L. (Ed.). (1962). *8mm sound film in education.* New York: Teachers College, Columbia University.

Forsdale, L. (1962). 8mm sound film and education. In L. Forsdale (Ed.), *8mm sound film in education* (pp. 3-11). New York: Teachers College, Columbia University.

Foshay, F. P. (1959). *Interaction in learning: Implications for television* (report of a seminar held at NEA headquarters 1/31-2/3, 1959). Washington, DC.

Foucault, M. (1977). *Discipline and punish: The birth of the prison.* New York: Pantheon.

Four years of network broadcasting: A report by the Committee on Civic Education by Radio of the National Advisory Council on Radio in Education and the American Political Science Association. [undated] University of Chicago Press.

Frazier, A., & Wigren, H. (Eds.). (1960). *Opportunities for learning: Guidelines for television.* Washington, DC: National Education Association.

Freeman, F. N. (1924). *Visual education: A comparative study of motion pictures and other methods of instruction.* Chicago: University of Chicago Press.

Freire, P., & Macedo, D. (1987). *Literacy: Reading the word and the world.* New York: Bergin & Garvey.

Fry, E.B. (1963). *Teaching machines and programmed instruction: An introduction.* New York: McGraw-Hill.

Fund for the Advancement of Education. (1961). *Decade of experiment: The fund for the advancement of education 1951-1961.* New York: Author.

Fund for the Advancement of Education. (1964). *Four case studies of programed instruction.* New York: Author.

Gable, M. A. (1951, September). Television in the Philadelphia schools. *The Instructor, 61*(1), 41, 45-46.

Gagné, R. M., & Briggs, L. J. (1974). *Principles of instructional design.* New York: Holt, Rinehart & Winston.

Gagné, R. M., & Briggs, L. J. (1974). *Principles of instructional design.* New York: Holt, Rinehart & Winston.

Gardner, H. (1993). *Multiple intelligences: The theory in practice.* New York: Basic Books.

Gentile, J. R. (1967). The first generation of computer-assisted instructional systems: An evaluative review. *Audio-Visual Communication Review, 15*(1), 23-53.

George. W. H. (1935). *The cinema in school.* London: Sir Isaac Pitman & Sons.

Glaser, R., Damrin, D., & Gardner, F. (1960). The tab item: A technique for the measurement of proficiency in diagnostic problem-solving tasks. In A. A. Lumsdaine & R. Glaser (Eds.), *Teaching machines and programmed instruction: A source book* (pp. 275-285). Washington, DC: National Education Association.

Gooden, A. R. (1996). *Computers in the classroom: How teachers and students are using technology to transform learning.* San Francisco: Jossey-Bass.

Goodlad, J. I. (1968, Spring). The future of learning and teaching. *Audio-Visual Communication Review, 16*(1), 5-15.

Goodlad, J. I. (1984). *A place called school: Prospects for the future.* New York: McGraw-Hill.

Goodlad, J. I., O'Toole, J. F., Jr., & Tyler, L. L. (1966). *Computers and information systems in education.* New York: Harcourt, Brace & World.

Goodman, S. M. (1947). *Curriculum implications of armed services educational programs.* Washington, DC: American Council on Education.

Gordon, D. (1942). *All children listen.* New York: George W. Stewart, Publisher.

Gordon, G. N. (1977). Instructional television: Yesterday's magic. In J. Ackerman & L. Lipsitz (Eds.), *Instructional television: Status and directions* (pp. 147-151). Englewood Cliffs, NJ: Educational Technology Publications.

Grierson, J. (1935). Foreword. In W. H. George (Ed.), *The cinema in school* (pp. 5-8). London: Sir Isaac Pitman & Sons.

Hajovey, H., & Christensen, D. L. (1987, May). Intelligent computer-assisted instruction: The next generation. *Educational Technology, 27*(5), 9-14.

Halsey, J. (1936, May). An experiment in geography teaching. *Educational Screen, 15*, 137-140.

Harrison, M. (1938). *Radio in the classroom: Objectives, principles, and practices.* New York: Prentice-Hall.

Hart, G.L. (1948). Navy training films program. In D.L. Bock et al. (Eds.), *New tools for instruction* (pp. 15-22). New York: Hinds, Hayden & Eldredge, Inc.

Hawkins, J. (1996). Dilemmas. In C. Fisher, D. C. Dwyer, & K. Yocam (Eds.), *Education and technology: Reflections on computing in classrooms* (pp. 35-50). San Francisco: Jossey-Bass.

Hays, D. G. (1923, February). Visual education: Its scope, purpose and value. *Educational Screen, 2*, 56-60.

Heddinger, F. M. (1967, January). Will big business and big government control R&D? *Phi Delta Kappan, 48*(5), 215-219.

Hedges, W. S. (1930). Commercial sponsorship of educational programs. *Education on the Air, 1*, 44-61.

Herbert, J., & Foshay, A. W. (1964). Programmed instruction in the Manhasset junior high school. In *The Fund for the Advancement of Education, Four case studies of programed instruction* (pp. 17-27). New York: The Fund for the Advancement of Education.

Herzog, H. (1941). *Children and their leisure time listening to the radio. A survey of the literature in the field.* New York: Office of Radio Research, Columbia University.

Hill, F. E. (1942). *Tune in for education: Eleven years of education by radio.* New York: National Committee on Education by Radio.

Hintz, W. B. (1888). *Illustrative blackboard drawing.* Proceedings of the 59th annual meeting of the American Institute of Instruction. Boston: American Institute of Instruction.

Hoban, C. F., Jr. (1946). *Movies that teach.* New York: The Dryden Press, Inc.

Hoban, C. F., Jr. (1948). Significant developments in the production and use of educational motion pictures. In D. L. Bock et al. (Eds.), *New tools for instruction* (pp. 23-32). New York: Hinds, Hayden & Eldredge.

Hoban, C. F., Hoban, C. F., Jr., & Zisman, S. B. (1937). *Visualizing the curriculum.* New York: Cordon.

Hoek, F. (1934, January). An enrichment in a course of study. *Educational Screen, 13,* 22-25.

Hoffman, N. (1981). *Woman's "true" profession: Voices from the history of teaching.* New York: McGraw-Hill.

Holaday, P. W., & Stoddard, G. D. (1933). *Getting ideas from the movies.* New York: Macmillan.

Holtzman, W. H. (Ed.). (1970). *Computer-assisted instruction, testing, and guidance.* New York: Harper & Row.

Hood, L. C. (1953, January). Television in the elementary school. *The Instructor, 62*(5), 33.

Horm, A. (1927, November). A neglected aspect of the educational film. *Educational Screen, 6*(9), 411-412, 440.

Hurn, C. J. (1993). *The limits and possibilities of schooling: An introduction to the sociology of education* (3rd ed.). Boston: Allyn & Bacon.

Illich, I. (1970). *Deschooling society.* New York: Harper & Row.

Import, M. S. (1969, January). Computers in NYC schools . . . from a teacher's viewpoint. *The Instructor, 78*(5), 34.

The influence of education. (1854, November). *New York Teacher, 3*(2), 76-77.

Jackson, P. W. (1968). *The teacher and the machine.* Pittsburgh: University of Pittsburgh Press.

Jackson, R. H. (1853, May). Letter to the editor. *Pennsylvania School Journal, 1*(17), 433.

Jackson, S. L. (1940). *America's struggle for free schools: Social tension and education in New England and New York, 1827-42.* Washington, DC: American Council on Public Affairs.

Jefferson, T. (1955). *Notes on the state of Virginia.* (Ed. by William Peden). Chapel Hil: University of North Carolina Press. (Original publication 1787)

Jensen, J. (1990). *Redeeming modernity: Contradictions in media criticism.* Newbury Park, CA: Sage.

Jones, G. R. (1996). *Cyberschools: An education renaissance.* Englewood, CO: Jones Digital Century.

Judd, C. H. (1918). *The evolution of a democratic school system.* New York: Houghton-Mifflin.

Judd, C. H. (1923, April). Education and the movies. *Educational Screen, 2,* 151-154.

Kaestle, C. F. (1983). *Pillars of the republic: Common schools and American society, 1780-1860.* New York: Hill & Wang.

Kanner, J. H. (1958). Teaching by television in the army: An overview. *Audio-Visual Communication Review, 6,* 172-188.

Kanner, J. H., Katz, S., Mindak, W., & Goldsmith, P. (1958). Television in army training. *Audio-Visual Communication Review, 6,* 255-291.

Kanner, J. H., & Marshall, W. P. (1963). Television in basic training: The improvement of training by television. *Audio-Visual Communication Review, 11,* 191-199.

Kanner, J. H., Runyon, R. P., & Desiderato, O. (1955, Summer). Television as a training and educational medium. *Audio-Visual Communication Review, 3*(3), 163-172.

Katz, M. B. (1987). *Reconstructing American education.* Cambridge, MA: Harvard University Press.

Keppel, F. (1967, January). The business interest in education. *Phi Delta Kappan, 48*(5), 187-190.

Kilpatrick, W. H. (1918, September). The project method. *Teachers College Record, 19*(4), 319-335.

Kilpatrick. W. H., Bode, B., Childs, J. L., Hullfish, H. G., Dewey, J., Raup, R. B., & Thayer, V. T. (1969). *The educational frontier.* New York: Arno Press & the *New York Times.*

King, W. H. (1954, June). What teachers expect from educational television. *The Instructor, 63*(10), 19-20.

Kliebard, H. M. (1995). *The struggle for the American curriculum, 1893-1958* (2nd ed.). New York: Routledge.

Klemm, L. R. (1988, Feburary). Chips from an educational workshop in Europe. *Journal of Education, 27*(5), 70.

Knapp, L. R., & Glenn, A. D. (1996). *Restructuring schools with technology.* Boston: Allyn & Bacon.

Knapp, M. M. (1928, October). Radio reading. *The Instructor, 37*(10), 70.

Kohl, H. R. (1969). *The open classroom: A practical guide to a new way of teaching.* New York: Vintage Books.

Kozma, R. B. (1987, November). The implications of cognitive psychology for computer-based learning tools. *Educational Technology, 27*(11), 20-25.

Kozol, J. (1991). *Savage inequalities: Children in America's schools.* New York: Crown.

Kurland, N. D. (1969). Review. *Audio-Visual Communication Review, 17*(4), 452-454.

Lambert, R. S. (1930). The use of radio in the development of international understanding. *Education on the Air, 1*, 120-124.

Lawler, R. C. (1929, April). Broadcasting: An oral English device. *The Instructor, 38*(6), 11.

Lazarus, A. L. (1956, January). Pupils' TV habits. *Educational Leadership, 13*(4), 241-242.

Levenson, W. B. (1945). *Teaching through radio.* New York: Farrar & Rinehard.

Lewin, W. (1927, December). Photoplays for vocational guidance. *Educational Screen, 6*(10), 452-454.

Lewis, D., & McFadden, D. L. (1945). *Program patterns for young radio listeners in the field of children's radio entertainment.* Washington, DC: National Association of Broadcasters.

Lilley, I. M. (Ed.). (1967). *Friedrich Froebel: A selection from his writings.* New York: Cambridge University Press.

Loftus, J. J. (1942). Introduction. In D. Gordon (Ed.), *All children listen* (pp. 1–12). New York: George W. Stewart.

Logan, R. K. (1986). *The alphabet effect: The impact of the phonetic alphabet on the development of western civilization.* New York: St. Martin's Press.

Long, M. S. (1952, April). Television has a part in modern education. *Educational Leadership, 9*(7), 412-417.

Lowery, S., & DeFleur, M. (1995). *Milestones in mass communication research* (3rd ed.). New York: Longman.

Lumsdaine, A.A., & Glaser, R. (Eds.). (1960). *Teaching machines and programmed learning: A source book*. Washington, DC: National Education Association.

Lynd, A. (1950). *Quackery in the public schools*. New York: Grosset & Dunlap.

Mann, H. (1848). *Eleventh annual report of the Massachusetts Board of Education*.

Marchand, P. (1998). *Marshall McLuhan: The medium and the messenger*. Cambridge, MA: MIT Press.

Marchant, J. (Ed.). (1925). *The cinema in education*. London: George Allen & Unwin.

Marvin, C. (1988). *When old technologies were new: Thinking about electric communication in the late nineteenth century*. New York: Oxford University Press.

McBride, J. (1977). A working model for instructional television. In J. Ackerman & L. Lipsitz (Eds.), *Instructional television: Status and directions* (pp. 65-74). Englewood Cliffs, NJ: Educational Technology Publications.

McCarty, H. B. (1934). The Wisconsin radio plan in practise [sic]. In T. F. Tyler (Ed.), *Radio as a cultural agency: Proceedings of a National Conference on the use of radio as a cultural agency in a democracy* (pp. 18-23). Washington, DC: The National Committee on Education by Radio.

McKee, B. (1967, December). Letter to the editor. *The Instructor, 77*(4), 9.

McLuhan, M. (1962a). 8mm in context: The modern media and externalized senses. In L. Forsdale (Ed.), *8 mm sound film in education* (pp. 16-25). New York: Teachers College, Columbia University.

McLuhan, M. (1962b). *The Gutenberg galaxy*. Toronto: University of Toronto Press.

McLuhan, M. (1967). *The medium is the massage*. New York: Touchstone Books.

Mercer, C. H. (1930). Foreign-language instruction by radio. *Education on the Air, 1*, 365-377.

Mercer, J., & Becker, S. (1955, Summer). The disenchantments of educational tv. *Audio-Visual Communication Review, 3*(3), 173-182.

Meredith, J. C. (1971). *The CAI author/instructor*. Englewood Cliffs, NJ: Educational Technology Publications.

Meyrowitz, J. (1985). *No sense of place: The impact of electronic media on social behavior*. New York: Oxford University Press.

Mikaelian, S., & Thompson, R. B. (1968, March). Evanston tried . . . Computer report cards. *The Instructor, 77*(7), 129.

Moore, E. L. (1931, May). Class radio programs. *The Instructor, 40*(7), 62.

Morehead, H. (1955, December). Television and learning. *Educational Leadership, 13*(3), 167-179.

Moreo, D. W. (1996). *Schools in the great depression*. New York: Garland.

Morgan, A. (1934). Radio as a cultural agency in sparsely settled regions and remote areas. In T. F. Tyler (Ed.), *Radio as a cultural agency: Proceedings of a National Conference on the use of radio as a cultural agency in a democracy* (pp. 77-83). Washington, DC: The National Committee on Education by Radio.

The movies and the schools. (January, 1927). *Educational Screen, 6*(1), 5.

Muffoletto, R., & Nelson Knupfer, N. (Eds.). (1993). *Computers in education: Social, political and historical perspectives*. Cresskill, NJ: Hampton.

Munson, E. S., & Warren, C. A. (Eds.). (1997). *James Carey: A critical reader*. Minneapolis: University of Minnesota Press.

Murphy, J., & Gross, R. (1966). *Learning by television*. New York: The Fund for the Advancement of Education.

Myers, S. E. (March, 1928). A visual study of the Panama Canal. *Educational Screen, 7*, 30-32.

Nasaw, D. (1979). *Schooled to order: A social history of public schooling in the United States*. New York: Oxford University Press.

National Center for Education Statistics. (1999, February). *Internet access in public schools and classrooms: 1994-1998*. Washington, DC: National Center for Education Statistics.

National Commission on Excellence in Education. (1983). *A nation at risk: The imperative for educational reform*. Washington, DC: U.S. Government Printing Office.

National Education Association. (1958). *Television in instruction: An appraisal*. Washington, DC: National Education Association.

National Program in the Use of Television in the Public Schools. (1960). A report on the second year 1958-59. New York: Author.

National Telecommunications and Information Administration. (1999). *Falling through the net: Defining the digital divide.* http://www.ntia.doc.gov/ntiahome/fttn99

N.E.A. broadcasts weekly radio programs on "Our American Schools." (1933, January). *The Instructor, 42*(3), 5.

Neill, A. S. (1960). *Summerhill: A radical approach to child rearing.* New York: Hart.

New York City Board of Education. (1924). *Educational radio program: Report of the educational activities carried on over the radio.* New York: Author.

New York City Board of Education. (1962). *Closed circuit television: A report of the Chelsea Project.* New York: Author.

Newsfront. (1968, January). *The Instructor, 77*(5), 6.

Nickerson, R. S., & Zodhiates, P. P. (1988). *Technology in education: Looking toward 2020.* Hillsdale, NJ: Erlbaum

Nineteenth Annual Report of the Superintendent of Common Schools for the Commonwealth of Pennsylvania for the Year Ending June 1852. (1853). *Pennsylvania School Journal, 1,* 346-352.

Noble, D. D. (1991). *The classroom arsenal: Military research, information technology, and public education.* New York: Falmer.

Nye, D. (1994). *American technological sublime.* Cambridge, MA: MIT Press.

Oettinger, A. G. (1969). *Run, computer, run: The mythology of educational innovation.* Cambridge, MA: Harvard University Press.

O'Neil, H. F., Jr. (Ed.). (1981). *Computer-based instruction: A state-of-the-art assessment.* New York: Academic Press.

Ong, W. J. (1958). *Ramus, method, and the decay of dialogue: From the art of discourse to the art of reason.* Cambridge, MA: Harvard University Press.

Orndorff, M. (1923, February). Slow motion photography. *Educational Screen, 2,* 79-81.

Packard, F. A. (1969). *The daily public school in the United States.* New York: Arno Press & the New York Times.

Pagen, J. (1970, February). Computerized instruction: Here to stay! *The Instructor, 79*(6), 114-115.

Papert, S. (1980). *Mindstorms: Children, computers and powerful ideas.* New York: Basic Books.

Payne, G. E. (1938). Editor's introduction. In M. Harrison (Ed.), *Radio in the classroom: Objectives, principles, and practices* (pp. xv-xvi). New York: Prentice-Hall.

Pea, R. D. (1985). Beyond amplification: Using the computer to reorganize mental functioning. *Educational Psychologist, 20*(4), 167-182.

Pea, R. D. (1988). Putting knowledge to use. In R. S. Nickerson & P. P. Zodhiates (Eds.), *Technology in education: Looking toward 2020* (pp. 169-212). Hillsdale, NJ: Erlbaum

Pea, R. D. (1993). Learning scientific concepts through material and social activities: Conversational analysis meets conceptual change. *Educational Psychologist, 28*(3), 265-277.

Perelman, L. J. (1993). Luddite schools wage a wasteful war. In T. Cannings & L. Finkel (Eds.), *The technology age classroom* (pp. 5-7). Wilsonville, OR: Franklin, Beedle & Associates.

Perkinson, H. (1968). *The imperfect panacea: American faith in education, 1865-1965.* New York: Random House.

Perry, A. (1929). *Radio in education: The Ohio School of the Air and other experiments.* New York: The Payne Fund.

Pestalozzi, J. H. (1977). *How Gertrude teaches her children.* Washington, DC: University Publications of America, Inc. (translated from 1898 edition)

Phillips, C., & Hill, E. (1969, February). Pupil-made computer tests. *The Instructor, 78*(6).

Postman, N. (1961). *Television and the teaching of English.* New York: Appleton-Century-Crofts.

Postman, N. (1979). *Teaching as a conserving activity.* New York: Delta Books.

Postman, N. (1985). *Amusing ourselves to death: Public discourse in the age of show business.* New York: Penguin.

Postman, N. (1995). *The end of education.* New York: Knopf.

Postman, N. (1999). *Building a bridge to the eighteenth century: How the past can improve our future.* New York: Knopf.

Postman, N., & Weingartner, C. (1969). *Teaching as a subversive activity.* New York: Dell.

Pressey, S. (1926, March 20). A simple apparatus which gives tests and scores—and teaches. *School and Society, 23,* 373-376.

Pressey, S. (1932, November 19). A third and fourth contribution toward the coming "industrial revolution" in education. *School and Society, 36,* 668-672.

Pressey, S. (1960). Development and appraisal of devices providing immediate automatic scoring of objective tests and concomitant self-instruction. In A. A. Lumsdaine & R. Glaser (Eds.), *Teaching machines and programmed learning: A source book* (pp. 69-88). Washington, DC: National Education Association. (Original publication 1950)

Rahmlow, H. F., Fratini, R. C., & Ghesquiere, J. R. (1980). *Plato.* Englewood Cliffs, NJ: Educational Technology Publications.

Ramo, S. (1960). A new technique of education. In A. A. Lumsdaine & R. Glaser (Eds.), *Teaching machines and programmed learning: A source book* (pp. 367-381). Washington, DC: National Education Association.

Ramsey, C. P. (1967, October). Selected for review. *Educational Leadership, 25*(1), 93-97.

Ravitch, D. (1983). *The troubled crusade: American education 1945-1980.* New York: Basic Books.

Reed, T. H. (Ed.). (1933). *Government in a depression: Constructive economy in state and local government.* Chicago: University of Chicago Press.

Research abstracts. (1953). *Audio-Visual Communication Review, 1*(1), 61-63.

Resnick, L. B., & Johnson, A. (1988). Intelligent machines for intelligent people: Cognitive theory and the future of computer-assisted learning. In R. S. Nickerson & P. P. Zodhiates (Eds.), *Technology in education: Looking toward 2020* (pp. 139-168). Hillsdale, NJ: Erlbaum

Resnick, L. B., & Klopfer, L. E. (Eds.). (1989). *Toward the thinking curriculum: Current cognitive research.* Washington, DC: Association for Supervision and Curriculum Development.

Resnick, L. B., & Klopfer, L. E. (1989). Toward the thinking curriculum: An overview. In L. B. Resnick & L. E. Klopfer (Eds.), *Toward the thinking curriculum: Current cognitive research* (pp. 1-18). Washington, DC: Association for Supervision and Curriculum Development.

Reverence for the past a hindrance to progress. (1896, June). *Journal of Pedagogy,* pp. 93-94.

Rheingold, H. (1993). *The virtual community: Homesteading on the electronic frontier.* New York: Harper Perennial.

Rickover, H. G. (1959). *Education and freedom.* New York: E. P. Dutton & Co.

Riedel, M. W. (1941). Films and little children. In R. Bell, L. F. Cain, & L. A. Lamoreaux (Eds.) *Motion pictures in a modern curricu-*

lum: A report on the use of films in the Santa Barbara schools (pp. 13-23). Washington, DC: American Council on Education.

Rigney, J. W., & Munro, A. (1981). Learning strategies. In H. F. O'Neil, Jr. (Ed.), *Computer-based instruction: A state-of-the-art assessment* (pp. 127-159). New York: Academic Press.

Robinson, I. E. (1930). Educational obligations of the broadcaster. *Education on the Air, 1,* 3-8.

Rock, R.T., Jr., Duva, J.S., & Murray, J.E. (Undated). *Training by television: A study in learning and retention.* Port Washington, NY: Special Devices Center, U.S. Navy.

Ross, E. D. (1976). *The kindergarten crusade: The establishment of preschool education in the United States.* Athens: Ohio University Press.

Roszak, T. (1994). *The cult of information: A neo-luddite treatise on high-tech, artificial intelligence, and the true art of thinking* (2nd ed.). Berkeley: University of California Press.

Roy, I. (1954, November). Television at home for science at school. *The Instructor, 64*(3), 111.

Rural choirs. (1931, October). *The Instructor, 40*(10), 13.

Saettler, P. (1990). *The evolution of American educational technology.* Englewood, CO: Libraries Unlimited.

Saettler, P. (1954, Spring). Historical overview of audio-visual communication. *Audio-Visual Communication Review, 2*(2), 109-117.

Salomon, G. (1988). AI in reverse: Computer tools that turn cognitive. *Journal of Educational Computing Research, 4*(2), 123-139.

Sandholtz, J. H., & Ringstaff, C. (1996). Teacher change in technology-rich classrooms. In C. Fisher, D. C. Dwyer, & K. Yocam (Eds.), *Education and technology: Reflections on computing in classrooms* (pp. 281-299). San Francisco: Jossey-Bass.

School broadcasting. (1933). League of Nations, International Institute of Intellectual Co-operation. Paris.

School radio programs. (1929, January). *The Instructor, 38*(3), 7.

School radio users win prize trips. (1930, June). *The Instructor, 39*(8), 7.

Schramm, W. (1964a). Introduction: Interim report. In *The Fund for the Advancement of Education, Four case studies of programed instruction* (pp. 8-15). New York: The Fund for the Advancement of Education.

Schramm, W. (1964b). Programed instruction in Denver. In *The Fund for the Advancement of Education, Four case studies of programed instruction* (pp. 29-40). New York: The Fund for the Advancement of Education.

Schramm, W. (1964c). Programed instruction today and tomorrow. In *The Fund for the Advancement of Education, Four case studies of programed instruction* (pp. 97-115). New York: The Fund for the Advancement of Education.

Schramm, W., Lyle, J., & Parker, E. B. (1961). *Television in the lives of our children.* Stanford, CA: Stanford University Press.

Segal, H. P. (1985). *Technological utopianism in American culture.* Chicago: University of Chicago Press.

Siepmann, C. A. (1948). Radio and films in education. In D. L. Bock et al., *New tools for instruction* (pp. 1-6). New York: Hinds, Hayden & Eldredge, Inc.

Siepmann, C. A. (1958). *TV and our school crisis.* New York: Dodd, Mead & Company.

Silberman, C. E. (1970). *Crisis in the classroom: The remaking of American education.* New York: Random House.

Silberman, H. F. (1967, April). Using computers in education: Some problems and solutions. *Educational Leadership, 24*(7), 630-639.

Sizer, T. R. (1996). *Horace's hope: What works for the American high school.* New York: Houghton-Mifflin.

Skinner, B. F. (1960). Teaching machines. In A. A. Lumsdaine & R. Glaser (Eds.), *Teaching machines and programmed learning: A case book* (pp. 137-158). Washington, DC: National Education Association.

Skornia, H. J. (1955, Spring). What can you do about educational television? *Audio-Visual Communication Review, 3*(2), 83-90.

Sloan, D. (Ed.). (1984). *The computer in education: A critical perspective.* New York: Teachers College Press.

Smith, K. (1999). *Mental hygiene: Classroom films 1945-1970.* New York: Blast Books.

Smith, K. U., & Smith, M. F. (1966). *Cybernetic principles of learning and educational design.* New York: Holt, Rinehart & Winston.

Smith, M. H. (Ed.). (1961). *Using television in the classroom.* New York: McGraw-Hill.

Snedden, D. (1927). *What's wrong with American education?* Philadelphia: J. B. Lippincott Company.

Snyder, T., & Palmer, J. (1986). *In search of the most amazing thing: Children, education, and computers*. Reading, MA: Addison-Wesley.

Sponberg, R. (1967a, November). Drill and practice by teletype . . . from a computer 2000 miles away! *The Instructor, 77*(3), 124-125.

Sponberg, R. (1967b, August/September). You and CAI. *The Instructor, 77*(1), 170-171.

Sponberg, R. (1968, May). Teacher-written TLU. *The Instructor, 77*(9), 101.

Spring, J. (1986). *The American school, 1964-1985: Varieties of historical interpretation of the foundations and development of American education*. New York: Longman.

Spring, J. (1989). *The sorting machine revisited: National educational policy since 1945* (updated ed.). New York: Longman.

Stack, H. (1936, March). Teaching safety through visual education. *Educational Screen, 15*, 82-84.

Stark, J. R. (1967, January). Educational technology: A communications problem. *Phi Delta Kappan, 48*(5), 194-198.

Sterritt, G. M. (1971, August/September). Using CAI as a learning incentive. *The Instructor, 81*(1), 133-135.

Stoll, C. (1999). *High tech heretic: Why computers don't belong in the classroom and other reflections by a computer contrarian*. New York: Doubleday.

Storen, H. F. (1953, February). Use of the air waves—a victory for education. *Educational Leadership, 10*(5), 322-324.

Talbott, S. L. (1995). *The future does not compute: Transcending the machines in our midst*. Sebastopol, CA: O'Reilly & Associates.

Taylor, R. (Ed.). (1980). *The computer in the school: Tutor, tool, tutee*. New York: Teachers College Press.

Thornburg, D. G. (1991). Strategy instruction for academically at-risk students: An exploratory study of teaching "higher-order" reading and writing in the social studies. *Journal of Reading, Writing, and Learning Disabilities, 7*, 377-406.

Thornburg, D. G., & Pea, R. D. (1991). Synthesizing instructional technologies and educational culture: Exploring cognition and metacognition in the social studies. *Journal of Educational Computing Research, 7*(2), 121-164.

Tuveson, E. L. (1968). *Redeemer nation: The idea of America's millennial role*. Chicago: University of Chicago Press.

Twelfth Annual Report of the Board of Education of the City and County of New York. (1854). New York: William C. Bryant.

Tyack, D. B. (1967). *Turning points in American educational history.* Waltham, MA: Blaisdell.

Tyack, D. B. (1974). *The one best system: A history of American urban education.* Cambridge, MA: Harvard University Press.

Tyack, D. B., & Cuban, L. (1995). *Tinkering toward utopia: A century of public school reform.* Cambridge, MA: Harvard University Press.

Tyler, T. F. (Ed.). (1934). *Radio as a cultural agency: Proceedings of a National Conference on the use of radio as a cultural agency in a democracy.* Washington, DC: The National Committee on Education by Radio.

Tyner, K. (1998). *Literacy in a digital world: Teaching and learning in the age of information.* Mahwah, NJ: Erlbaum.

Tyson, L. (1933). Preface. In T. H. Reed (Ed.), *Government in a depression: Constructive economy in state and local government* (pp. v–vii). Chicago: University of Chicago Press.

Tyson, L. (1930). Contributions of radio to higher education. *Education on the Air, 1,* 135-149.

U.S. Surgeon General's Scientific Advisory Committee on Television and Social Behavior. (1971). *Television and growing up: The impact of televised violence.* Rockville, MD: National Institute of Mental Health.

Van Allen, R. (1968, November). Individualized instruction or learning? *The Instructor, 78*(3), 33, 86, 92.

Van Schaick, F. (1941). Films and safe conduct. In R. Bell, L. F. Cain, & L. A. Lamoreaux (Eds.), *Motion pictures in a modern curriculum: A report on the use of films in the Santa Barbara schools* (pp. 65–84). Washington, DC: American Council on Education.

Vygotsky, L. S. (1978). *Mind in society: The development of higher psychological processes.* Cambridge, MA: Harvard University Press.

Walker, D. F. (1996). Toward an ACOT of tomorrow. In C. Fisher, D. C. Dwyer, & K. Yocam (Eds.), *Education and technology: Reflections on computing in classrooms* (pp. 91-106). San Francisco: Jossey-Bass Publishers.

Waller, J. C. (1934). A summary of the achievements of educational radio. *Education on the Air, 5,* 29-44.

Washington County, Maryland, Board of Education. (1964). Washington County closed circuit television report.

Watson, P. G. (1972). *Using the computer in education: a briefing for school decision makers.* Englewood Cliffs, NJ: Educational Technology Publications.

Weber, J. J. (1928). *Picture values in education.* Chicago: The Educational Screen.

Weizenbaum, J. (1976). *Computer power and human reason: From judgment to calculation.* New York: W. W. Freeman.

Welter, R. (1971). *American writings on popular education: The nineteenth century.* New York: The Bobbs-Merrill.

Wilkins, L. (1924). Modern languages in the high schools. In *New York City Board of Education, Educational radio program: Report of the educational activities carried on over the radio* (pp. 157-158). New York: Board of Education of the City of New York.

Willey, W. R., & Van Bortel, F. J. (1953, Fall). A conceptual framework for programming educational television. *Audio-Visual Communication Review, 1*(4), 252-260.

Winsip, A. E. (1927). Moving pictures in the classroom. *Journal of Education, 105*(20), 533.

Woelfel, N. (1942). Radio education during the crisis. *Journal of the Association for Education by Radio, 1*(5), 1.

Wood, G. C. (March, 1923). Some problems relating to the use of motion pictures in the secondary school. *Educational Screen, 2,* 110-112.

Young, M. F. (1993). Instructional design for situated learning. *Educational Technology Research and Development, 41*(1), 43-58.

Zook, G. F. (1934). Introductory remarks. In T. F. Tyler (Ed.), *Radio as a cultural agency: Proceedings of a National Conference on the use of radio as a cultural agency in a democracy* (pp. 1-2). Washington, DC: The National Committee on Education by Radio.

AUTHOR INDEX

323

SUBJECT INDEX

Printed in the United States
18747LVS00001B/166-234